THE MOUNTAINS
OF THE BUDDHA

Javier Moro

Translated by Asha Puri

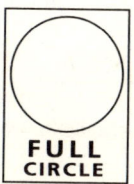

THE MOUNTAINS OF THE BUDDHA
© All Rights Reserved, 2000
First Indian Edition, 2000
ISBN 81-7621-075-7 *(Hardcover)*
ISBN 81-7621-070-6 *(Paperback)*

Published by **FULL CIRCLE**
Head Office: **18-19, Dilshad Garden, G.T. Road, Delhi-110 095**
Tel: 228 2467, 229 7792, Fax: 228 2332
e-mail: gbp@del2.vsnl.net.in
Editorial Office: **J-40, Jorbagh Lane, New Delhi-110 003**
Tel: 462 0063, 461 5138, Fax: 464 5795

All rights reserved in all media. No part of this publication
may be reproduced, stored in a retrieval system,
or transmitted, in any form or by any means, electronic,
mechanical, photocopying, recording, or otherwise,
without the prior permission of FULL CIRCLE.

Designing, Typesetting
    Print Production: **SCANSET**

Printed at Nu Tech Photolithographers, Delhi-110 095

PRINTED IN INDIA

CONTENTS

1. LONG LIVE THE DALAI LAMA! 1
2. THE SOLITUDE OF THE MONARCH 45
3. DAYS OF MOON AND WIND 79
4. THE YEAR OF THE EARTH PIG 139
5. THE REALM OF THE GODS 181
6. WHEN HORSEMEN GALLOP ON WHEELS 225

   Epilogue 256

   Final Note 260

   Acknowledgements 261

   Bibliography 263

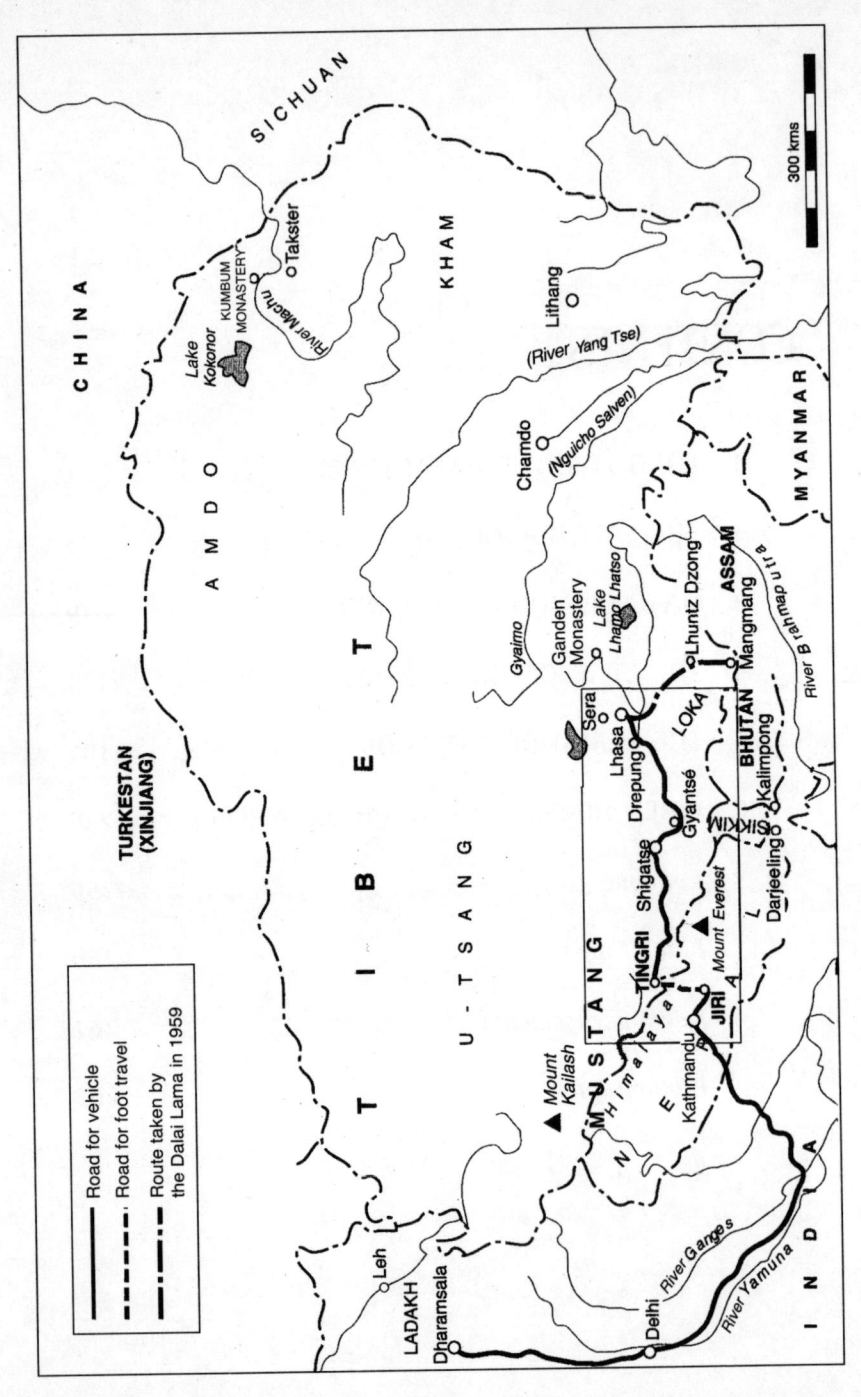

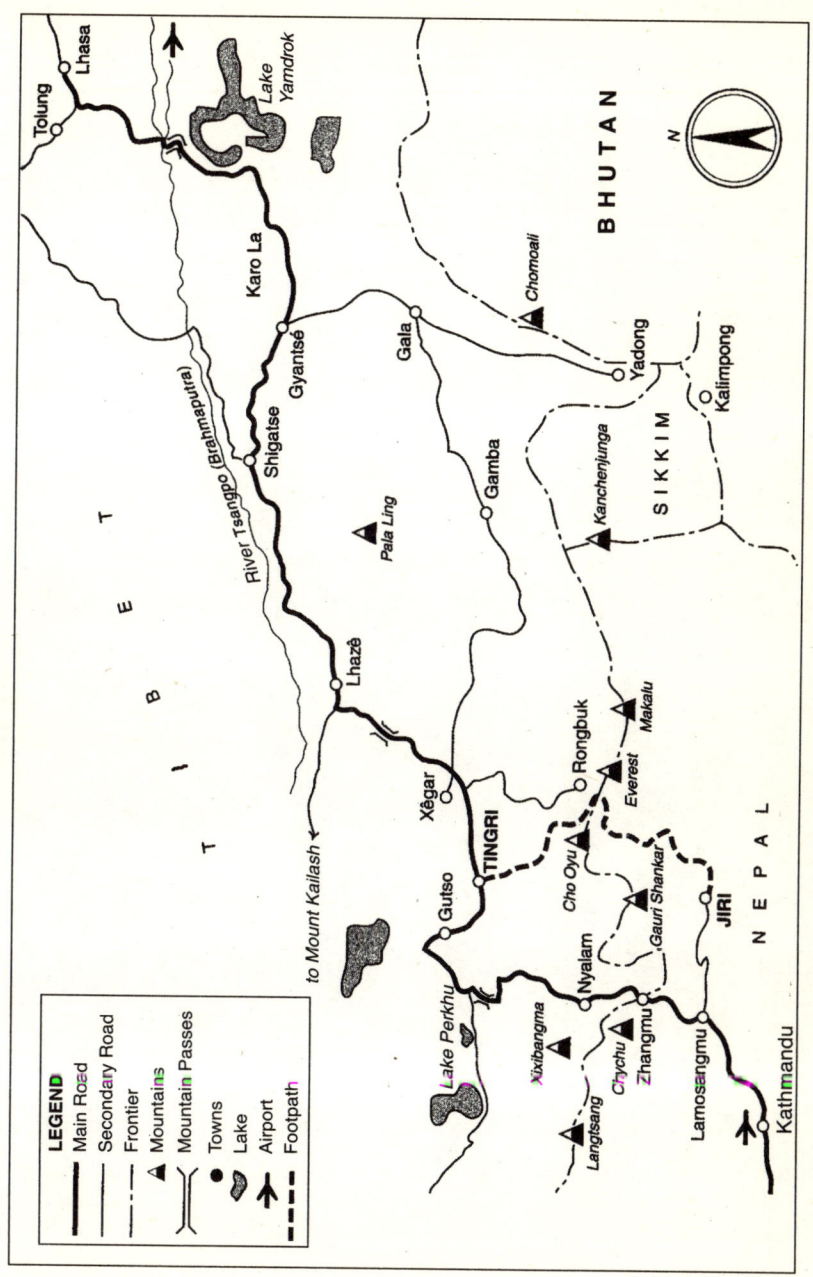

1

LONG LIVE THE DALAI LAMA!

I

n Tibet, the roof of the world, an immense land where snow clad rocky peaks touch the skies, there was hope and excitement in the air. The news had spread like wildfire. Everyone was talking about it in hushed tones: peasants from distant villages, soldiers at faraway campsites, monks and merchants from remote townships. They went from house to house to wake their sleeping neighbours, friends and relatives, hugged them and told them of the best news heard in a long time in the land of snows. Every nook and cranny of Lhasa, the legendary forbidden city, was buzzing with it. It traveled to temples and monasteries, houses and narrow streets, worn out hospitals, avenues without sidewalks and awkward concrete buildings. It reached bars where drunken Chinese clients lingered till dawn, discotheques packed with tourists and women willing to sell their bodies, the only deluxe hotel the capital boasted of, as far as the surrounding caves in which the hermits live. When the Tibetan Unit of All India Radio announced the news, the reaction was instantaneous. Many a face lit up with joy and hope, but there were others who were angry, if not downright affronted. The time was 6 a.m. and the day was October 5, 1989.

However, the dull sound of the monastery gong echoing across the building failed to rouse young Kinsom that day. She was sleeping soundly on a wooden cot with just a blanket on, despite the freezing cold. A sweet, cloying smell permeated

 The Mountains of the Buddha

her dreams. A little while later she felt a gentle hand stirring her:

"Wake up, wake up ... We are going to burn incense and make offerings of Tsampa."

"Why? What has happened?"

"His Holiness the Dalai Lama has been awarded the Nobel Prize. Soon Tibet will be free!" her friend replied, as she continued to wave her joss sticks around the bed.

Kinsom had never heard of the Nobel Prize, but from the other novice's enthusiasm, she gathered it was something important. "Ani Choki says we are no longer alone in the world. Now many people from many countries will do their best to see that His Holiness comes back to Lhasa..."

Ani Choki was the oldest of the nuns. A wisp of a woman, with bright penetrating black eyes peering out of a wrinkled, lined face, she was considered to be a fount of wisdom. It was she who took the decision to rebuild the convent on the ruins of the ancient monastery destroyed by the Chinese during the Cultural Revolution. She took on the task of selecting novices for the reconstruction work as well as organizing prayer and meditation sessions. More than two hundred girls lived, studied, prayed and worked in this sisterhood, which was located at a day's walk from Lhasa, perched a top of a hill, far removed from the hustle and bustle of the world.

Young Kinsom got up, stretched her limbs and settled her purple tunic. For a few moments she gazed through the window that had no pane at the walnut and apricot trees in the valley. In the distance, the golden light of the sun's first rays formed a halo around the bluish contours of mountain peaks that reared up in the north.

Strong, tall and slim, Kinsom exuded health. The biting cold made her cheeks glow. She had a flat nose and black, laughing eyes. Her head was shaven, a sign of the vows she had taken. Her shy smile revealed a set of sparkling, even teeth. Born to a family of shepherds, she had inherited the

Long Live the Dalai Lama!

nomadic temperament of her forefathers. She was not afraid of physical labour and worked unstintingly to help rebuild the monastery stone by stone. Like the other girls, she would occasionally grumble about not having enough time to study Buddhist scriptures. She learnt how to read and write when she was twenty. But such was her thirst for knowledge that she never hesitated to ask for help from anybody who had something to teach her. That day, however, her mind was not on her books. It was a day of celebration.

The steady hum of the morning prayers gave way to the chattering of excited voices. In spite of repeated warnings, it was impossible to contain the wave of happiness following the announcement that the Nobel Peace Prize had been awarded to Tibet's highest spiritual authority. Kinsom pulled out a crumpled photograph of the Dalai Lama from under her rickety old bed and clutched it against her tunic. Without stopping to serve herself a bowl of tea from the kitchen, she ran out to the verandah and joined in the impromptu celebration. Along with the others, she chanted pro-independence slogans and threw in the air, handfuls of *tsampa* or barley flour, which is a Tibetan staple. The juniper branches in her hands filled the verandah with a bluish smoke which had a strong aroma. 'Long live the Dalai Lama! Free Tibet!', chanted the more intrepid ones, all the while looking from the corner of their eyes at the three Chinese policemen, who could do no more than look on impassively. Clad in blue sheepskin jackets, they were part of a contingent that lived next to the monastery. It was their job to keep an eye on the activities of the convent: they kept track of the number of novices, made sure the nuns met only on the appointed days and conducted the much hated re-education sessions. But nothing had prepared them for that day. They stood as helpless bystanders, unable to deal with the biggest challenge ever posed by this community.

 The Mountains of the Buddha

Later in the day, as the nuns were praying in the altar room in front of a golden statue of a distant serene Buddha, they gave a start at the sound of vehicles screeching to a halt at their doorstep. All of them knew what lay in store for them. A dozen Chinese soldiers in green uniforms burst into the room, followed by the three policemen. Armed with machine guns and clubs, they shouted through a loudspeaker for the exit to be blocked. They began to hurl abuse at the nuns and hit them with their clubs. Not a cry escaped the lips of the terrified nuns who were used to having their privacy invaded by the Chinese authorities. Kinsom had enough presence of mind to hide the photo of the Dalai Lama in the folds of her tunic. In the bright morning light, she could see the figures of the policemen barking orders in the doorway. She remembered the door joint she had been fixing and was amazed at how she could think of something so ordinary at such a time. It must be a defence mechanism to counter fear, she thought to herself.

The Commanding Officer began to insult the Dalai Lama, calling him a fraud, an impostor and a lackey in the service of the imperialists. It was always the same litany, Kinsom was to recount later, "In the 're-education' sessions they kept disparaging him. But how can we forget the veneration in which our parents hold the Dalai Lama. We knew they were telling lies. They never succeeded in intimidating us."

After he had finished his tirade, the Commanding Officer formally accused the two eldest nuns — one of whom was Ani Choki, the founder — of fomenting revolt. They were beaten, handcuffed and dragged down the staircase like dogs. The remaining nuns began to weep and implored them not to take their seniors away in such a manner. A cry escaped Kinsom's lips. She felt a strong bond with her teacher; it was Ani Choki who had accepted her in the convent when she had come from her village as a young girl. The elder nun had become not only her teacher, but also her friend.

Long Live the Dalai Lama!

Four days after their raid on the monastery, the police returned with the photographs of fourteen nuns. Fortunately for Kinsom, hers was not there. All the fourteen were expelled. From that day onwards, the arrested nuns were forbidden to carry any external sign of their faith for the rest of their lives. They were put under house arrest in their respective villages and had to report to the local Chinese Commissioner. They were not allowed to mix with neighbours nor could they participate in community events. Ration cards and work permits were denied to them. They became a burden on their families and lived isolated from the rest of the world. This was the punishment meted out to rebels.

All Tibetans are under surveillance, monks and nuns all the more so, as they have always been at the forefront of the struggle for independence, undeterred by the bloody repression. From the day the Chinese occupied Tibet, the religious community has been associated with all the initiatives and demands for independence. Aware of the spiritual and political influence of the Tibetan clergy, the Chinese had been particularly repressive in dealing with its members, branding the most active among them as counter-revolutionaries. Later, even though freedom of religion was to be granted officially, access to the few monasteries and convents that survived the Cultural Revolution had become increasingly restricted. The police descended upon them at the slightest provocation, as on that fateful October morning. Furthermore, Political Commissars organized re-education sessions that used to so annoy Kinsom and her friends. Sometimes, day after day, week after week, young Tibetans were forced to spend entire afternoons watching video propaganda extolling the virtues of the Motherland.

Those who had not been expelled were forced to endure three sessions of 'self-criticism' a day. They were beaten, threatened with arms and warned that the monastery would be closed down. "We were told that so many restrictions were

 The Mountains of the Buddha

going to be imposed on us that 'not even the birds could sing' ", recalled Kinsom. We were only allowed to say a few prayers and perform some rites. Every movement of ours was watched and our cells were searched after each re-education session."

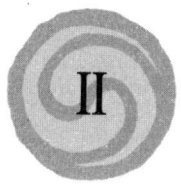

Many Tibetans continued to resist both actively and passively, the Chinese occupation of their homeland. For these heroic people, the Nobel Prize being awarded to the Dalai Lama was a shot in the arm. The fight for freedom which began in a small way, – confiding in tourists, pasting posters at night, distributing photographs and speeches of His Holiness and holding spontaneous demonstrations in monasteries – took on a more forceful character after the Dalai Lama's address to the US Congress in the September of 1987. In his speech to the representatives of the most powerful nation in the world, the leader of the Tibetan people proposed a peace plan based on dialogue with the Chinese authorities. He suggested: transforming the whole of Tibet into a zone of peace, free of nuclear waste; he pleaded for the abandonment of China's population transfer policy in the land of snows; lastly, he asked Beijing for a commitment to set free the tens of thousands of Tibetan political prisoners languishing in jails. In exchange, the Dalai Lama offered to give up Tibet's demand for independence provided the Tibetan people were guaranteed full autonomy within the Chinese nation. This was more than a concession, it was a radical change of stance. The Dalai Lama's proposals were received with unprecedented warmth in the United States. This infuriated the authorities in Beijing who immediately accused the North American Congress of interfering in the internal affairs of China. To make the Chinese position with respect to the peace proposals absolutely clear, the government organized, a few days later, a massive public trial in the Tibetan capital. Fifteen thousand Tibetans were rounded up in the Triyu Trang stadium where they were to witness eight Tibetans being sentenced to life imprisonment and two to death.

Three days after this mock trial, the Chinese authorities faced an unexpected challenge. It occurred on a sunny Sunday morning when groups of foreign tourists were peacefully strolling through the heart of the old city in the precincts of the Jokhang Temple. This is an architectural complex comprising several minor temples, numerous little chapels and altars which house amongst the most ancient and sacred cult objects of the Himalayas, including a seventh century Buddha image. The Jokhang is not meant to overawe the devotee. Its warm intimacy, rather, is conducive to solitude and meditation. There are small low-roofed rooms full of mystery with little statues of Buddha shining in the light of oil lamps. This is the real spiritual centre of Tibet. It was ransacked and stripped of its countless artistic treasures during the Cultural Revolution. A part of the temple was converted into an enormous pigsty by the Red Guards and the monks quarters were renamed Guesthouse No. 5. Hurriedly rebuilt, the temple was decorated with plastic frescoes and plaster statues, some of which were painted in gaudy colors. In spite of everything, the Jokhang complex remains the most popular religious centre of Tibet. Hundreds of pilgrims from all over the Himalayas throng here after long and arduous journies by bus, truck, on horseback or even on foot. They prostrate themselves at the entrance, the gray flagstone floor of which has acquired a sheen through centuries of devotion.

  The Mountains of the Buddha

At ten o'clock that morning, twenty-six monks, wrapped in large, deep crimson tunics, ran around the temple, waving the blue, red, white and yellow flag of free Tibet. They stopped between the statues of the two roaring lions in the square and, to the astonishment of passers-by, shouted: "Chinese go away! Free Tibet!" After that, they ran around the temple five more times and disappeared. The whole demonstration hardly lasted twenty minutes. This was the first time since the sixties that anything like this had happened. For the monks it must have taken a lot of courage to dare to come out in the open and defy the invaders of their country. Their fate, needless to say, was no different from that of all those that Beijing calls traitors.

But this was only the tip of the iceberg. Hardly a week later, on October 1, 1987, as the Chinese were commemorating the thirty-eighth anniversary of the People's Republic, forty monks came out of the Jokhang, shouting slogans and waving flags for independence. The demonstrators were arrested and taken to the police station, a three-storeyed building which looks onto to the same square. And then the unexpected happened. Pilgrims walking around the temple and reciting mantras gathered outside the police station. Within minutes, their numbers swelled. While they blocked the entrance to the police station, thousands of their compatriots invaded the square and began pelting stones at the building. A hundred policemen armed with AK-47 rifles appeared but when they saw the infuriated mobs their courage deserted them and they did not dare fire. They were faced with thousands of men, women and children shouting anti-Chinese slogans. They could no longer contain themselves and had to give vent to the resentment that had been building up in them for the past thirty years — thirty years of occupation, destruction, and repeated attempts to exterminate Tibetan culture and religion.

A twelve-year old boy came upon a rifle dropped by a fleeing policeman. Rather than using it to shoot the policeman, he picked up the rifle by the barrel and smashed it to bits

Long Live the Dalai Lama!

on the ground. The boy's reaction is illustrative of the Tibetan way of thinking, shaped by centuries of Buddhism which is essentially a philosophy of peace: arms are not to be used against the enemy but to be destroyed. The police were petrified. Faced with this widespread rebellion, the men on duty betrayed their fear. To protect themselves, they called for a dozen armed vehicles to surround the building.

The vehicles were set on fire by the demonstrators. The fire spread to the building and, in no time at all, flames consumed the outer walls of the police station. Soon, the square was reverberating with the sound of automatic rifles. Witnesses' accounts tell of a policeman standing on the terrace of the police station, who was the first to open fire on the crowd. The machine guns came next. Several Tibetans fell to the ground. The pavement was covered with blood. Then an act of great heroism galvanized the battered crowd. Braving the flames, a forty-five year old monk entered the police station to try to rescue the detained. He came out of the building with severe burns all over his body. Jampa Tenzin's courage and valour made him a hero. The crowd hoisted him up in the air and passed him about triumphantly in the streets of Lhasa. His fists were clenched in a victory sign even as large pieces of singed flesh stuck to his arms. Thanks to his daring, most of the detainees were able to escape. Those who remained were executed while trying to flee.

Many Tibetans approached the tourists, asking them to take photographs and tell the world about their plight. Chinese shopkeepers in the neighbourhood were harassed. Tibetans kept pelting stones for several hours so that the firemen could not get near the police station. At one o'clock in the afternoon there was a loud crash: the roof of the police station had collapsed in a cloud of dust and fire. The crowd broke out into applause. During the night, small trucks without number plates were seen moving around the Tibetan quarters, stopping

10   *The Mountains of the Buddha*

outside some houses and carrying off frightened residents to an unknown destination. The repression which followed and, indeed, lasted for some time, was brutal.

A few months later, Beijing was keen to use the opportunity provided by the Monlam Chenmo festival — the most important prayer festival of Tibet — to improve its image and show the world a peaceful, stable Tibet. The authorities hoped that the success of the festival would make the recent events recede in public memory. By the middle of February 1988, thousands of pilgrims reached Lhasa; so did a reinforcement of six thousand riot control policemen. No vehicle was allowed to enter the capital without a permit. "In the monasteries", said Kinsom, "the Chinese police organized innumerable sessions to educate us about the history of Tibet, about our patriotic feelings and the perils of separatism. Like many monks of the larger monasteries, I decided not to participate in the main festival celebration. We had no desire to celebrate while so many of our companions were languishing in jail." Finally, the Chinese had to forcibly bring in monks from all the four corners of Tibet. On the penultimate day, the day of the main festival, hundreds of monks in the Jokhang square, were getting ready to perform the ceremony known as the welcoming of the Buddha of the future. Just as the Chinese authorities were busy congratulating themselves on the successful organization of

Long Live the Dalai Lama!

the Monlam, a group of Lamas broke away from the crowd, approached the VIP stand and asked for the release of their compatriots. The Chinese officials, more out of fear than anger, left the stand amid the noise and chants of hundreds of monks who had started to shout, fists clenched: "Free Tibet, free Tibet!" Some younger monks climbed onto the stand and caught hold of the microphones: "We want independence for Tibet! Long live the Dalai Lama!" The monks, being filmed by the video cameras of the security forces, knew that there was not the slightest possibility of being able to escape the wrath of the occupiers.

The thousands of Tibetans who joined in this spontaneous demonstration also knew this. As they sang patriotic songs, some threw stones at the police cars from the roof of the Jokhang Temple while hundreds of monks walked around the square. It seemed as if there was no force on earth capable of stopping this demonstration. But it was not long before two thousand policemen moved in, armed to the teeth. They surrounded the square and threw tear gas shells. About a hundred monks were detained. The Tibetans faced the police the whole afternoon with machine guns rattling in the background. A young monk, a mere boy, threw a stone at the security forces before falling with a bullet in the eyes. There were three people who actually witnessed the policeman aim at and shoot the child. As young and old alike confronted the police, the women helped by piling up stones. On the following morning, when the security forces entered the Jokhang Temple to arrest all the monks there, people set ladders against the walls to help them escape. For seventeen whole hours Lhasa had been the scene of violent clashes. Hundreds were arrested that night and taken to Lhasa prisons where they were interrogated and tortured. However, in spite of the arrests and terror that had gripped the capital, fifteen nuns decided to carry on. Covering themselves with cloaks to protect themselves from the blows they knew they were

 The Mountains of the Buddha

going to receive, they went to demonstrate in front of the Jokhang Temple. Before being arrested, they managed to shout: "Long live the Dalai Lama! Free Tibet!"

The demonstrations continued despite the brutal repression, the climate of fear and, the extreme vigilance of the Chinese security forces. A sense of solidarity born out of the feeling that they were on the verge of being exterminated by the occupiers pushed the Tibetans into showing the world that they were ready to lay down their lives in self-defence. "However brutal and violent, repression cannot silence the voice of justice and freedom," the Dalai Lama had declared from his refuge in the Indian city of Dharamsala on the other side of the Himalayas.

Looking at the way the situation was developing, the Chinese declared martial law. Tibet was sent into near total isolation. Beijing imposed a wall of silence; the scarce news trickling out of the country spoke of continuing demonstrations, fear, arrests, torture, terror and death. Into this oppressive atmosphere of despair came the news of the Nobel Peace Prize being awarded to the Dalai Lama. Given this background, it was easy to understand the euphoric outpouring of the people and their overwhelming desire to shake off the yoke of the oppressor even though they knew their success would be short lived – the time it takes an incense stick to burn. At this crucial juncture, the Prize raised the morale of all Tibetans. It also served as a warning to those who, in desperation, wanted to turn to violence because they felt that peaceful means would lead them nowhere. In a world plagued by violence, non-violence had received a powerful boost.

However, for the Chinese, the Nobel Prize came as a humiliation, a big blow to their pride, as not a single citizen of the People's Republic had ever won a Nobel Prize. In private, Chinese leaders had to concede that thirty years of communism had in no way diminished the prestige of the Dalai Lama. In fact, the very opposite seemed to have happened: his absence had only magnified his aura in the eyes of his people. The insults and disparagement had hardly scratched the surface. The monk Tenzin Gyatso, the Fourteenth Dalai Lama, incarnation of the Buddha of Infinite Compassion, Lord of the White Lotus, Ocean of Wisdom, was and continued to be, whether in his country or in exile, the true sovereign of the land of snows, the God King of all Tibetans.

oung Kinsom cherished the dream of meeting the Dalai Lama one day. She admired all those who had dared, with single-minded purpose, to cross the mountain passes and brave the uncertainties of the weather to meet the Dalai Lama. It was a long and arduous journey across the Himalayas. At every step there were vigilant border guards to contend with. But the glow one felt in the presence of His Holiness more than made up for it all. Countless refugees, aged and infirm, shaken by the violent upheavals, had died in peace, happy at just having caught a glimpse of him. On countless occasions, Kinsom had heard stories of compatriots who owed their survival to the ceaseless protection of this monk; his mere presence had helped them move ahead in life to overcome their personal suffering and provided them opportunities to give the best of themselves, regardless of the price they had to pay. Kinsom too wanted to be blessed by him. Perhaps her dream would never come true but she clung on to it with all the strength of her youth. "Who knows?

 The Mountains of the Buddha

Maybe one day...", she thought to herself as she accompanied three of her friends to Lhasa one morning in the January of 1990. While they walked towards the city centre, they counted the 108 beads of their rosaries and chanted the mantra *Om Mani Padme Hum* (Praise to the Jewel at the heart of the Lotus) – a mantra omnipresent in Tibet. It is carved on stones lying on the roadside and tall mountain rocks; it is written on multicoloured prayer flags flying in the wind; it is recited on entering a dwelling or monastery and in the never ending psalms of the pilgrims. It is one of the first things a child learns to say. Century after century, in one life after another, this litany has been repeated in Tibet for more than a thousand years and has acquired a timeless quality. It represents the aspirations of each and every Buddhist as it symbolizes the body, the word and the pure spirit of a Buddha – one whose spiritual level has attained the highest degree of consciousness: enlightenment. Enlightenment is a state where all suffering and anxiety have been suppressed and immortal peace and joy have at last been discovered.

So lost in thought was Kinsom as she walked along that her companions had to keep pushing her back on the footpath to save her from being knocked down by cyclists. From behind the mountains, the sun had spread its rays across the city which stretches over an immense plateau situated at an altitude of 3700 m. Like all those who enter the capital on foot, Kinsom and her companions could see the golden roof and impressive facade of the Potala Palace. In other times it had been the official residence of the Dalai Lama and the seat of government. This peculiar monumental structure looms large over the city – a reminder of the time when the roof of the world had been a veritable melting pot in a truly unique civilization. Except for this majestic symbol, there is very little left of Lhasa's past glory. Traditional houses have all but gone, and the old quarters are constantly being pulled down, giving way to concrete buildings built by workers brought over from

China. Nightclubs, bars and brothels for the soldiers and policemen stationed in the city line the straight parallel roads. Even so, Lhasa does not resemble other Chinese cities. The city centre still retains its old-world, medieval charm. Smiling monks, grimy peasants, jugglers and acrobats gather here. It is a small square, friendly, bright and sunny, with spectacular mountain views and the sound of tiny bells tinkling in the pristine air; even the chaos and dirt add to its hospitable appeal. The barking of stray dogs and the cries of children only heighten the sense of quietude. Lhasa is also a swarm of dialects, a crowded marketplace filled with strong smells, carts full of assorted objects, mountains of fruit and vegetables, handcarts with mounds of rancid butter, bags full of tea and street stalls selling filthy cuts of sun dried yak meat.

Before making her purchases, Kinsom wanted to go by the Jokhang square. She liked going there to see the jovial monks and friendly pilgrims who gave the holy city a colourful, cosmopolitan air. In choosing Lhasa as their meeting point, pilgrims from all over the Himalayan region enriched the life of the city. Prostrating themselves till their foreheads touch the ground, they circle the temple clockwise. They lie down on steps, in the streets, on the banks of the river, in the surrounding hills, never losing their good humour. For many Tibetans, this is a secret confirmation of the fact that, in spite of the Chinese invasion of their city, its spirit remains unscathed.

While crossing the sun filled square, Kinsom and her companions passed by three Chinese policemen guarding the Red Flag. In the obscurity of the altar rooms, filled with fine clouds of incense, they joined the praying pilgrims; the most devoted ones blew a trumpet made out of a human femur that resembled a flute; others drew water in bowls made from a skull top. Young Tibetans prayed, prostrated themselves and then sprinkled the sanctuaries with small bits of one jiao banknotes and grains of barley. Before leaving the recesses

 The Mountains of the Buddha

of the temple, they emptied small quantities of yak butter in the tiny lamps.

As she strolled along the streets around the temple, through a maze of stalls selling prayer flags and stone encrusted yak bones, the familiar melody of a traditional song suddenly caught Kinsom's attention. With her friends, she followed the trail of the singing voices till she came upon a cluster of Tibetans — peasants and pilgrims standing and listening, rapt, to a venerable old man who sang:

> Never shall I forget the face of my parents.
> Oh jewel of wisdom,
> My country they never sold, they robbed.

Kinsom and her companions joined in the chorus. Then they started singing satirical songs, poking fun at the Chinese. Amidst much laughter and merriment, a street side fiesta was soon under way. The youngest in Kinsom's group was impatient to leave, but Kinsom wanted to stay a little longer. She wanted to enjoy one of those rare moments of reprieve, shared joy and freedom so hard to come by. Indeed, the Tibetans with their legendary good humour can always be counted upon to find, even when they are weighed down by daily chores and the yoke of oppression, a few moments of magical respite and enchantment. Then only the present matters, for it is like a precious jewel that must be treasured and cherished. Herein lies the strength of a people that are steeply rooted in a religion that makes destruction a necessary condition for rebirth; compassion its golden rule, and; the transience of beings and objects its main article of faith.

Unfortunately, the police did not take long to break up the festivities. People began to run in all directions; some shouted slogans, while others pelted stones. They were in a mood to fight against the injustice meted out to them. The venerable old Tibetan stayed put, humming the refrain of his song, watching all that was going on around him with complete detachment. Dark and tanned, his eyes were like two black beams lost in the wrinkles of his face. His dirty gray hair fell over his shoulders. A policeman ordered him to keep quiet but the old man continued undaunted, a defiant look in his eyes. The police raised their clubs and in spite of taunts from the crowd watching at a distance, they dealt several blows to him on his face and body. The old man staggered but continued to stand. He began to bleed from the mouth, nose and ears. His voice was reduced to an inaudible hum, but he continued to smile. Some people shouted: "Leave him in peace!"; others hurled abuse at the Chinese. However, neither side was willing to back off. The old man kept on singing and the police kept on beating him. The old man was bent double until he almost collapsed on the ground, struggling not to fall on his knees as the police kept hitting him with sticks on the back. Kinsom had had enough, she could not bear it any longer. She pulled off her muffler and waved it about as if it were a flag. "Chinese go away! Free Tibet!", she shouted several times. Her companions did not try to hold her back; they were so angry that they joined her shouting. The attention of the policemen fell on the nuns who ran away. Practically all of them managed to save themselves, thanks to the help of those living nearby who opened their doors to them so that they could hide. The youngest of the nuns escaped arrest because a peasant woman who had a vegetable stall hid her under her apron. Kinsom ran towards a crossing to find a hiding place but the police were following on her heels. All of a sudden she felt a blow on her head. She felt as if it were exploding and she collapsed to the ground.

V

When Kinsom opened her eyes, she was sprawled in the trailer of a military truck which moved along, blowing its horn non-stop, until it reached the outskirts of Lhasa. Her face and neck were covered with marks of dried blood. Stunned as she was, her head was throbbing. But that was nothing compared to the pain she felt in her arms. When she tried to move, she realized that she was handcuffed. Each pothole on the roadway caused a contraction which seemed to tear at her wrists and dislocate her shoulders. From where she was, she could see the butt of the soldiers' rifles, building tops, lamp-posts, treetops and an expanse of clear blue sky. How she wished she could vanish in thin air. The truck continued for about twenty minutes more and when she saw the watch tower, Kinsom felt her pulse miss a beat with fright. The place brought shivers down the spine of most Tibetans. Merely mentioning the Gutsa prison brought to mind the fate of thousands of compatriots who had suddenly disappeared in its entrails never to be heard of again. For those who had had the good luck to leave its doors alive, the memory of this hell had them breaking out into uncontrollable sobs, very often bringing on a nervous breakdown. This complex of gray rectangular buildings set in an arid plateau surrounded by high walls is the most visible symbol of the brutality used by the Chinese authorities to subjugate the Land of Snows.

As she kicked and struggled with all her might, the guards pushed Kinsom into the admission room, where a uniformed woman searched her thoroughly. She took all her belongings including the shopping money, made her sign a receipt and noted her name in the entry register. Then she was taken by the guards who locked her in the interrogation chamber, a vast hall furnished with metal tables and chairs. Kinsom trembled at the sight of the whips, ropes, electric wires and iron hooks hanging on the ceiling. All the stories she had heard about the Chinese and what they were capable of doing to prisoners flitted into her mind. She had heard these stories in the village from her uncles, relatives and companions in the monastery. They were handed down from generation to generation – a necessary duty to be performed for the generations to come.

A Chinese official bulging in a tight green uniform once again took down her particulars. He had three *gonyi-pa* – a word that literally means double-faced and is used to describe Tibetans who collaborate with the Chinese – under his command. Kinsom knew that they were the worst of the lot, as they were willing to go to any length to curry favour with their superiors.

"Who was with you?", one of the *gonyi-pa* asked her.

Kinsom did not reply, partly because she had no desire to do so and partly because she was too dazed to answer.

"Did you know them?"

"No."

She was dragged to an iron chair and handcuffed to it. The technique used had been perfected over the years by the People's Liberation Army; it consisted of crossing a piece of rope around the victim's chest and then fastening the arms, stretched upwards behind the victim's head. The rope was then slung under the victim's armpits, and jerked downwards. Kinsom bent in pain and let out a guttural cry: they had dislocated her shoulders. So painful was this form of torture, called the airplane, that many prisoners lost control over their bowels and bladder.

"Who organized the demonstration?"

   The Mountains of the Buddha

Kinsom was crying in pain. The guards realized that she was on the verge of fainting and released the rope. They started hitting her on the face, chest and feet; with each blow they asked the same question. Kinsom repeated her answer: that the street meeting was an impromptu one. As this was not what her torturers wanted to hear, one of them pulled out the preferred instrument of torture in Chinese prisons: an electric prod of the kind used for branding cattle. They applied it to the chair. Kinsom was trembling, she arched her upper body and fainted. When she recovered consciousness, the guard started again. Another one hit her. She fainted again.

"Who was with you? Who gave you the order to demonstrate?"

It was inconceivable to the Chinese authorities that the nuns were demonstrating of their own volition. Their action must have been part of a larger plot to undermine 'the prestige of the Motherland'. They wanted names, names and more names. As Kinsom would not open her mouth, they decided they would have to do something about it. They forced her mouth open and inserted the electric cattle prod until it touched the back of her throat. It seemed to Kinsom that her cheeks were bursting, her tongue was smouldering and that her eyes had all but fallen out of their sockets. When they removed the prod from her mouth, she noticed pieces of broken tooth which she had thrown up in blood stained vomit. But she would not talk. At last, bleeding all over her body, her tongue so swollen that it did not fit in her mouth, covered with bruises, Kinsom heard the voice of the official saying the session was over. They untied her, put handcuffs on her wrists, fetters on her ankles and took her out. Since she refused to talk, she was sentenced to solitary confinement and denied the right to enter into contact with any of the other prisoners.

She was put in a small cell, about three metres long and two metres wide. A thick concrete slab served as a bed and the recess in the wall, fitted with thick iron bars, as a window.

Her meals were passed to her through a small hatch. There was a bucket half filled with dried turd, a reminder of the previous occupant. Kinsom does not remember to this day how long she remained motionless and glassy eyed, trying to regain her breathing. She had to move to counter the cold but her body was so stiff, her joints so painful that even the effort of breathing was unbearable. One morning, when she finally woke up from her stupor, she saw her daily ration being pushed through the hatch. She managed to raise herself somehow, drag her shackled feet and pick up with trembling hands a bowl of black tea and some grayish mush. She was starving and parched with thirst but, because of the terrible condition her mouth was in, she could not swallow even a drop of water. She warmed her hands on the bowl and with the tea washed her face and neck.

The icy solitude of her cell was occasionally broken by the sound of distant voices barking orders or the cry of a fellow prisoner. Memories from her childhood flitted into her mind – the relish with which her younger brother would drink the warm milk that she had just drawn from the *dzomo*, a gentle creature that was a cross between a cow and a yak. Their joy at receiving visits from the holy men, who reached the township frozen to the marrow and begging for food. They were half clad, just like Milarepa, the great yogi and best known ascetic of Tibetan Buddhism, who was capable of meditating for days on end in the snow and frost of the Himalayas wearing only a cotton robe. They prayed the whole day and sometimes through the night, not only for the family's prosperity, but also for the freedom of their country and the health of the Dalai Lama. They said their prayers in front of the family altar, which was hidden to avoid denunciation. There had always been an altar in her parents' home, even during the worst years of the Cultural Revolution. For Kinsom, who had grown up in an environment where religion was considered an inseparable part of life, these holy men were

 The Mountains of the Buddha

veritable heroes. They had renounced the world and chosen the most difficult path of all, defying the ban on religious life imposed by the Communists in the first thirty years of their rule over Tibet. Later, when the Chinese granted some religious freedom, a monk would periodically visit her parent's home. He would conduct the ceremonies on festive occasions and make offerings twice a year. He was also a healer, always willing to tend the ailments of this semi-nomadic population. From him, Kinsom heard for the first time, in detail, a story which would remain engraved forever in her memory. It was the story of a Prince called Siddharth, a family man with a child, who at the age of twenty-nine, left the palace where he had lived since his birth to go to the city. There, he came across an old man bent with age, a man suffering from plague and a dead body that was being carried to the crematorium. These three encounters — the revelation of old age, illness and death, common to all mankind — proved to be decisive for the world: the Prince gave up his palace, his family and royal obligations. Henceforth, he would devote all his energies to the search of a new light that would enable human beings to free themselves from their suffering. In the course of his travels across North India, the Prince questioned many wise men. For six years, he led a life of extreme asceticism in the mountains but, he found this was leading him nowhere. At last, he discovered the peace and certainty he sought within himself, sitting in the shade of a spreading *bo*-tree. There, the mystery of death, rebirth and the annihilation of suffering in the world was revealed to him. It was much more than a mystical experience: he had penetrated the ultimate reality of all things. He had become the Buddha or the Enlightened One.

To travel, to learn, to know and to perfect oneself is an ideal all Tibetans cherish. Kinsom was no exception, even though she could not read or write, as there was not a single school for miles around. In the solitude of the mountains, she pondered over the teachings of the monk and slowly her dreams for the future began to acquire shape. "The awakening", the friendly monk had told her, "cannot be learnt, but the path leading to it can. For this, study occupies a very important place in the life of Buddhists."

Kinsom, tired of spending day after day in the mountains in the sole company of the animals, announced one day to her family that she was thinking of embracing the religious life. Her father, an elderly man with a weather-beaten face and a deceptively fragile frame, could not hide his displeasure. All the good man said was: "We need you here". Kinsom, however, did not want this life; she had never wanted to marry or have children. She had talked about it with her friends, daughters of shepherds and peasants like herself, who also wondered, about the future of their occupied land. What was the point of having children if one could not feed them properly? If they had to be like pariahs in their own country, unable to study in their mother tongue, condemned to be fringe dwellers by the Chinese? Certainly there was no place for motherhood in Kinsom's plans for the future, made in the solitude of the valleys and woods. She wanted to spend her passage on earth to improve her *karma*. In Buddhism, this notion is of paramount importance. Individual destiny is the sum of one's deeds, good or bad, in this life and the previous ones. Our deeds can be compared to invisible threads weaving our existence. Good deeds have good effects and bad deeds are an obstacle to spiritual realization. Kinsom knew that fate meant to reap what one had sown. It was perhaps for this reason that she wanted to do something exalted so that she could move ahead on the path of enlightenment. In this life she had the opportunity to accumulate at least one good *karma* which could help others. She was not very clear how she was to go about this but felt intuitively that if she followed the path of *Dharma* and the teachings of Buddha, sooner or later, she would discover light.

Had it not been for the support of her mother, who since childhood had told her that religious knowledge was all she

   The Mountains of the Buddha

could carry with her after death, Kinsom would have found it extremely difficult to oppose her father and follow her vocation. Her mother worked on her husband to let their daughter choose her own path. Like most Tibetan peasant women, she combined gentleness with strength of character and was fully prepared to give up her daughter for a higher cause. Kinsom remembered vividly the day of her departure. She saw her mother standing on top of the path, her jet-black hair tied in a plait, her laughing eyes and her smile revealing two missing teeth. She was waving as prayer flags fluttered in the wind, producing a strange sound like the distant rumbling of thunder before the storm.

Now, in the darkness of her cell, Kinsom tried to imagine the life of her parents at that moment. Were they with the animals in the mountains covered with pine trees whose delicate fragrance filled the air? Were they looking for the delicious berries that grew in the woods? Had they heard about her arrest?

VI

The cell door opened amidst the jangling of keys and locks. They were ready to take her off once again. Kinsom was unable to tell how much time had elapsed since the last session. All she knew was that she was feeling better physically even though she was gripped with cold and hunger. She refused to drink the foul soup they pushed through the hatch at mealtimes.

They took her to the chamber where she had been interrogated the last time by the same team. The official started to explain to her in a friendly voice that he needed the names of the other rebellious nuns of her convent. Kinsom said they had joined the group singing in the street simply out of curiosity. She could not give any names because she had acted on the spur of the moment. The official repeated the charges against her. She was accused of being anti-Communist, anti-Chinese and, what was even more serious, of secessionist activities for which she could get a very stiff sentence, even death. Kinsom stared at the floor. The official, realizing that his words had had no impact, called one of the torturers. The man ordered the young girl to take off her clothes. She did not budge and was dealt a series of blows. She was told she no longer had the right to wear the habit. All she deserved were the rags they would give her to cover her body. She would not be allowed to cut her hair or undertake any kind of religious activity. Then they pulled off her tunic. She stood completely naked while they fondled her breasts, her thighs, her pubis with the guards mouthing obscenities. Finally the official called the men to order. He was a professional and could not tolerate any deviation on the part of his subordinates. They stopped fondling her and ordered her to bend her body forward, striking blows on her head till she lost her balance. Pushed into a corner of the room, humiliated and in pain, all Kinsom wanted was to die. How she wished she could jump out of the window. She recalled the parting advice of her father, resigned to the fact that his daughter was leaving her home to strike out her own path. He had advised her against going to a Lhasa convent. Instead, he had said that she should seek the solitude of the mountains; this would be more useful to her in her religious practice. He knew that convents and monasteries were dangerous places for they had become bastions of the resistance. She had listened to him and had gone to the mountains. But her father did not know that even the remotest mountain ranges had not been spared the chaos and violence of this world. She wanted to tell him that there was no escape, no salvation in the land of snows — there was only death and destruction. "Look father, see what they have done to me..."

Once again the official spoke. In dulcet tones he offered her protection, hinting that she could return to the convent if she cooperated. She was offered money, even though past experience had shown that nuns were impervious to such inducements. "I would rather die and have my body cut up and fed to the vultures than denounce my sisters", thought Kinsom. Tired of waiting for an answer, the official left the room, his briefcase tucked under his arm. Kinsom began to tremble for she knew the worst was still to come. "It was awful", recalls Kinsom. "The *gonyi-pa* are unbelievably cruel. They forced me to lie down on the table. While one opened my legs, another inserted an electric prod in vagina. They played with it as if it were a toy that amused them thoroughly. While applying electric shocks, they were laughing and joking. I felt my insides were being torn apart. I fainted. To bring me back to consciousness they threw a bucket of cold water in my face. One of them said to me, 'Now you are no more a nun, only trash'. He was not wrong, for I was a wreck, a heap of bleeding flesh. By raping me with that prod they had broken my vows of purity and chastity. My body was nothing more than a bag of bones, a raw wound. I was like an animal in a slaughter house. They took me back to the cell and for the next nine days they would let me out only to torture me. They did everything they possibly could. They kept me hanging naked by the feet for a whole night, threw buckets of urine in my face and forced me to eat a *momo*, a Tibetan patty, stuffed with excrement. They were neither men nor beasts; they were machines."

To put an end to this nightmare, there were times when Kinsom was tempted to reveal the names of her companions.

But she always found the strength to refrain. For she knew that if she spoke, she would lose everything: her dignity, her self-respect and the right to call herself a human being. Her silence was her last refuge. Her lips would remain sealed even if they dragged her to death. "They can rape my body every day", said Kinsom to herself, "but as long as I do not speak they will never be able to rape my soul. I remembered what I had been taught and knew that this alone was what mattered. The purer my mind became the greater were my chances of securing a good reincarnation. Then I could follow the path of *dharma* in an exemplary manner, attain nirvana and even Enlightenment..."

On returning to her cell, one of the guards, a middle aged Chinese woman with an angular face and two school girl plaits, gave her a coarse patched garment to wear and returned her her shoes. These, however, hardly afforded any protection against the biting cold and her physical debility. She was trembling and broke into spasms; her skin was cracked and her entire body was stinging with sores. The guard felt sorry for her and in a surprising act of commiseration gave her a muffler and vest.

For her thirty days in solitary confinement, Kinsom's only reliefs were the patch of sky she could see from her makeshift window – the only way she could tell whether it was night or day – and, the evening stroll to the lavatory to empty the urine bucket.

One evening on her way to the lavatory, she could not help herself. She walked up to the guard and asked her in a low voice: "Aren't you ashamed of treating people like this?" The woman stared fixedly at her.

For a moment, Kinsom thought she was going to get a slap in the face because she had dared to break the rule of silence. Then, she thought, after all, what more could they do to her? The woman in uniform just accompanied her back to her cell and closed the door. When the food came through the hatch, to her surprise Kinsom discovered two *momos* in the bowl instead of the usual one. This raised her spirits. Even the hardened Chinese had a heart.

Her physical condition continued to deteriorate. Her wounds could not heal because of continuous torture. Much more worrying was the problem of incontinent urination. Suddenly, she would feel a warm uncontrollable flow between her legs, which exasperated her. This was the result of the electric prod in the vagina. Kinsom knew some prisoners had never been able to recover the control of their bladders and sphincters. Her spirits flagged. She was not allowed to attend her own trial and the future seemed to hold nothing but more torture for her. She fell into a state of stupor. The words of the official threatening her with capital punishment echoed in her mind. She stared at the dirt spots on the wall with only one thought in her head: they were going to execute her. She imagined the other prisoners, locked up in identical dark cells, waiting for death. At night, her dreams were chaotic: images of her as a child flying a kite superimposed on scenes of her arrest, life in prison and beatings. Whenever she was awake, death always seemed her only refuge. She had contemplated hanging herself with the rags they had given her to wear, though she eventually discarded the idea. There had been a case of a nun throwing herself from a bridge while being transferred to another prison, but that was the exception. Kinsom, like most Tibetans, thought that suicide was even more abhorrent than the greatest suffering. According to the teachings of her religion, a person who committed suicide could not hope to be reborn in human form or continue his spiritual development for the next five hundred lives. Suicide would mean turning one's back to the reality of the world. Had she not been taught that suffering is universal and persists throughout the life of all sentient beings, culminating in death? Was this not the supreme law of life? Day after day, the same drama is enacted in nature: the bird of prey is swallowed by the predator, plants compete with each other for the sun's rays... Wherever there is beauty there is bound to be strife and pain. In Buddha's teachings there is no saviour, no superhuman force, no promise of supernatural intervention. So Kinsom had nothing to clutch onto in the hopeless solitude of her cell. In any case, what could the gods do? Even if they were merciful protectors, they had not rid the world of suffering as they themselves were not free from it. One thing alone was true: man's struggle against pain. In this struggle each one stood alone and victory was only possible through purely human methods. Kinsom's faith offered no absolute truth, no dogma, just the means to attain salvation. She knew she had to guard against falling into futile despair. She had to follow the example of Buddha. What mattered was controlling the mind. It was through meditation that the Buddha found the way to annihilate pain, indissociably linked to all human existence. Such is the power of the mind that one can in, stages, reach one's inner essence, that part which is unchanging and immortal and can be found in the nature of all things. What the Christians and Jews call God; the Hindus, Shiva, Brahma and Vishnu, the mystics, the occult essence; the Buddhists call Buddhahood. Like all other religions, Buddhism is based on the conviction that there is one Fundamental Truth and that this life provides us with a sacred opportunity to move towards it.

Kinsom, who had ceased her meditation since she entered Gutsa, forced herself to recite mantras rather than dwell on her troubles: she tried to dispel the cold, hunger, pain and the persistent thought of death. It was only in the silence of the night that she managed to withdraw from the turbulence of her thoughts and experience her innermost being that was like a jewel hidden in the mud. She sought inner silence because "only when the waters are still can you see at the bottom of the pool". She began to think of her battered body as a mere temporal cloak for her spirit, which she would shed to be reborn at another level of existence. Does Buddhism not teach the transience of all things and the value of detachment, both from the self and others? Does it not say that nothing should be taken seriously, for the ultimate truth is found in bliss and wisdom, not pain and ignorance? Is not being happy the most important value? Kinsom used these long spells of silence to recall the words of her mentor. Slowly, she was able to lift the veils from her mind and find the serenity she so needed to survive if only to face the the next day. In the state she was in, it took her all her mental strength to look beyond her own suffering. She had to summon great courage to remain insensitive to her own pain.

VII

The small patch of sky that she could see from her cell became her lifeline. At night she would stare out of the small recess and hold on to the twinkling stars; she felt her gaze join the cosmic light. Sky and earth, time and eternity merged into one. This mystery converted itself into strength, illuminating the mind and bringing warmth to the body. During the day, looking at this turquoise blue frame on which a pale crescent moon occasionally floated was like breathing pure air — an experience of the Absolute. This opening was her only link with the beauty of the world, far away from the cries of prisoners, the shouts of the guards, the damp, dirty walls of her cell. She was aware that without this tiny recess defended by thick iron bars she would have been buried alive.

And the others, she wondered, did they also have this privilege? How many more people had been thrown into labour camps and prisons in Tibet? How many more bodies had been battered with clubs, prods and batons? How many more of her companions were dying because they had refused to speak like her, or worse still, had spoken. How many more would have to endure this endless night of torture?

And what had become of her mentor, the venerable Ani Choki, whom the police had dragged away on the day of the Nobel celebration? Was she in one of the Gutsa cells, just a few metres away? Had they sent her to a re-education camp? Was she still alive? But the question that preyed upon her mind was the one she dared not ask: had they done to Ani Choki what they had done to her?

Soon after leaving her parents' home, Kinsom had arrived at the monastery — a heap of ruins — where she had met Ani Choki for the first time. Ani Choki and a group of eight elderly nuns, all of whom had seen better days before the monastery had been destroyed by the Chinese, had remained there. They were hanging on to the place with all the strength of their faith. From their tents, they had started the reconstruction work. They were the ideal role models, the best friends and guides Kinsom could ever hope to have. In spite of their advancing age, they had taken upon themselves the task of reconstruction. Every day they would go out and ask for help and return with material and food. First, they set up the kitchen, then a pole for the banners with prayers inscribed on them. They survived by cultivating barley and tending sheep as well as on the offerings made by those who did not fear to frequent the monastery once again. They were educated women who knew the sacred texts by heart. The Red Guards, in a fit of anger, had burnt their holy books. The nuns were now patiently rewriting them, drawing upon the innermost recesses of their memory to do so.

Ani Choki had admitted Kinsom immediately, pleased to have a pair of young, willing hands to help. She had warned her that life would be hard, but she had also promised to teach her to read and write and, if there was time, to study Buddhist philosophy with her. What more could Kinsom, a poor ignorant daughter of the mountains, lost in the wilderness of her land, have asked for? That very night she was given shelter in one of the mountain caves which she shared with other novices, all delighted at the prospect of living like the legendary hermits. During the day, these women built the walls of the monastery, using mud and stones. It took them two hours to climb up the steep path, carrying wood, bamboo and other materials on their backs. Life was by no means easy but Kinsom preferred it to that of a shepherd.

There were about thirty young girls in all. Daughters of nomads, they lived a life of complete austerity without the slightest of comforts. Whenever there was a snowstorm at night, Kinsom and her companions had to remove the snow with their bare hands. If it rained, they had to abandon their flooded caves and beg for shelter. "It was like my life as a nomad", said Kinsom. The novices meditated and recited mantras in the open, even in temperatures that sometimes fell to minus fifteen degrees. Kinsom would always remember the *puja* or prayer held when she entered the convent. Some women sang psalms; Kinsom had never heard anything as beautiful ever before. In this land of martyrs where everything including the biting cold was a struggle, they sang, their breath turning to frost, the greatness of the human spirit and the mountains echoed their song as if they too were taking part in the ceremony. In the beauty of that moment, the long saga of destruction — of temples, men and minds — and the shadows that loomed large over Tibet were forgotten. In that moment, something had escaped the suffering and folly of

Long Live the Dalai Lama!

human history as in the mute lips of the statue of the Buddha of Infinite Compassion around which the novices had gathered.

Later, when she had become familiar with the rudiments of the alphabet, she had taken her vows. For the purpose, two Lamas came from a nearby monastery. They sat on the ground and started reciting mantras to the sound of trumpets and cymbals. The day before, Kinsom had had her hair shaved, a symbolic gesture by which she had renounced vanity and marked her transition from the material to the spiritual plane, freed from the tyranny of her sex. She had pledged before the Lamas to follow the precepts of purity, chastity and renunciation. Henceforth, she would have to cultivate serenity and friendship, renounce anger and greed, behave with equanimity, treat all human beings with compassion and not allow herself to be overwhelmed by joy or grief. She would have to strive to discipline her mind and endeavour, at all times, to follow the path of enlightenment. When the music came to an end, Kinsom had raised her head, reassured, and looked up through half open eyes, because of the dazzling sun, at the Lamas wearing yellow tunics over the usual crimson ones. She returned their smile and took her vows to embrace the Buddhist faith based on the principle of the three refuges: refuge in the Buddha or wisdom; in *Dharma* or the doctrine; in Sangha or the community of the faithful.

These memories came back to her and proved to be invaluable. They were the foundations on which Kinsom would base her struggle to keep the flame of her existence alive. The example of Ani Choki and the elder nuns helped her find a meaning to her suffering. Tibetan Buddhism has had its share of great women, independent, intelligent and strong, who, without renouncing their faith or succumbing to physical and mental deprivation, had borne the harshest of trials. They were women who had paid no heed to social convention or the opinion of their family and friends. They had led an errant life, remaining steadfastly true to the goal of spiritual realization. They were women who had fought for their rights, their traditions, their country and their religion. Impervious to contempt and ridicule, they had attained an equal status with men. In fighting against the repression of the invaders, they had gained the respect and veneration of all their compatriots.

Among the novices, the miraculous powers of the elder nuns was the subject of daily gossip. More than one young girl claimed to have been cured just by touching the clothes or an object belonging to one of the elder nuns. Rumour had it that they could look into the past, present and future. That they could, like the great *yoginis* of the past, survive on water alone, as they possessed magical powers: they could extract vital essences from plants, and even stones. It was for this reason they had stayed on at the monastery in spite of its being destroyed. They could, through sheer will power, prolong their lives and decide the moment of their death. The young novices believed that their elders were capable of achieving the same feats as the great nuns of the past: such was their concentration that they could pass through walls and leave their footprints on rocks. A common practice among yogis was producing heat in the body. The great mystic Milarepa was an adept in this art. The elder nuns told the tale of how, before the Chinese invasion, in the very same convent they were now rebuilding, a ritual ceremony would take place on the fifteenth day of the twelfth month of the Tibetan calendar. The nuns used to go out at dawn in short skirts, with fine white linen cloth draped around them and take a round of the building. They would remove their tunics in each one of its four corners, soak them in frozen water and then promptly put them back on again. The Lamas and their disciples followed the proceedings from the flat terraced roof of the monastery with ritual music playing in the background. People from all over the countryside came to watch this heat-producing feat; they left with their faith and devotion reinforced.

Kinsom had also dreamed of performing such esoteric feats, but Ani Choki put paid to any idea she may have had of doing so. Acquiring occult powers, said Ani Choki, was an obstacle to the realization of the ultimate goal: enlightenment. She told Kinsom of how Buddha had asked one priest to leave the monastery for having performed a miracle in public. The only worthwhile miracle was the transformation of the human heart. On another occasion, Buddha thought little of an exercise in levitation performed by a disciple; he lamented over the time wasted by another yogi who had misspent twenty years of his life learning to walk on water, when a boatman could have carried him across the river for a little money.

Her mentor told Kinsom that times had changed. For most nuns, such practices and philosophical studies were no longer a priority. What mattered was to ensure that day-to-day religious life carried on as usual: wearing the habit, holding religious processions at sacred places, observing rites and reciting prayers. To fight against oppression was the main goal. What better path to enlightenment could there be than to sacrifice one's life for one's people? Hoisting the Tibetan flag and shouting slogans were the new creed specially as they had the support of the majority. The Tibetan religious community has proved its resilience as well as its capacity to mould tradition to the needs of religious and political freedom. The figure of the Dalai Lama provides a powerful symbol, combining religious freedom and independence, like the two wings of a bird poised for flight.

VIII

A powerful beam of light invaded Kinsom's cell and aroused her from her dreams. "My time has come", she said with the resignation of one who had accepted her fate. As was their habit, the guards pulled her out roughly; two guards had to carry her on their shoulders to another section of the prison because she was so weak. The young nun, who was expecting a bullet in the neck any moment, thought that they were moving her closer to the morgue to spare themselves the effort of carrying her there. She knew just how practical the Chinese could be. And how money minded they were. She knew they would send her parents a bill, the normal practice in the event of a prisoner being executed. The price of bullets would be indicated with macabre precision on a dirty sheet of paper stamped with the prison seal. The price of the food and the cell rent would also be included. She knew that her family would not be able to pay and that her mortal remains would not be given to them.

That day Kinsom was proved wrong. They took her to a room where she found herself before the official who had conducted her interrogation.

"Have you thought about the questions we asked you?", he barked. Kinsom nodded and said, "Yes, and I have nothing to add. I acted alone on an impulse, after praying in the Jokhang Temple. I do not know any of the others who had gathered there to sing. There was no conspiracy."

"Why were you demonstrating?"

Long Live the Dalai Lama!

"Because you Chinese are destroying us," she replied, looking him in the face.

"Now I am done for," she thought to herself. The insolence of her reply and her arrogance would be yet another charge, yet another reason for further torture. Kinsom waited, though she expected at any moment to be knocked to the ground, kicked in the ribs, paralyzed with an electric prod, and finally released from the suffering of this world with a bullet in the back of her neck. But nothing happened. The official pulled out a sheet of paper from his briefcase: "For your counter-revolutionary and secessionist activities, the People's Tribunal..."

Kinsom came near the table and listened carefully. The official continued: "...You have been sentenced to three years imprisonment."

He had hardly finished saying this when the guards caught her by the arms, raised her to her feet and carried her through the interminable corridors of the Gutsa prison. Her initial reaction was one of relief: she been spared another beating, she was happy to be alive. But then the full import of her sentence hit her. The idea of spending another three years in this hell plunged her into deep despair. If one month of prison had done this to her, how could she bear three more years? Three years of living behind these wretched walls with the constant smell of blood, dampness and disinfectant; three years of being beaten, listening to the guards barking orders and swallowing foul soup. Three years seemed an eternity for a twenty year old with the temperament of a nomad who had been brought up in the open air of the steppes. What terrible sin had she committed against the millions of sons and daughters of the People's Republic of China? She had done no violence to anyone. For thirty seconds, just thirty seconds, she had shouted "Free Tibet". And for that they were punishing her for three cruel years? Monks usually got two years for demonstrating, why then were nuns being given

The Mountains of the Buddha

three? They had won equality in the eyes of their countrymen, but not in the eyes of the Chinese.

All Kinsom's carefully prepared defences crumbled. Thirty-six months in Gutsa was a fate worse than death. And then she did something she had vowed never to do before the Chinese: she broke down and cried. So loud were her sobs that they convulsed her body. Her legs could no longer bear the weight of her emaciated frame and she fainted. The guards had to drag her to block number three. They dropped her in a community cell like a piece of limp luggage. There she lay, exhausted by her tears, on the blood and urine stained floor, forced to live, wanting to forget and longing for death.

"I had never heard anybody cry like that," said Yandol, small, graceful and feminine. She was one of the inmates of the new cell. Fifteen years old, she had a round face and light honey-colorred eyes which gleamed with mischief. Kinsom's new cellmates gathered around her, consoling her and hugging her. But her sobs just would not stop. "Even today they wonder how I could have shed so many tears!", Kinsom would recall.

Yandol's head was still shaven. "She must be a nun," thought Kinsom to herself. As Yandol held Kinsom's head, she told her she was from the Shugsep convent. Kinsom tried hard to smile but the effort was too much for her and tears just kept flowing down her already wet cheeks. Her mouth was deformed and her vision so blurred that she could hardly see the other prisoners. Yandol told her the worst was over. "Do not lose heart," she said. "We will all leave the prison together." Gradually, as she lay falling asleep in Yandol's comforting arms, her spasms stopped, her breathing became more regular and her tears dried. "She was really in a terrible shape," said Yandol. "Her mouth was full of sores, her body covered all over with weals and scabs. Her arms and legs were like sticks, she had chilblains, her teeth were broken and she had wounds on her head."

Long Live the Dalai Lama!

The other women carried her to a filthy, rickety old bed — a luxury compared to the concrete slab of her solitary cell. Yandol then began to massage her with skillful, delicate hands, moving in a measured, unchanging rhythm. First she rubbed her ribs, then her back till she reached her shoulders. One of the women started humming an old lullaby, as old as Tibet itself; mothers must have sung it long before Buddhism when Tibet was still the land of a thousand gods. She sang in a low voice so as not to arouse the suspicion of the guards. Yandol kept massaging her hands, her arms, sliding her locked fingers around her neck to make the blood flow again. Then in a quick succession of deft strokes, Yandol's agile fingers brought life back to her feet, her heels, her soles, her head, her neck, her face, her nose, her back. After this Kinsom was made to do a series of exercises with her arms, a revitalizing ritual, bringing her sublime relief. Soon, that ugly, filthy cell became livable, filled with light and warmth. Kinsom closed her eyes and gave herself up to sleep, her mind going back to the high plateaus she had known. She could see vividly the tanned faces of her parents, brothers and sisters; she could smell the rancid butter of the female yak, the *dri*, sheepskin pelts, the warm yak dung fumes in the kitchen; she could feel the soft wool of the sheep, see carpets of sweet smelling flowers, idyllic spots in which resplendent skies shone, valleys blessed by the smiling sun. For the first time since she had entered Gutsa, Kinsom enjoyed the repose of deep sleep.

Yandol's story was very different from that of Kinsom. She was the daughter of a family of well-to-do traders from Tolung, a village near Lhasa. She had gone to school. There she had learnt Chinese, but nothing about her own culture and religion. She was very keen on entering a convent and her parents, a religious minded couple, approved of her plans. They were happy that their daughter would continue her studies and, at the same time, receive religious instruction, which most Tibetans consider to be the most worthwhile asset a person can acquire during one's life on earth. Their daughter was fortunate indeed. Once in the convent, Yandol soon stood out for her exceptional capacity to assimilate the complex teachings of Buddhism. She dreamed of leading the life of a true nun and being a political activist. She had romantic ideas about her role in the struggle against the invaders. In the autumn of 1991, she set forth alone to the capital to protest. She had given the matter much thought. It was not the number of demonstrators that mattered but the strength of her faith. She felt even a solitary act of protest would have symbolic value, create awareness and make people react. In the Jokhang square on October 1, the Chinese National Day, this pretty, shy girl clenched her fist and shouted, "Long live the Dalai Lama!" Her heroism got her two years in prison.

In Gutsa, she was forced to stand on one foot for a whole day. They hit her repeatedly to get her to tell them the name of the organizer. All they got was a peal of laughter in reply. They threatened her with an electric prod, but they did not use it. "In fact," recounts Yandol, "the Chinese official conducting the interrogation seemed to be a good man. He advised me in a low voice to speak as little as possible. He said that I would do well to stick to my original story. I did just that. So in comparison to the others they did not hit me too much. Though some of their blows were so hard they still buzz in my ears." Yandol was the exception. All the others had received the same treatment as Kinsom. Yandol knew this from the size of the scars and the condition of the prisoners, who seemed more dead than alive when they returned to the cell. She finally realized that she had escaped the worst of the torture not because of her tender years but because she had had the incredible good luck of getting a humane interrogator. In the jails of Tibet, age was not an extenuating factor. To chain the prisoners, rings were fixed on one wall of each cell; the lowest one, hardly a few feet above the ground, was meant for children. There was a thirteen year old girl chained in a corner of Yandol's cell. Unable to withstand the torture, she swallowed seven nails in an attempt at suicide.

The only thing that the prisoners could look forward to was the monthly visit from their near and dear ones, although they were allowed no more than ten minutes. At last, Kinsom was allowed to meet her parents, this time in flesh and blood rather than in her dreams. When she saw them standing in front of her, she had to use all her strength to contain her emotions. Her parents too had to struggle to hide their shock at the heartbreaking condition their daughter was in. It was only at this meeting that Kinsom learnt that they had come the previous month after a five day long journey only to be told by the officials that their daughter was incommunicado. Worse still, they were reprimanded for having allowed their daughter's mind to deviate.

Like everything in the prison, the rules and regulations were fixed according to the changing moods of the guards. Very often families like Kinsom's, after having travelled for days on end over mountains and through valleys to spend a few moments with their loved ones, were turned away, but not before the food parcels they had brought for them had been confiscated. It was also quite common for family members to be beaten up and thrown out at the door.

Even that day, Kinsom's parents were lectured by a Political Commissar, who insisted they persuade their daughter to reform. However, when they finally did see her, all they spoke of was her brothers and sisters, the flock, life in the mountains, the snow, the avalanches as well as of the arrests of other peasants' daughters after they had joined the monastery. Kinsom felt a tug at her heart to think that these childhood friends also had to suffer the same barbarism. She tried her best to look cheerful in front of her parents. She told them that now things were better, that she was being properly treated. She was going to work in the hothouse and they had nothing to worry about.

Her mother was, however, not deceived. She could scarcely recognize her daughter who had once been a picture of good health. There she stood before them: pale, gaunt, sunken cheeks, swollen gums and teeth broken by means the good woman chose not to reflect on. They had brought her the ten kilos of food permitted by the regulations. Like many of her companions in jail, Kinsom suffered constant stomach cramps brought on by unhygienic food. In spite of her initial resistance, she had little choice but to eat the foul soup in which insects floated. Now she held all the delights of Tibetan cuisine in front of her: there was a mound of *momos* and small cakes like *tigmos* and *petsels*. All the pleasures of life seemed wrapped up in that parcel of food. Then the time came to say good-bye. A clasp of hands, "we'll come back soon", the jangling of locks, turning back for one last look and their daughter was handcuffed and taken away. Once again the father would have to show his identity papers at the exit to shouting Chinese officials, once again they would walk through interminable corridors, and as they left the building, the mother would let a tear fall on the earth, like a brilliant frozen crystal. They knew instinctively what lay on the other side of the grill: shattered bodies and souls gone astray.

In the meanwhile, Kinsom had a violent scuffle with the guards who were trying to take away her precious food parcel from her. Clasping the precious parcel to her body, she returned to her cell and shared some of the joy it contained with her companions in distress.

Prison life had not changed from the days of the penitentiary of old. For Kinsom, Yandol and the others it was a daily source of humiliation and shame. The guards did not even allow them to empty every day the bucket which served as a collective toilet in their cell. They had to put up with the filth and stench of mornings without water. The only way they could preserve the last shreds of their dignity was to wash themselves with tea. They could not externalize their faith.

Long Live the Dalai Lama!

Just about anything was a pretext for arbitrary punishment. On nights when the guards had too much to drink, they mistreated the prisoners. Some of them, full of the kung fu movies they had seen, used the prisoners as punching bags. Others who took their inspiration from another kind of film, deflowered these "stubborn whores" with electric prods.

Gutsa is one of the cornerstones of the policy of social and cultural annihilation that is being pursued in Tibet. China, a civilization with a passion for refinement, has given much to the world: porcelain, matches, mechanical watches, paper money, gun powder, the tea ceremony, the aroma clock, the first catalogue of stars. But like the alternation of the Ying and the Yang, of light and darkness, the Chinese have used their talent to varying purposes: to raise harmony to an art of living and as much to perfect torture and genocide. In 1990, the humanitarian organization Asia Watch described Tibet as a huge laboratory used by the Chinese armed forces to test the techniques of torture. After forty years of colonization, Tibet, a country with more than two thousand years of history behind it, stands on the brink of annihilation. Behind the majestic mountains that isolate it from an indifferent world, the Land of Snows continues to be martyrized; its suffering is no less than that caused by Stalin's purges, Hitler's genocide of the European Jews or, the extermination of the Cambodian population by Pol Pot's Khmer Rouge. The holocaust in Tibet is an unequal combat between the brute force of those who wield political power and the peaceful protest of a profoundly religious people. Their determination to shake off the yoke of the oppressors through purely non-violent means is what makes their struggle unique in the world.

2
THE SOLITUDE OF THE MONARCH

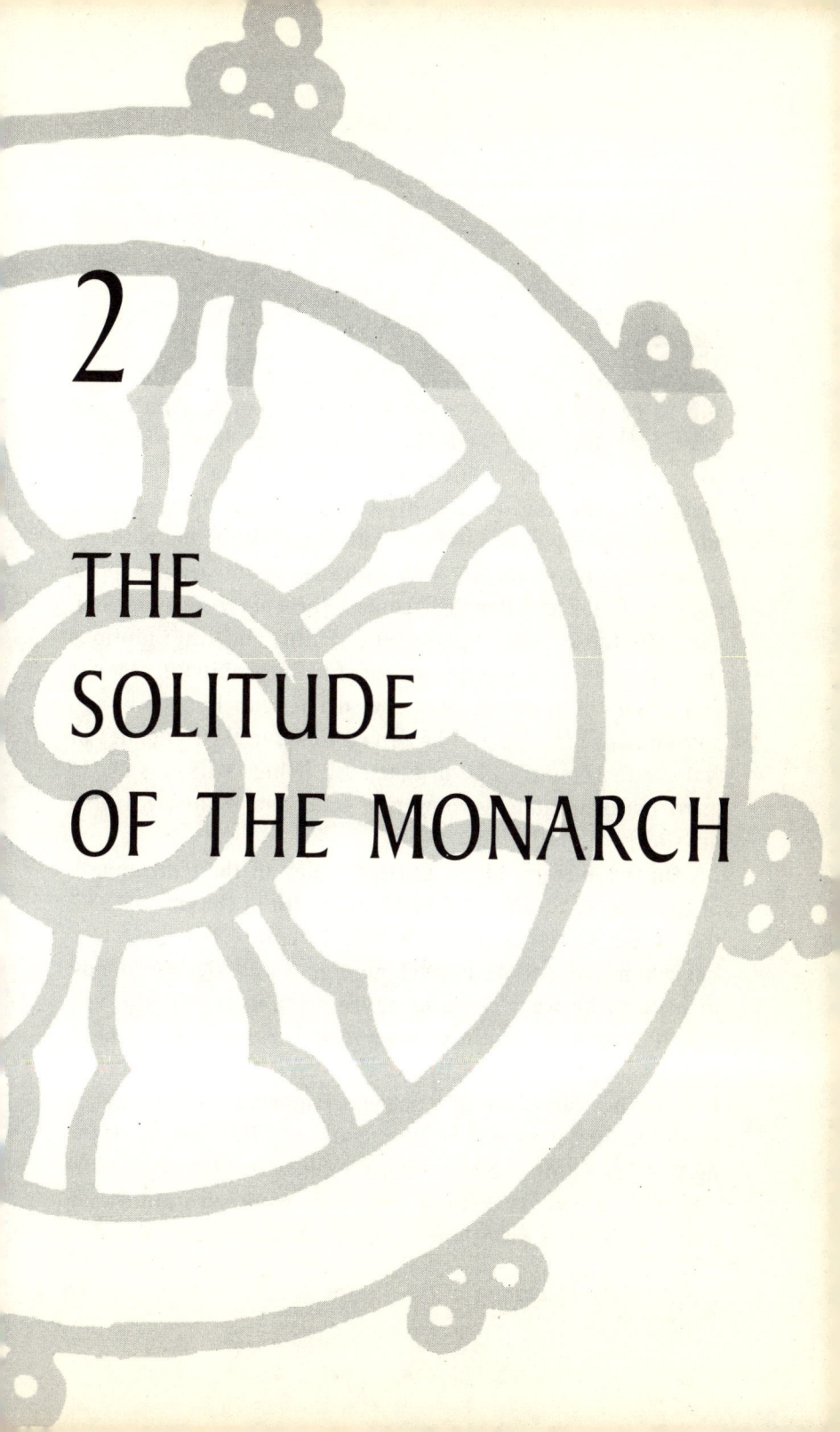

I

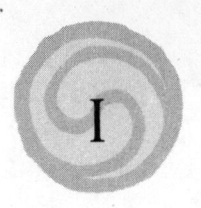

A prophecy had foretold the terror in the year 1933. In the seclusion of the Potala Palace, the thirteenth Dalai Lama, sensing his death was near, set out to write his political testament: "It may well happen that here, in the centre of Tibet, religion and secular administration will be attacked both from within and without. Unless we can guard our own country, it will soon happen that the Dalai and Panchen Lamas, the Father and the Son, and all those who uphold the Faith and the glorious reincarnations will disappear and fall into oblivion. Monks and their monasteries will be destroyed. Religious and government officials will be forced to serve their enemies or wander the country like beggars. All beings will be sunk in great hardship and overpowering fear, and nights will drag on slowly in suffering."

On the evening of the thirteenth day of the tenth month of the Year of the Water Bird, that is, 17th of December 1933, the thirteenth reincarnation breathed his last. For those who knew him well, he was an intelligent man, and loyal to friends. In history, he went down as a visionary monarch who was able to keep in check the expansionist designs of the Chinese, proclaiming for the first time the sovereignty of his country. Because he was aware of what was happening in the outside world, he understood that Tibet could not live forever in the peaceful isolation it had known for centuries. The reforms he initiated reflected a genuine desire for modernization. Harsh and humiliating punishments were abolished; for the first time, bank notes began to circulate in Tibet; a modest army was raised; a telegraph line was set up linking Lhasa to Gyantse; a small hydro-electric plant was built in the capital and an official from Sikkim was called upon to organize the first police force. Tibetan passports were restored and recognized internationally.

Even so, after his death, Tibet continued to live in seclusion, with little or no contact with the outside world other than occasional skirmishes with Mao's soldiers who were fleeing Nationalist troops. All over the country, however, monks in their temples were getting ready to undertake the meticulous search for the fourteenth incarnation of the Buddha of Infinite Compassion. They knew that for the past four hundred years, the Lord of Infinite Compassion, in a continuous cycle of death and rebirth, had always returned to watch over his people.

In the month of December of 1933, strange cloud formations — elephants and dragons pierced by rainbows — kept floating past the north-eastern side of the holy city of Lhasa. Another uncommon occurrence took place in the funeral chapel where the mortal remains of the deceased lay: overnight a giant fungus grew on a pillar made out of a dead tree trunk. What was stranger still, it grew on the north-eastern column of the shrine. According to custom, the body of the deceased had been seated in the lotus position in the burial vault of the Norbulingka Palace. Traditionally the face is turned southwards, as this is considered auspicious. But one morning, the monks discovered that the face had turned to the north-east!

In the interim, the National Assembly had appointed a Regent to govern till such time as the Lion Throne, the symbol of supreme spiritual and temporal power, was not returned to its rightful occupant. In keeping with his customary duties, the Regent issued instructions for the search to begin. Ceremonies and prayers all over the country were supposed

The Solitude of the Monarch

to ensure the speedy return of the Precious Protector. The chief oracles were consulted and their predictions recorded in the utmost secrecy. The Regent himself decided to undertake a journey in the company of some eminent Lamas to the sacred lake of Lhamo Latso, situated at a hundred and fifty kilometres south-east of Lhasa. Popular belief has it that in the waters of this lake visions of the future can be seen. Accordingly, the select group took up residence in a monastery near the lake in order to consult with the divine powers.

The Regent, after a few days of meditation while contemplating the blue waters of the lake, saw with great clarity three letters of the Tibetan alphabet: A, K and M. Some days later, he had a dream in which he saw a gold and jade monastery roof; houses in a little village at the end of a lost valley, a humble granary with a turquoise roof, gutters of an unusual shape and a white and brown dog frisking about on a verandah. But many elements were still missing. Back in Lhasa, the oracles were consulted and it was decided in the utmost secrecy to send out three search parties in different directions.

Ke-Tsang Rimpoche, a high dignitary from the Sera monastery, headed the small delegation travelling to the north-east. Their caravan had been on the road for two months when, at a distance, they saw the Kumbum monastery. The sacred lake had guided them well: this famous monastery had gold and jade roofs. The letter A, they thought, must refer to Amdo, the name of the region, and K to Kumbum. Just as this thought occurred to them, a majestic rainbow shone in all its splendour over the monastery to welcome them.

The emissaries proceeded with the greatest circumspection as they continued their search for further clues. After consultations, it emerged that the path to be followed was the one that lead to the village of Takster, near the Chinese border.

Monks from Kumbum guided the envoys who had disguised themselves as traders so that they could judge things for themselves. They walked across lush barley and rye fields amidst lofty hills covered with dark green grass. To the south of the Takster village rose an eternally snow capped mountain, considered sacred by the local people. They crossed juniper and poplar forests, walked through peach, plum and walnut groves, their eyes feasting on an infinite variety of berries and scented flowers. Crystal clear water gushed out of springs, cascading down the mountainsides; wild birds and animals — bucks, monkeys, the occasional leopard, bears and foxes — moved freely without the slightest fear of humans. In the midst of all this natural beauty, the Karma Rolpai Monastery stood out in the distance: the letters K and M referred perhaps to this monastery. Its golden roofs, its emblem — the wheel of religion flanked by copper stags on either side — gave the entire region an aura of sanctity; and the prayer flags fluttering from the village rooftops only heightened this perception.

The moment they entered the village the notables recognized the house with the turquoise roof. It faced the holy mountain and was made of stone and mud. There was a yard in the middle in which stood a tall flagpole at the top of which was a banner sending a thousand prayers to the skies. What distinguished it from the other houses were its gutters made of dry juniper branches. As soon as the members of the search party saw this, they knew that the Dalai Lama was not far off. Without revealing the purpose of their visit, they asked for shelter for the night. To avoid being detected, Ke-Tsang Rimpoche, who was in charge, pretended to be a servant while the other members acted as if they were in authority.

The father of the family was a small well-built man, dressed in a cape, a leather belt and high leather boots. He had a passion for horses and was delighted with the one he

The Solitude of the Monarch

had just bought. He had a way with horses; the local people said that he had the gift of being able to heal them. The mother, who had born sixteen children of which only seven survived, was kindness itself. She immediately offered them *tsampa* or barley flour, and salted tea with yak butter, the national drink of Tibet. While the family was talking to the visitors, the servants were told to make tea for themselves in the kitchen. Ke-Tsang Rimpoche now had an opportunity to look around. The house was no different from others in the region: a kitchen that served as a living room, a chapel where the family met at dawn to make offerings, the parents' and the guest's room, a well stocked larder and a byre for the cattle. It smelt of hay, fresh grass and animal sweat. For furniture, there were several brightly coloured cupboards made of the same wood as the floor of the house. The senior Lama tingled with emotion as he saw the white dog with brown spots. Then he stumbled on a little child of around two years old. Ke-Tsampe Rimpoche kneeled down and the child immediately tried to snatch the rosary the monk was wearing around his neck. Made of a hundred and eight wooden pearls, the rosary had belonged to the Great Thirteenth. "I'll give it to you, if you tell me who I am," the Lama said to him. Pat came the child's reply: "You ... Sera Monastery."

Who was this child who could guess so correctly? The old monk was deeply moved when he placed the rosary around the child's neck. This first contact proved to be interesting though it could by no means be considered conclusive. Without letting on a thing, the old Lama decided to return to Lhasa the very next day to inform the government of the result of his search. In the doorway, the child was waiting for the party. He asked them to take him along with them to the capital. It was no mean task convincing the child that the time was yet not ripe. His childish impatience could only be calmed by the promise of a speedy return.

The Mountains of the Buddha

A few months later the emissaries returned, this time in their official capacity. The old monk Ke-Tsang Rimpoche, wearing a golden hat and a purple tunic, was immediately recognized by the child's parents as the humble servant of last winter. As the impressive procession drew near, they understood that their offspring could be an incarnation of a Lama. In Tibet this was not unusual; Tibetans knew that the soul, like old clothes discarded for new ones, left the body when it died to enter another. They also knew that the most erudite of the great Lamas had the ability to choose the time of their death and the place of their rebirth. In the years that followed the death of a *tulku* or reincarnated master, his disciples would go out in search of his next incarnation. Had not their first born been recognized as the reincarnation of the Abbot of Kumbum? Perhaps history was repeating itself. The mother recalled that on the day before she gave birth to her son, she dreamed of blue dragons greeting. The neighbours felt honoured that such high reincarnations were born in their humble village. They had not forgotten that the Great Thirteenth, on his way back from a pilgrimage, had been compelled to spend the night in a nearby monastery. He had left behind a pair of worn out boots, a sure sign that he would return sooner or later. But neither the villagers nor the boy's parents suspected that this mischievous little boy who came from a family of humble peasants could be the fourteenth Dalai Lama. And the dignitaries took great care to hide it.

II

On this occasion, the sole purpose of the delegation that arrived at the doorstep of the modest Takster farmhouse was to meet the child alone and put him through further tests. The monks had come with two identical black rosaries, one of which belonged to the Great Thirteenth. Without a second's hesitation, the child picked up the right one and put it around his neck, not even bothering to look at the other. When questioned about his past life, the child's responses were quite convincing. He was shown several groups of similar objects some more beautiful than the others but had no difficulty in identifying those that belonged to the thirteenth Dalai Lama. However, when two walking sticks were placed in front of him, the child had some doubts. The monks held their breath in complete silence and remained outwardly impassive. First, the child picked up the wrong stick, the one with the iron knob. Then, after examining it for a long time, he put it aside and firmly grasped the other one as if he would not let it go. The dignitaries heaved a sigh of relief and Ke-Tsang Rimpoche immediately explained why the child had hesitated: though the thirteenth Dalai Lama had used the second stick till the end of his days, the first one had also belonged to him before he gave it to an old monk. Ke-Tsang Rimpoche had forgotten this but the child made him remember. With his heart in his mouth, the old man pointed to the *damaru* – small ritual drums with pellets. The child clutched onto the humblest looking one, the right one, and beat it the way it was supposed to be beaten during meditation. The men sitting around him did not dare utter a word. To conclude, the child was submitted to a physical examination to look for the distinctive attributes of an incarnation of the Buddha of Infinite Compassion: big ear lobes, slanting eyes, eyebrows curving up at their ends, streaks on the legs like those of a tiger skin and lines in the form of a conch shell on the palm of the hand. As the last doubts were cleared, one of the monks, looking at the Child God, the master he had lost and now rediscovered, began to weep with joy: "We were so moved that we could neither breathe nor keep still nor speak." Immediately, a messenger was dispatched to the capital to inform the Regent. And life went on as usual for this family of humble peasants who had to wait several months before receiving the official confirmation that their son was indeed the highest reincarnation.

The village of Takster was situated in the Amdo province. Though it formed a part of Tibet, it was under Chinese tutelage and the governor had clearly indicated his desire to play an active role in selecting high dignitaries. To protect the child from the Chinese, the Lamas asked the parents to take him as soon as possible to the Kumbum Monastery. At sunrise one morning, he was stirred out of bed and packed off on horseback to this huge monastery. Later, he recalled that he was seated on a throne the moment he arrived. The monks received this little peasant boy who had just turned three as if he were a prince, a great master. When his parents left, he cried, feeling alone and abandoned. This is how he began his difficult apprenticeship of solitude and discipline. Much later, he was to recall that this first separation from his parents was one of the saddest periods of his life.

After being apprised of the results of the search, the National Assembly met in Lhasa and confirmed that the Buddha of Infinite Compassion was indeed back among the

Tibetans. Preparations for the enthronement began. Messengers were sent to the British government in India, to Peking, to the King of Nepal and the Rajas of Sikkim and Bhutan to announce the good news and invite them to the ceremony. Simultaneously, the final arrangements for the journey of the new incarnation to Lhasa were being made.

The child's joy at leaving the monastery and travelling with his family was not shared by his parents. Without knowing what fate held in store for them, they had been compelled to leave behind all that they cherished: their village, their home, their lands, their animals, their friends. They knew that their son was a high reincarnation, but no one had told them that he was the Fourteenth Dalai Lama. At last, in the sixth month of the year of the earth hare, that is, the summer of 1939, the time had come for this ruddy, playful child who had just turned four to embark on the greatest journey of his life. He travelled in the company of about fifty people – his family, the members of the search party, officials, innumerable muleteers and guides, and three hundred mules and horses. The caravan advanced slowly through the most beautiful and wild landscapes in the world. They passed by Lake Kokonor, a sparkling mirror that reflected snow capped peaks. Like a column of insects, the caravan painfully crawled up mauve and orange peaks covered with snow. Often they would splash through frozen meltwater streams. Every few days, they would pass by tiny settlements, some nestling in lush green pastures, others holding fast onto a hillside as if secured by invisible hooks. From time to time, they could see from afar a monastery perched on top of a cliff. But for the most part, it was an arid, empty space with terrible dust-laden winds and wild hailstorms. For the young child travelling in a palanquin carried by a pair of mules, everything was fascinating: herds of yaks, packs of wild donkeys, turquoise lakes, emerald fields with deer and antelopes fleeting past wraithlike. And when he looked up, he saw flocks of cackling geese soaring towards the sky. The child could hardly believe his eyes: amidst shared laughter with his brother he was contemplating the infinite, not knowing that he was to be its lord and master.

They were a fortnight away from Lhasa when on an autumn day, a delegation of senior officials came to escort him to the capital. One of them welcomed the party in the traditional manner, offering them *katas* or silk scarves. Later, the venerable Ke-Tsang Rimpoche told the boy's parents that their son was the reincarnation of the Dalai Lama. Overwhelmed, the peasant couple stood dumbstruck, with a sense of disbelief that usually accompanies great news. Nothing had prepared them for the change that was about to come into their lives. Was this happy, playful boy quarreling with his brother till they almost fell out of their palanquin the Child King in person? At first, they felt a wave of great joy. Later, this joy was tinged with pride and reverential fear that would never leave them for the rest of their lives.

A little further on, another group of about a hundred men, headed by a minister of the Tibetan government, reached the caravan. The minister read out the joint proclamation of the Regent and the National Assembly in which it was declared officially that the child from Takster was the fourteenth Dalai Lama. Then, his mother, in accordance with the instructions she had received, removed his peasant's clothes and made him wear the monastic habit of yellow satin with gold brocade and placed on his head a pointed cap whose ear-flaps fell to his shoulders. Ceremonial advisors were pressed into service and the child gave his first audience, showering his first blessings with his small hand. He seemed calm, not finding it in the least strange that his parents, brothers and sisters now called him *Kundun* or 'the Presence'.

The journey continued in a golden palanquin, carried by sixteen noblemen, dressed in large green satin tunics and red velvet hats. The state astrologer, musicians, monks and

The Solitude of the Monarch

ministers headed the procession; behind followed the Regent, the prime minister and the family of the Dalai Lama, wide-eyed as they were yet to recover from their surprise, followed by a large number of abbots and officials. In every village or city the caravan stopped, it was received by processions of Lamas and monks, banners aloft in the heavily scented air. Thick, fragrant, protective fumes rose from braziers of jasmine and juniper wood placed at intervals of thirty metres. There were people who played flutes, drums and cymbals. Attired in their best, clergy and lay people alike joined their palms to welcome the child prodigy – their leader, their son, their father, their God. The little one looked on serenely, his eyes taking in everything. All these people were there for him. Flowers, incense, music, people with tears in their eyes trying to get a glimpse of him... how amazing all this was!

At a distance of three kilometres from the city gates, Abbots from the monasteries of Sera, Drepung and Ganden, the three pillars of Tibetan Buddhism, representatives of foreign countries and the elite in its full regalia were awaiting the procession in the center of a huge encampment where stood the carved wood throne meant for the new Dalai Lama. Two strong arms lifted the child draped in a cloak and placed him on the throne atop six feet high yellow cushions. From his lofty perch, smiling, the child from Takster watched the ceremony being performed by one of the state oracles to confer upon him the spiritual leadership of his people. After the soldiers of all the regiments of the Tibetan army had presented arms to the little God King, the interminable procession continued its march towards the holy city. A high official was pointing out the sites of Lhasa to the tired parents of the child. These were places every Tibetan had heard about. In the distance were the Chakpori hills with their famous medical schools. Then they passed by the Drepung Monastery, the largest in the world, a city in itself consisting of a whole host of stone buildings and hundreds of shrines whose golden pinnacles soared towards the sky. It was as if the ten thousand monks living there had bowed to the ground to pay homage to the sacred column. At the entrance of the city could be seen the British delegation building, hidden behind a grove of willow trees, and the gate of the holy city crowned by three *chortens* or white sanctuaries in which the ashes of the great Lamas were kept. When the child's mother looked up at the Potala Palace, her heart trembled. She knew that her son would have to spend most of his life here. In the dazzling light of the sun's rays reflected on the golden roof, monks were playing three-metre-wide oboes to herald the arrival of the procession. The whole of Lhasa was out on the streets; for men and women, young and old, the arrival of this majestic procession symbolized dynastic continuity, which alone could provide stability and preserve the Tibetan religion and way of life. Each and every Tibetan now felt that their future and happiness were secure and that is why they turned out in such large numbers. Boarding houses were packed and travellers slept in stables and verandahs. Nothing could hold back the popular outpouring of joy, not even the whips and the large sticks of the policemen who could barely conceal their nervousness.

"The day of joy has come," some people were shouting while the rest of the crowd pushed and shoved to catch a glimpse of the new reincarnation. The child King could not fail to hear the enthusiastic cries of his people. "I felt as if I was in a dream," the Dalai Lama was to say much later. "There was an unforgettable fragrance of wild flowers and the music of freedom and happiness in the air." Did he already know that between life and dreams there is but a thin veil, translucent and mobile? A veil that only poets, wise men and children can see through.

When they at last reached the Sanctum Sanctorum of Tibetan Buddhism, the Jokhang Temple, located in the heart of Lhasa, the child humbly bowed before the sacred images.

He surprised all those present with his poise and his patience. In spite of the solemnity of the occasion, the little monk exuded great charm and charisma. He endeared himself to all with his stoic acceptance of the elaborate ceremony. He did not flinch at the ordeal of having his hair shaved off in public or when they told him that henceforth his name would be Jetsun Jamphel Ngawang Lobsang Yeshi Tenzin Gyatso — Sacred Lord Glorious Gentle Eloquent Compassionate Defender of the Faith Ocean of Wisdom. The procession ended at the Norbulingka Palace, the summer residence of the Dalai Lama. There Tenzin Gyatso or Kundun, as this son of humble Takster peasants was now to be called, was installed in the magnificent apartments of his predecessor. "I had the strange feeling that I had at last come home," confessed the Dalai Lama much later.

III

His family was provided a new sixty room residence that looked onto a magnificent park; "splendid, impressive and majestic" were the words used by the eldest son of the family to describe it. The youngest son, however, after a few weeks of his arrival, spent his time in the apartments that had belonged to the Fifth Dalai Lama on the seventh floor of the Potala Palace. It seemed that these rooms had not been touched for centuries. The food placed next to an altar as an offering to the Buddhas was invariably devoured by rats. The child began to appreciate these creatures who gave him company during the solitary winter nights when it was so cold that his body became numb.

Nearly half a kilometre long, this three-storeyed building with a thousand rooms and halls, channels and corridors, steep staircases, and old chapels seemed more like a museum than the home of a child. In the rooms were preserved valuable rolls of parchment some of which, were more than a thousand years old. Entire chambers were filled with objects that had belonged to the first kings of Tibet: sumptuous gifts from Chinese and Mongolian emperors and treasures acquired by his predecessors. Also kept here was the antique armour that had not been used for centuries. The libraries contained the annals of Tibetan culture and religion, seven thousand thick volumes, some of which weighed as much as twenty kilogrammes. Many of them had been written on palm leaves imported from India. Two thousand volumes of Buddhist writings were illuminated with gold, silver, turquoise and coral ink, each line written in a different colour. In the basement were countless warehouses in which butter, tea and cloth were stored to be distributed by the government among the army, the monasteries and the officials. But it was the centre of the Palace that was the most impressive. There lay a row of tombs of all the Dalai Lamas who had come before the child from Takster.

It was in this imposing setting that young Tenzin Gyatso was brought up entirely in the company of monks. They called him the Precious Protector, the Wish Fulfilling Gem, or simply the Presence. Very few were allowed to speak to him directly. He met his family every four to six weeks and his father practically every morning because it was his habit to attend the tea ceremony. The Child God appeared in public only to preside over lengthy ceremonies of religion and state. Except for one occasion, when he almost fainted with anxiety because he had to intone a prayer before twenty thousand monks at the Jokhang Temple, the young Dalai Lama seemed at home in his role. "I enjoyed the show", he was to recount later.

At the age of six, his education became much stricter:

The Solitude of the Monarch

morning prayers, meditation, writing lessons, memorization, dialectics and meetings with the representatives of the government held in accordance with a rigid protocol. In the afternoons he had some free time. Of all the gifts he received, the ones that fired his imagination were a Meccano set given to him by the chief of the British commercial mission in Lhasa and a telescope. Whenever his preceptor would give him some spare time, the child would run to the flat-roofed terrace to gaze at things other than the skies. He had a magnificent view of the city: the Chakpori hills with its medical schools on one side and the residence of his family on the other. He watched his father's horses and his brothers and sisters playing in the garden. He missed them, especially his mother and sisters. He also remembered his friends and the animals along with all those who had made his days in the village so happy. It was not always easy to be the Presence. Perhaps on account of his previous lives he had understood, even at that young age, that the more powerful one was, the greater were the responsibilities. People looked to their leader for poise, gentleness and rectitude, and for this he needed to develop his inner strength. In Tibet, as elsewhere, mere scholarship was not enough to make a man wise. Accordingly, his teachers imparted not just book learning but also taught him how to develop discernment that comes with the intelligence of the heart. After each lesson, Tenzin Gyatso meditated over what he had learned during the day. It took him a long time to still his mind, for it would jump in all directions like a monkey in a cage. But gradually he learnt how to distance himself from his thoughts. Knowledge alone was not enough. True understanding came from being able to feel the reality of the world from within.

In his cloistered world, he turned to his telescope to satiate his unbounded curiosity. Standing on the flat-roofed terrace of the Potala, he would watch pilgrims prostrating themselves in front of the Jokhang. Through the window, he could make out the figure of a woman carrying her newly born. He also befriended the prisoners. At five o'clock in the evening, the prisoners from the small prison of Shol were allowed a little free time on the verandah. How astonished they were to learn the identity of this elfish silhouette that was pointing at them and greeting them every evening! From his gilded prison, Tenzin Gyatso must have felt a deep bond with these captives, whom he considered his friends. They in turn would prostrate themselves whenever they saw him on the terrace.

Each time there were parties in the city, the revelers would run and hide when they saw the Dalai Lama appear so as not sadden the heart of the Child God, who could never take part in such festivities. "When I was ten or eleven," the Dalai Lama recounted, "I would sit and read religious texts with my tutor in a small, dark room facing the north. Beneath us lay a road where children would return home herding animals and singing Tibetan opera songs. I wished I was with them. If I were there, I used to imagine, that would be something truly fantastic." But this was not for him. His exceptional destiny required solid preparation, a spartan education and solitude. Only through study and meditation could he achieve his goals in the long run; he had to learn how to control his thoughts, till he and his mind were one, far from the noise and distraction of the world. For this, he had to develop his innermost perception.

As winter drew to an end, the Dalai Lama left the Potala Palace for the Norbulingka in a procession marking the official start of summer. The Regent, cabinet ministers and Commander-in-Chief of the army, sword drawn in salute before the palanquin of the God King, made their way through an emotional crowd, held back by the long whips of the bodyguards. To the people's delight, the Child God's parrots and nightingales sang and squawked in their cages while his brilliantly caparisoned horses, decked in yellow saddles, bridles and bits of gold, pranced behind their grooms. Monks blew shrill, high-pitched horns and the regimental bands played the popular Irish song, "It's a Long Way to Tipperary" which was considered to be almost a Tibetan tune even though the words had been long forgotten. As the Tibetan language lacked military vocabulary, the army used martial terms and marches introduced by the British instructors who had been called in by the Great Thirteenth, fearing the threat of a Chinese invasion.

Founded in the eighteenth century by the Eighth Dalai Lama, the Norbulingka or Jewel Park had become a favourite picnic spot among city dwellers who often came to bathe and relax in its two-square-kilometre walled park, dotted with temples and palaces. In summer, the entire government shifted to the Norbulingka, enjoying the peace and tranquility of the Palace. Deer, peacocks and pheasants moved freely among the pavilions. Fishes in the ponds would swim to the surface whenever they sensed the presence of the Child God. Gardeners worked hard to maintain the flower beds and exotic plants. In the Jewel Park, the Dalai Lama spent the happiest moments of his childhood. Reading the copies of the National Geographic and Life magazine collected by his predecessor, he grew fascinated by modern inventions. He would spend his time first dismantling watches and film projectors and then putting them back together from memory. Later he tried his hand with both the Austin's and the orange Dodge, the only motorized vehicles in all of Lhasa. After the death of the Great Thirteenth, they were no longer seen on the roads. The young Dalai Lama repaired them with the help of the only two other people who knew how to drive in the city. When no one was looking, the Dalai Lama would hop onto one of the cars and drive off through poplar groves and gardens, occasionally hitting a tree or a railing, much to the consternation of his tutors and surprise of the servants. It was also at this time that his interest in history and the modern world was aroused

The Mountains of the Buddha

by what he had read in the magazines and he began to study these subjects on his own.

Then one day, an Austrian mountaineer by the name of Heinrich Harrer arrived in the city after his escape from a British internment camp in India. On their very first meeting, the Child God bombarded Harrer with all manners of questions. After years of solitary meditation and analysis, suddenly all his unanswered queries came pouring out. How does an engine work? What is a kangaroo? What is a nuclear bomb? It was Harrier who opened his eyes to the world. Curiously enough, no one in the Dalai Lama's immediate circle, neither monks nor lay people, had the faintest idea of what life beyond Tibet was like. There was no one who could read or write in English or in any other language of a country with a free press which allowed ideas, opinions and world events to circulate freely. Harrier worked on the English of the young monarch, whose knowledge of the language was confined to what he had been able to pick up from the National Geographic and Life; he taught him mathematics, geography and interesting things like the structure of the atom or why Vienna time was seven hours behind that of Lhasa. The young monarch instructed Harrer to set up a film projection room. From among all the films there was one that the Dalai Lama never tired of watching: the documentary on the life of Mahatma Gandhi. Acceding to the wishes of the child, Harrier screened it about a dozen times. The Austrian mountaineer was captivated by the personality of Tenzin Gyatso. "He was modest, he would look at everything with wonderment. Even a merchant's son would be far more spoilt than he", wrote Harrier in his memoirs.

But history abruptly cut short this friendship. On October 7, 1950, thirty thousand soldiers of the Chinese army, one of the largest and most powerful military machines in the world, launched a simultaneous attack from six different directions. Just two months earlier, an earthquake had devastated the entire south-eastern region of Tibet, changing the course of the Brahmaputra or the Tsang Po, flooding hundreds of villages and causing untold destruction and loss of life. The Tibetans, of course, reacted in their own inimitable fashion to this omen: they read the holy books in public, put up more prayer flags, doubled their offerings and burned mounds of incense. In the words of Heinrich Harrier, people were convinced that the power of religion alone was enough to protect them. In fact, life in Lhasa carried on as usual even after the news of the invasion. The inhabitants of the city were making the most of the last few days before winter set in; they would go down to the river and bathe in the shade of willows and poplars swaying gently in the warm breeze. Classical Tibetan operas were being staged all over the city. The parks were full of people singing, dancing and drinking. Immaculate lawns glittered with jewel-bedecked wives of ministers and aristocrats, dressed in colorful aprons. Waiters served endless rounds of *chang* – Tibetan beer – in engraved silver cups; women would hide their laughter, covering their lips painted with Elizabeth Arden lipstick just imported from Calcutta, and young aristocrats recited verses to applauding crowds. The magnitude of the disaster had still not sunk in: they were oblivious to the fact that nothing would ever be the same again. When he heard the news of the invasion, Harrier thought to himself that this time the Tibetans were going to need much more than prayers to save themselves.

IV

Young Tenzin Gyatso would be called upon to govern a country the size of Europe, yet his education had taught him little about the world save for a few rudiments he had acquired from Heinrich Harrier. Perhaps because he was aware of his ignorance, of all that he still had to learn, he was filled with a terrible sense of anguish when he heard from the sweeper monks at the Potala that overnight the walls of Lhasa had been plastered with posters demanding his immediate enthronement, which in the normal course of things was to have taken place after a few years. Spiritual leadership is conferred to the Dalai Lama at the age of four but temporal powers are only handed over when he attains majority. Through the sweepers, the Child God of Tibet was able to learn about what was happening in the streets. Popular songs were asking that he be enthroned. The fact that the people looked upon him as a saviour weighed him down. He was neither prepared nor old enough to face the challenge. But the Chinese communists were already there right in the heart of Tibet.

The roof of the world had everything the Chinese wanted: space, mineral riches and virgin forests. Last but not least, the strategic situation of Tibet. Tibet was considered to be of utmost importance. He who owns Tibet, owns the heart of Asia. As the words of the Great Thirteenth echoed in his mind, Tenzin Gyatso could not help but shudder. He sensed that this was going to be a tragic ordeal for his country; without arms and steeped in a pacifist faith as it was. Never before had he spent so many sleepless nights.

The Solitude of the Monarch

Given the trying circumstances, the tension was palpable as the State Oracle, the traditional adviser to the government, replied to questions put to him. In an urgently convened meeting at the Potala Palace, the sight of him entering into a trance was impressive indeed. His body shook and got contorted under the influence of the spirit. All of a sudden he jumped out of his ceremonial chair. He placed a *kata* or white silk scarf at the feet of the Dalai Lama and then uttered a sentence that was to change the course of the young monarch's life : "The time has come. He must rule." With these words the boy had become a man. The oracle had placed in the hands of Tenzin Gyatso the reigns of a country at war. The Child God was only fifteen years old.

The first news of Chinese activities in the occupied zone came from the Kumbum Monastery where he had spent eighteen months after being recognized as the reincarnation of the Supreme Protector. The emissary who came was none other than his brother, now an Abbot in the monastery. The Chinese had imposed harsh restrictions on the monks; his brother had been reduced to a virtual prisoner in his own monastery. The Chinese had tried their level best to indoctrinate him and attempted to buy him over. He was given permission to go to Lhasa with the sole purpose of convincing the Dalai Lama to submit before the Chinese authorities. In case the Dalai Lama refused, his brother had been instructed to murder him, for which he was promised a handsome reward.

Tenzin Gyatso was aghast. The little he knew about the Chinese and their communism had been gleaned from a copy of Life magazine. His brother's insistence that the only hope for Tibet was to launch, with foreign help, an armed struggle against the Chinese filled him with apprehension. Although the Buddha had forbidden all forms of violence, there were some circumstances in which it could be condoned. For his brother, this was one such circumstance. He had decided to break his vows and travel abroad to seek help. He begged the

The Mountains of the Buddha

Dalai Lama to do the same, but Tenzin Gyatso had other worries on his mind. There were only ten days left for his enthronement. To celebrate the event, he had wanted to fulfill an old dream: to grant general amnesty. The idea of empty prisons pleased him though it was with a heavy heart that he bid farewell to the inmates with whom he had shared a fragile friendship. When he went back to the terrace all he saw through his old telescope was some dogs sniffing about in search of scraps of food. A page had turned in his life.

The day began with a splendid feast in the presence of all the members of the Government and the few foreign representatives stationed in Lhasa, all glittering in their magnificent attire. The ceremonial proceedings seemed to last an eternity and Tenzin Gyatso had the greatest difficulty in refraining from asking for a chamber pot. Instead, he was handed the Golden Wheel, the symbol of temporal power. Trying times lay ahead of the young monarch who would have to do his utmost to save his country from disaster. In keeping with tradition, he appointed two Prime Ministers, one from the clergy, the other from the laity. Then he dispatched delegations to the United States, Great Britain and Nepal in the hope of winning their support. A delegation was also sent to China in an attempt to negotiate a withdrawal. Unfortunately, all his efforts drew a blank: it seemed as if the doors were closing on Tibet and there was no hope left. The world did not want to hear anything about this country that had lived withdrawn in its shell for thousands of years. As the Chinese reinforced their positions in the East, the government feared for the life of the monarch. Whatever be the fate of the roof of the world, its most precious asset, its guide and protector could not be allowed to fall in the hands of the enemy. In the utmost secrecy Tenzin Gyatso's flight to southern Tibet was planned. From there he could take refuge in India, should the situation warrant it. That was what the Oracle had said.

The Solitude of the Monarch

V

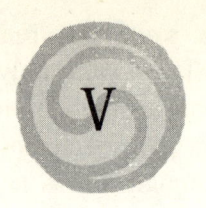

On the night of the 18th December, 1950, the high dignitaries who met in the Potala drank a last cup of tea in silence. Then they refilled their cups and put them down untouched — a symbolic gesture indicating their desire to return soon. The caravan left the Palace in the dead of night under a starry sky of the kind that can only be seen on the roof of the world. The day before, a convoy had been sent ahead, carrying more than fifty cases of gold and silver deposited in the Potala vaults. The Dalai Lama felt both excitement and sorrow, excited at the thought of the journey, sad that he had to leave his people. He traveled incognito, disguised as a lay person, for the government feared that if the people recognized him, they would stop him from fleeing. Abandoned to their fate, the people of Lhasa sank into despair and fear as the capital was thick with all kinds of rumours. "Communists eat human flesh." "They have three hands and funny mouths." "Men and women, they are all the same."

In the meanwhile, the grave teenager, wearing a cassock and fur cap that almost covered his eyes, continued his journey, mounted on a gray horse. From time to time, he would get off his horse and stop to speak with his people. Never had Tenzin Gyatso been closer to them than in those ten days. He saw how concerned they were about him. He wanted to be worthy of their trust. And he was discovering his country like the travellers of yore who had ventured into Tibet. Before him stretched out vast, open spaces with clumps of vegetation, fantastic rock formations, awesome peaks, the horizon hidden by a blinding light and stillness broken only by the sound of the wind. This land of gods and titans, occupying a plateau the size of Western Europe, seemed to belong to another planet. At an altitude of about four thousand metres above sea level, the air is so thin that its density is one third of the normal density of the earth; three-fourths of the world's humidity is trapped in the territories that lie at the base of the high plateau mountain ledges. The seven million inhabitants of Tibet were descendants of nomadic tribes related to the Mongols. Legend had it that this land had been the Tethys Sea. When the sea dried up, a monkey and a witch made their abode there. The monkey was a manifestation of Chenresi, the Buddha of Infinite Compassion. From his union with the witch were born six sons, the first Tibetans. They grew and multiplied, fought and appointed kings and generals. But the Tibetans had to wait for the reign of the thirty-third monarch, Songtsen Gampo, to unite and form an empire that would be the largest in Asia. Paradoxically, Trisong Detsen, the thirty-seventh monarch, who extended the empire to its furthermost limits, was also the man who sowed the seeds of its decline. Though the royal family had always been favourably disposed towards Buddhism, a foreign religion, the new king imposed with a vengeance its creed of non-violence on his people who in the past had practiced a form of indigenous shamanism called Bon. The Tibetans pursued peace with the same zeal as they had shown for the martial arts. This change of heart was brought about by Buddhism which teaches that suffering is an inseparable part of life; only when we understand the illusory nature of existence can we free ourselves from the ceaseless cycle of pain and attain Buddhahood. Mahayana Buddhism, which was adopted in Tibet, emphasized that attaining enlightenment was a collective task: not just the individual but all sentient beings had to be relieved of their suffering. Compassion, non-attachment and

The Solitude of the Monarch

wisdom became the characteristic of the Tibetan soul. Hunting, fishing, even killing an insect became a matter of thought. Prayer wheels moved to the hum of mantras and rows of little sacred flags fluttered in the sky. The mantra *Om mani padme hum* was engraved on thousands of stone piles and spire-shaped sanctuaries. The entire countryside seemed like a live network of shrines, connected to each other by never ending streams of pilgrims.

While the Dalai Lama was travelling on one of innumerable mountain paths to the Indian border, an incident occurred that almost put an end to his journey. A group of monks on a pilgrimage recognized him and begged him to return. "It was an extremely tense moment," the Dalai Lama was to recount. "Many monks had tears in their eyes that spoke of their anguish and despair. They could not bear the thought of my leaving them." The monarch's preceptor had to throw himself down on the track, pleading to let them continue. The monks finally agreed but not before extracting a promise from the Dalai Lama to return soon.

In the blinding light of the high mountains, the young monarch continued his journey. Nature seemed to be reminding him that like the seasons, all things must come and go: joy and suffering, war and peace.

News was still awaited from the delegation sent to Peking, headed by Ngabo Ngawang, Governor of the Chamdo region. The Dalai Lama had hoped that his envoy would be able to make the Chinese authorities understand that the Tibetans did not want "liberation" but good relations with their neighbour. Above all he wished to avoid the loss of life that would be the inevitable outcome of any takeover of Lhasa by the People's Liberation Army. He had not expected a miracle; yet nothing had prepared him for the news he heard on Radio Peking on the night of the 23rd of May, 1951. Sitting in a room of a monastery near the Indian border, the Dalai Lama heard the flat voice of the news reader. The Government of the People's Republic of China and the "local government of Tibet", the voice blandly announced, had just signed a seventeen point agreement for the "liberation" of Tibet. Tenzin Gyatso was dismayed. Against its will, the Tibetan delegation had been forced into signing an agreement, converting the Land of Snows into a de facto Chinese territory.

A little while later, a telegram from the head of the delegation to Peking confirmed the news; at the same time came the announcement that the new Governor of Tibet, General Chiang Chin-Wu, was on his way to meet the Dalai Lama. Given the gravity of the situation, several people including the Dalai Lama's brother advised him to seek refuge in India. In a letter from Calcutta, his brother wrote: "The United States are ready to help us. If they are fighting communism in Korea, they will do likewise in Tibet." But then he also received messages from both his Prime Ministers, begging him to return to the capital as soon as possible. His people needed him.

It was a difficult dilemma for a teenager. Exile and help from the United States meant war. His entire non-violent upbringing revolted against such a course of action. Convinced that hope lay in dialogue with the enemy, he decided to go back to Lhasa, reunite with his people and wait for the Chinese delegation to come.

On July 16, 1951, a messenger brought news to the monastery of the imminent arrival of the Chinese. What would a communist leader be like, wondered the monarch. He came out onto the balcony with his telescope to see what was happening. Clouds of mist were rising from the far end of the valley. Soon he saw three men wearing dull gray uniforms in sharp contrast to the resplendent red and gold silk habits of the Tibetan dignitaries. The meeting took place in an atmosphere of cold civility. "The general was friendly, not very protocol bound," recalls the Dalai Lama. "He gave me a letter from Mao Tse-tung which began with the first

The Solitude of the Monarch

sentence of the 'agreement', welcoming me to the motherland. How I came to hate those words! While he was handing over the letter to me, I could not but help noticing the gold watch on his wrist. Later he asked me whether I intended to return to Lhasa. I told him that I would be coming back very soon. I was convinced that he would have liked us to travel together to make political capital of our joint return to Lhasa. I somehow managed to wriggle out of it, returning to Lhasa two days ahead of him."

On his return to the capital, the whole of Lhasa was out on the streets. But the joy of seeing the Precious Protector was mixed with the fear of what lay ahead. Three weeks later a contingent of three thousand soldiers of the People's Liberation Army arrived. Dumbstruck, thousands of Tibetans thronged the streets of the holy city to see these bedraggled men go by, waving red flags and portraits of their god Chairman Mao. Women had tears in their eyes. Men clapped their hands, as is customary in Tibet, to keep the demons at bay; some children even dared to throw stones. The slow, insistent thud of war drums woke the young monarch much before the soldiers reached the capital. From a terrace of the Potala, through his telescope, he followed the progress of the interminable column, enveloped in a cloud of dust. He felt very uneasy at the sight of the red flags. Was not red the colour nature used to express danger? Looking at them from close quarters, he realized that the soldiers were emaciated. They seemed overcome by fatigue, wounds and altitude sickness; he even felt sorry for his enemies. He was also struck by their military step and fixed, vacant stare. It was an unstoppable machine. The words of his predecessor kept ringing in his ears. With a heavy heart and telescope under his arm, he turned back to enter the Palace.

In the following weeks, another twenty thousand men arrived in Lhasa, empty handed. They grabbed everything they could lay their hands on, shattering the fragile economy of the Land of Snows. For the first time in the history of Lhasa, people suffered from starvation. Hostility against the Chinese grew. Even the monks would put their hands in the pleats of their habits as if they were going to hit out at the soldiers if they tried to come too close. Soon, songs poking fun at General Chiang and his golden watch could be heard all over the city. And when people found out that many of his officers wore costly fur linings under their uniforms, the Chinese appeared all the more ludicrous. It was at that time that a popular resistance movement sprung up, demanding the complete withdrawal of troops from both the Tibetan Government and the Chinese military authorities. The walls of Lhasa were plastered with posters asking the invaders to leave. The ineffectual Tibetan Government was inundated with a flood of complaints both from the people and the Chinese, furious at the reception they had got in the occupied capital. Gradually the tenor of the protests became more strident. The Chinese generals accused the Tibetan Government of supporting the rebels. Relations between General Chiang and the Dalai Lama's Prime Ministers became increasingly tense. Joint meetings would often end in acrimony, with the participants pounding their fists on the table and hurling insults at each other. The time for cold civility and diplomacy was over.

Things had come to such a point that Tenzin Gyatso actually thought of removing both his Prime Ministers whose lives were in danger. Continuing to oppose and anger the Chinese authorities would serve no purpose other than to nurture the vicious cycle of revolt and repression. This could only lead to violence. And violence, the young monarch reasoned, was senseless. It was not realistic to think that they could throw out the Chinese by force. If there was a show of force, the Chinese would win hands down and the victims would be the people, unarmed and disorganized as they were. Non-violence was the only

The Solitude of the Monarch

way of gaining a certain degree of freedom. But it was a long drawn out process that required patience. It meant passive resistance and non-cooperation.

With a heavy heart, he had to drop his loyal and honourable ministers though they fully understood his reasons for doing so. As they said their parting farewells, the God King placed the traditional silk scarves around their necks and all three of them had tears in their eyes. Tenzin Gyatso did not appoint any new Prime Minister: what was the point of offering fresh scapegoats to the Chinese who would simply direct all their wrath against them? Henceforth, the leader of the Tibetans had to confront the generals on a daily basis. The monarch, not even seventeen years old, was left alone to face the conquerors of his invaded kingdom.

Overburdened by his role and by a feeling of deep solitude, Ocean of Wisdom had only his smile as a weapon to fight the Chinese officials. He would smile -yet he would not give in. His aim was to avert a bloodbath. The officials who had thought the teenager would be easy to manipulate, were utterly irritated. But it was a role that was becoming increasingly difficult by the day. The economy had completely collapsed: nomads were prohibited from moving about, their trade was monopolized and they were forced to grow crops completely ill-suited to the high altitudes. More and more army barracks were being erected in the Land of Snows, while people were starving. But so far the blood-bath had been averted.

VI

In Shigatse, the second largest city of Tibet, the Chinese were preparing to reinstate the Panchen Lama, the second spiritual authority of the country, on his ancestral seat. He had been raised under the eye of the Chinese in a monastery near the border. On his way to Shigatse, he stopped in Lhasa, just in time to meet the God King at a brief official meeting. Both came from the same region, both had been recognized as high incarnations since early childhood. But history, once again, would split them apart. The Chinese did not let them exchange confidences, let alone pray together. On seeing him go, Tenzin Gyatso knew the Chinese would do their utmost to turn his spiritual son into his enemy. He could be the perfect instrument to counter the Dalai Lama, an acceptable alternative, a puppet in their hands. Unaware of the fact that Panchen Lamas had never held political power in Tibet, two years later, Mao orchestrated the triumphal return of the child from Shigatse, followed by an impressive retinue with all the trappings of power aimed at competing with the Dalai Lama's. But he soon fell from grace, because, in spite of everything, he remained faithful to his people. The tragedy of his life would become one of the most vivid symbols of the Tibetan drama.

The dismissal of the two Prime Ministers helped to ease somewhat the atmosphere in the Potala. On their part, the Chinese promised to grant religious freedom, build new hospitals, schools and roads. The propaganda however remained as sarcastic as ever. Wanting to help modernize Tibet was all very well but asking the people 'to unite to expel imperialist forces' was ridiculous, as only six Westerners were living in Tibet before the invasion, and they in any case had already left. The Dalai Lama's brother described the Chinese promises as 'honey on a knife: if you suck it, you will cut your tongue.'

Towards the end of 1953, Peking came to the conclusion that its attempts to set up a phony government to control the country and silence foreign critics had proved to be a fiasco. The Communist Party decided to abandon the seventeen point agreement, favouring instead direct intervention in all Tibetan affairs. The Dalai Lama was invited to the Chinese capital, where Chairman Mao intended to impose his decision on the young leader. Tenzin Gyatso accepted the invitation, despite strong domestic opposition: fears were expressed that he would never be allowed to return or he would fall victim to an attempt on his life. But Tenzin Gyatso did not want to lose this opportunity to try and convince the highest authorities of the invading power to soften their stand.

On the morning of July 11, 1954, tens of thousands congregated on the banks of the river to bid him a safe journey and a happy return. Bands were playing and banners fluttering in the wind while clouds of incense billowed on either side of the river. The God King walked down a white carpet till the river bank and boarded a yak skin boat. Once seated, his face protected from the sun by a yellow silk parasol held by a monk, he turned back to wave to his people. He saw that many were weeping. Others threatened to throw themselves into the river, convinced that they would never see him again. Tenzin Gyatso felt the same sorrow he had experienced four years earlier when he had embarked on his journey to a monastery on the border; sorrow because he was not able to do more to alleviate the suffering of his people.

He got into the orange Dodge that had been ferried across, followed by an impressive procession. His first stop was at Ganden Monastery. Forty kilometres away from the capital, this was the most beautiful of all monasteries in Tibet. Against the backdrop of snow-clad peaks stood resplendent golden roofed temples and elegant buildings with purple coloured walls. Ganden, which means 'paradise of happiness', was the third largest monastic university in Tibet. Its three thousand three hundred monks were responsible for preserving the literary and artistic heritage of the country, compiling the vast corpus of medical knowledge of their forefathers and perfecting the techniques of the plastic arts and architecture. It was here that Tibetan culture had flourished, in the cloisters of Ganden and other large monasteries, which at a certain point of history had housed one-fourth of Tibet's male population. Children entered at the age of seven but only the most gifted were allowed to carry on with higher studies, enabling some of them to become masters and Lamas. The others became builders, artists, artisans, cooks and servants while a group of monks were trained for administrative tasks. All of them strove to attain enlightenment by practicing rigorous mental discipline based on daily ritual, contemplation and meditation. Divine will regulated their lives, interpreted for them by the Lamas, monks who had attained the high position of master after twenty to twenty-five years of intense study and meditation. Ganden belonged to the Gelugpa tradition; members of this school to which the Dalai Lama belonged wore yellow caps. Students were made to memorize and debate for twenty years before being allowed to take the final 'doctor in divinity' examination. Their effort was surpassed only by that of the hermits who spent an entire lifetime in the isolation of a mountain hut or cave. Tended by a few disciples, they practiced physical and mental austerity of an extreme kind. But it was the four thousand *tulkus*, incarnate Lamas capable of deciding the time and place of their rebirth, who were the pre-eminent religious practitioners. Recognized in infancy by their followers, they were returned to their monasteries to once again take up the great Buddhist work of leading all beings to awakening. At the top of the spiritual hierarchy were the high emanations of the Buddha, among whom foremost was the figure of the Dalai Lama, the living incarnation of Chenresi, patron saint of Tibet and the holiest presence in the land.

Accompanied by grave Abbots who moved in a slow, deliberate way, Tenzin Gyatso went to pray before the tomb of Tsongkhapa, the founder of the Gelugpa School, located in a brown temple in the centre of Ganden. He noticed the statue of a buffalo's head, one of the protector divinities of Tibet. When he had first seen it, it was looking down with a rather subdued stare. "I was unprepared for the curious phenomenon that I witnessed," the Dalai Lama recounted later. "Before leaving Ganden, much to my surprise, I saw that the head of the buffalo had moved. It was now facing the east with a ferocious expression. Later, I heard that at the time of my escape into exile, the walls of one chapel at Ganden ran with blood." As they bid him farewell, the worried Abbots warned him that the Chinese would try and brainwash him. "They will never be able to do so," replied the Dalai Lama. "Can anyone snatch a man's memory from him?"

As there were few motorable roads in Tibet, the impressive Dodge had to be abandoned after a few kilometeres. The procession continued on mules. During the never ending journey, the words of the abbots kept coming back to the Dalai Lama. He could understand their anxiety but he had confidence in himself. Nobody could destroy what he had inherited from his past lives: a respect for wisdom and an understanding that happiness cannot not be imposed from outside by any regime no matter how powerful. And is not happiness the goal of every human being even of the Chinese?

3
DAYS OF MOON AND WIND

I

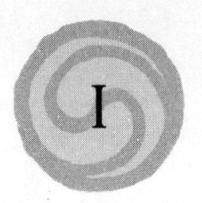

For the women inmates of the Gutsa prison, meeting the Dalai Lama had become more than a dream; it was now the cornerstone of their existence, the purpose that allowed them to bear their humiliation and suffering. Twenty-five months in prison had made them realize that living in Tibet after their release would be impossible. As it is, Tibetans were treated as second-class citizens in their own country; they would be complete outcasts. Life would be a prison without bars: village committees and Political Commissars would keep a close watch on them; they would not be allowed to practice their religion, learn from Lamas or progress on the path of inner realization. This was a jail from which there was no escape. The thought of suicide did cross their mind from time to time, as it seemed the easiest way out. But they always found the strength to overcome their despair and reject it.

They had to proceed step by step. First, they had to serve what remained of their sentences and leave Gutsa, only then could they think of escaping Tibet, which had become more than just an earthly prison. The only escape route possible was southwards, a path to intimidate even the bravest. But flee they had to, on foot, come what may. They had to keep moving on, moving on... This was a recurrent dream in the gloomy obscurity of their cells. Walking is a symbol of freedom and just the thought of it was bracing. From times immemorial Tibetans have traveled on foot, no bag or baggage to weigh them down, no attachment, no hatred, just a calm acceptance of their lot. Under the open skies, they have followed the pilgrim's trail across snowy peaks, secure in the knowledge that they had several lives ahead of them. For centuries, Tibetans have been visiting holy places – for them a pilgrimage is a metaphor, a wordily replica of the only worthwhile journey, the journey within. As the pilgrim moves towards the last horizon, he cannot see his ultimate destination though it is there in his innermost being. Many undertake the journey prostrating themselves, marking the spot on the ground that their heads touch, rising and then prostrating themselves again, thus, covering thousands of kilometres over a period of three, four or five years.

The rebels of Lhasa, the nuns imprisoned for having dared to shout "Free Tibet", would escape to tell the world of their plight and that of their capital city where even the slightest attempt at protest was brutally repressed. They would denounce the schools where Tibetan children could not learn Tibetan; they would speak of the new scourge of alcoholism and of the prostitution into which Tibetan women had been forced in order to survive. They would let the world know about the forced sterilizations and the struggle of a people who had become a minority in their own land.

In 1993, for six million Tibetans there were seven and a half million Chinese, a demographic onslaught that proved to be disastrous for Tibet. On the orders of the Communist Party, a massive influx of Chinese kept pouring into the land of snows. To lure them over to this 'frozen wasteland inhabited by savages', they were offered substantial incentives: three to four times their salary in China, interest free loans, accommodation, vacations, even a 'breathing subsidy' to compensate for Tibet's four-thousand-metre-high altitude. Entire forests were cut down to build houses for the Chinese. Five to six storey residential complexes with electricity and running water sprang up in all the cities, disfiguring the landscape. As for the Tibetans, they only got electricity if they lived near the Chinese quarters and that too for just three to

Days of Moon and Wind

four hours. The rest of the Tibetans had to do without light. Traditional Tibetan trades — restaurants, tailoring shops, building and carpentry — were taken over by the immigrants. The number of beggars swelled. But what was even worse was that some Tibetans began to doubt their own culture to the point of being ashamed of it.

A policy of systematic genocide was pursued. The inhuman birth control measures spared no one. In 1989, a report of the Shanghai Academy of Social Sciences[1] recommended the setting up a of special police force to carry out abortions on women belonging to national minorities with a population of more than five hundred thousand. Health teams travelled extensively across the country to ensure that the orders were carried out. Members of these teams received economic incentives to perform as many sterilizations and abortions as possible. There were horrific eyewitness accounts of truckloads of women including girls of thirteen and fourteen being forcibly taken away to clinics. In remote areas where there were no hospitals, groups of Chinese doctors and nurses went in jeeps, followed by a small truck carrying the equipment. They travelled for three to four months, going from village to village, in search of women carrying a third or fourth child, sometimes even a second one. On each trip, they 'attended to' two thousand cases. Reports of forced abortions on women in an advanced stage of pregnancy were confirmed with the discovery of three, four and five month old foetuses in the Chamdo Hospital garbage dump. The Chinese did not stop at that: babies born to two children families were killed. The mother would give birth to the child, hear it cry and rest for a while. When she woke up, she was told that her offspring had died in childbirth. A Tibetan doctor confirmed that well formed healthy babies were drowned in buckets of water just after birth. "The mothers went out of their minds," she said.

---

[1] As reported in "Tibet: Survival In Question", by Pierre Antoine Donnet (Zed Books, 1994)

The Mountains of the Buddha

When questioned by a human rights committee, a Chinese doctor admitted that he had been compelled to kill newly borns to fulfil his abortion quota. Failure to comply would have meant losing out on the economic incentives and demotion. Buddhism proscribes the taking of life in any form. For Tibetans, who are intensely devout Buddhists, these birth control measures were shattering.

Behind those walls that seemed to have absorbed all the world's suffering, Kinsom, Yandol and their friends dreamed of being able to speak out against the prison, the torture, the inhumanity. Escape had become a necessity. As her thirty-six month sentence came to an end, Kinsom realized that there was no point in trying to stay in Tibet. It was clear that she could not return to her convent or seek admission in any other. She would never be allowed to study or participate in the struggle for the survival of her people. She had no other choice but to leave, on foot, without papers. There was no question of the Chinese issuing her a passport; they knew she would denounce the atrocities of which she had been a victim and witness. However, she had got to hear of underground networks. She would have to find the right contact and the money to travel down to the Indian or Nepali border, braving mountain trails at altitudes which were, at times, higher than five thousand metres. Young Yandol – baby-face woman with the typical sallow Tibetan skin – shared this dream of freedom. She had visions of herself in Dharamsala, living in a Tibetan convent, meditating and educating herself to return one day to an independent Tibet. It was a wild dream, and in her moments of lucidity she was aware of this, but she needed it as much as she needed to breathe in order to survive in Gutsa.

Both Kinsom and Yandol were transferred to block No. 4 meant for political prisoners, who were for the most part clerics. This came as a relief to them because for a moment they had feared being sent to the common prisoner cells. But the Chinese were afraid that the secular prisoners might catch

Days of Moon and Wind

the 'reactionary fever'. They were put in a cell with seven other young nuns including Dawa[2] whose tragic story was well known both in the prison and resistance circles. Arrested in 1989, she was brutally tortured while in police custody. A policemen had cut off her left breast and the tendons of her big toe with a shaving knife. Put in solitary confinement, she received no treatment whatsoever. She lost a great deal of blood and her wounds got infected. When they put in her the same cell as Kinsom and Yandol, she stayed silent, her hands on her breasts, like a hounded animal, scared that one of the prisoners may be a spy. Kinsom gradually gained her trust, offering her food and covering her with whatever was available each time she shivered. Young Yandol managed to clean the wounds by pouring lukewarm tea on them, thereby detaching the cloth from her skin.

The first year, the prisoners had absolutely nothing to do except to wait for the monthly family visit. Any kind of physical, cultural or recreational activity was prohibited. They could not even speak in Tibetan or if they did, it was in hushed tones with one eye on the cell door. If anyone was caught in the act of meditation, their feet would be tied and they would beaten to pulp. Hours, days, weeks, months passed by in the same monotonous way. It was like a frozen film in which all you heard was Radio China, the coarse laughter of the guards, coughing, slamming doors and creaking hinges.

But they had friendship. The incarcerated women who had been complete strangers to begin with were now good friends. Members of the same family, they looked after each other. When they felt cold, they would huddle together to warm themselves. When they felt hungry, they would share the food their families had brought them. When they felt despair, they would turn to their faith. And when they felt afraid, they would dream of freedom. So strong was their bond that what happened to one was experienced by the others. At the time

---

[2] The story of Dawa is reported in "Les rebelles de l'Himalaya", by Philippe Broussard (Denoel, 1996).

of leaving, while her friends rejoiced, the one being released would cry. She cried because she was going alone towards an uncertain freedom, away from the warm haven that their filthy cell had become. Neither Kinsom nor Yandol had ever experienced anything like this before. They were united by the solidarity that comes from having to share the daily pain and suffering of prison life. The hardships of life had taught them detachment; yet their resolve to continue the struggle and their veneration for their troubled country and its supreme symbol, the Dalai Lama, remained unshaken.

II

Travellers down the ages venturing into the Land of Snows were often surprised by the courage and freedom of the Tibetan women. There is a Chinese legend which speaks of the existence of a land beyond the mountains governed by women, corresponding to modern day Tibet. There, men were servants and soldiers, never rulers. Power was in the hands of women, who also performed ritual sacrifice. Marco Polo and other travellers have described, in great detail, the delightfully savage customs of these women. They often had two or three husbands. The men, much to the astonishment of the Westerners, were not jealous to discover a stranger in their wife's bed. Such legends are based on ethnological evidence: even today many Tibetans practice polyandry, given the scarcity of women in remote areas. But it was not just the libertine propensities of Tibetan women

Days of Moon and Wind

that were discussed; they were described as women of character, far more independent than other Asian women. They were the brains of the household, and men the brawn. Their courage knew no bounds. For the French traveller Alexandra David Neel who traveled across Tibet in the early twentieth century, the serene courage of these women was amazing: "Few European or American women would have dared to live in the midst of a plateau, in small groups of four or five, sometimes even alone," she wrote. "Few would dare to undertake journeys lasting several months at different times of the year to lonely places in the high mountains where only bandits and savage animals prowled." These traits survived the Chinese invasion. The occupiers had come up against a people whose character had been forged by centuries of struggle for survival in a harsh natural environment that seemed to belong to another world. Because of the role women played in the home and upbringing of their children, they were closer to tradition than their menfolk. As such, young Tibetan women felt a greater sense of responsibility when it came to defending what remained of their old culture. Many felt the best way to do so was to combine their religious vows with political activism: nuns were better placed for political action than civilians because civilians had families to look after.

The only area in which women were not considered as equals was, surprisingly, religion. Nuns, less numerous than monks, had always played a marginal role, one that was never fully appreciated. In comparison to the monasteries, convents were poor, insignificant institutions, unable to maintain the same educational standards. Even the poorest families had to pay for the upkeep of their daughters who had entered the convent. When they did not have the means, nuns were forced to beg or enter the service of rich families in the city. There was a popular song that went: "If you want a teacher, make your son a monk. If you want a servant, make your daughter a nun."

Young Tibetan women became nuns for several reasons, some because it was a calling, others because their parents wanted them to do so or simply because they wanted to escape the hardship of everyday life. There were those who entered a convent to be with friends, others still who thought it represented social mobility. Wearing the habit of the Buddha often conferred a certain status, though real respect came from the dedication and sincerity with which they fulfilled their vows. For the nuns who lived isolated in the labyrinth of the convent's passageways and rooms, it was the means to gain access to the collective heritage of their country and the roots of their spirituality. Moreover, many young women saw in the religious way of life the path to self-awakening and an education in keeping with tradition.

Tibetan history has been marked by the teachings of many great masters. Few women, however, have been recognized for their erudition, though there are some *yoginis* whose lives continue to inspire nuns today. Biographical accounts speak of the liberation of a saintly woman to whom magical powers and miracles were ascribed. Every Tibetan has heard the stories of these *yoginis*, in which legend and historical fact are so closely interwoven that sifting one from the other is difficult. As in the case of a nun who meditated in a cave and never washed her habit. When she died, her disciples burnt her clothes and with a mixture of the ashes and sand made pills that were said to cure common ailments. And then there is the story of a pious woman living alone in a hut who could tell a person's past and future with great accuracy. Others lived for more than a hundred years, practicing *chulen*, that is taking herbs and small stones in place of normal food. Biographical literature also describes nuns whose bodies vanished at the moment of death and others whose bodies stayed for days on end after they had breathed their last. In Tibetan Buddhism, spiritual realization often occurs when a person is dying. The state of mind at that time can decide the

Days of Moon and Wind

quality of rebirth, for death is a mirror that reflects the meaning of life. As one dies, the power to meditate reaches unparalleled heights. A good Buddhist always hopes to die before his master so that he can be guided in his last moments through *bardo*, the interval between agony and death. It is then that a new form of life takes shape in the eternal cycle of birth and rebirth from which freedom can attained only through enlightenment. *Bardo* is a mirror where all comes back; so say the masters, to live well is to learn to die well to return and live better. In Tibetan tradition, the master's birthday is never celebrated, the moment of his death or enlightenment is. At the time of cremation of great adepts, supernatural signs are known to occur: appearance of a rainbow, showers of flower petals, emanation of sound, light and shimmering particles from the mortal remains of saints. When the pious nun Jetsunla was dying, those by her side recounted that the air filled with perfume and the sound of tinkling cymbals. While she was being cremated, rainbows covered the sky. There were others whose bodies gave out sweet odours. These pious women have been venerated by Tibetans down the ages.

If women have carved a niche for themselves in Tibetan Buddhism, it is thanks to the merit of these *yoginis*. In the land of snows, as elsewhere, men had arrogated the right to occupy all public and ecclesiastical offices, leaving no room for women. It was far easier for a monk to secure education, economic support and a high post than a nun. Furthermore, the final say in the running of a convent often lay with the head of a nearby monastery. But as the latter would rarely bestir himself, it was the nuns who were effectively in charge.

Recent events have overturned the secular hierarchies of the past. Today even novices, half women half girls, have emerged from the shadows to spearhead the resistance movement, demanding freedom and demonstrating on the streets of Lhasa. Now their countrymen looked on them with a new found respect. That women, traditionally relegated to the background, should put themselves in the first line of fire shows the despair of the people but also shows the womens' capacity to resist and the intensity of their faith. Within a few years, women gained the respect and recognition they had been denied for centuries. Of the hundred and twenty-six demonstrations in Lhasa between 1988 and 1994, fifty-five were organized by nuns. Theirs was a generation of rebels, ready to sacrifice their youth, for whom political activism went hand hand in hand with the search for enlightenment. They were convinced that sacrificing their lives for the cause would lead to a better rebirth, carrying them forward on their journey to Nirvana.

This explains the strength of their resolve. Buddhists believe that until the soul attains Nirvana, there can be no escape from the cycle of birth and death, this ocean of suffering called *samsara*, a flux in which matter is being constantly created and destroyed. This is a painful state, since men and women can be reborn at lower levels of existence, as animals for example. Given however that rebirth is determined by one's *karma* (sum total of good and bad deeds accumulated over various lives) and the degree of purity of the mind at the time of death, reincarnation, in a certain sense, is a choice. It is the power to control future birth, acquired by meritorious beings such as the Buddha, the Prince who lived like a pauper. When one has attained some degree of perfection, what the Buddhists call the 'subtle consciousness', the human spirit does not die in the usual sense of the term; it becomes worthy of being reborn in another body. The Buddhists believe the primordial pure state of consciousness to be a force that cannot be matched, the creative principle of existence and, in the ultimate analysis, the spirit of all that exists. This subtle consciousness resides in every individual and remains there until enlightenment. It is called 'the being' and assumes different forms of existence: animal, human and, eventually, Buddhahood. This constitutes the basis of the theory of rebirth. The subtle mind, having adopted various forms over the centuries, always tends towards enlightenment and Nirvana, a state of infinite rest, so vast that thinking of it or converting it into an object of desire makes one move away from it. Only when such perfection is attained is the self forgotten. The being is at one with the world and there is no thought, no doubt, no distance. On attaining a high level of spiritual realization, the mind can choose its next form, rebirth as a human, and hope to reach awakening. This was the reincarnation to which aspired the imprisoned nuns, convinced that deep within them lay something indestructible and unchanging that could never die. It was on this line dividing the ephemeral from the eternal that resided their secret, their strength, their willingness to sacrifice their all for the cause.

III

After fifteen months, the authorities decided that a stiffer dose of re-education was called for. Punishment was not enough: the deviant mindset of the prisoners had to be corrected through labour and indoctrination. One morning Kinsom, Yandol, Dawa and four other inmates were taken to the interrogation room. Going back there sent shivers down Kinsom's spine even as she admonished herself for feeling afraid. She thought she had become wiser, but the feeling of terror that overcame her made her realize what a long way she had to go before she could fully control her emotions. She prayed to the Goddess Tara, the epitome of wisdom emanating from the tears of the Buddha of Compassion, the Eternal Protector of Tibet. It was Tara who offered protection against fear and attachment, who helped to move away from *samsara* — the cycle of earthly life, primary emotions and the ocean of suffering.

As soon as the interrogation began, the nuns understood that this time they were not going to be subjected to electric shocks or the airplane. A Chinese official informed them that henceforth they would be considered as "students". They had been promised education for work by the Chinese. And the Chinese always kept their word. They would get better food provided they fulfilled their stiff production quota. Productivity, the Chinese said, had to be rewarded. Since there was no choice, the nuns merely lowered their heads in submission.

Little Yandol was sent to the kitchens. She had to leave her cell early in the morning and spend three hours among huge kettles, pots and pans, where on a slow fire she prepared black tea or cooked vegetable soup. When she thought no one was looking, she would add a little more oil or vegetables to the stew until one day they saw her doing so. After that, she became more careful but whenever she could she would throw that extra spoonful of oil into the brew. She had access to the food store and would often pinch a bit of flour or rice. She was finally caught red-handed and locked up in the deep freeze where the provisions were stored. Big hunks of meat on hooks stared at her from all sides. At first, she thought she had been relieved of her duties in the kitchen. But after a while, she began to get scared — perhaps they had forgotten all about her. Barely seventeen years old, she felt she would turn into one of those inert pieces of meat, convinced that they had left her to her fate to die of cold and starvation. She started pounding on the door. When she got no reply, she was filled with a terrifying sense of anguish. Her claustrophobia made her want to scream but her voice refused to come out. She was trembling all over when the door opened abruptly and a guard took her out. That one hour in the cold storage had seemed like an eternity. After her ordeal, she was pleasantly surprised to find that they were no other chores, no beating, no solitary confinement awaiting her. Alas, her joy was short lived! They had thought up a far more subtle form of punishment. They forced her to slaughter pigs and ducks along with the Muslim prisoners. Now a Buddhist, especially a cleric, is forbidden by religion to end any form of life. Poor Yandol shed tears of pain and anger, pain for the animals, anger because she had been forced to break her vows. Determined to get her own back, she continued to pinch food and pour a little extra oil in the soup despite the risk she ran. This was her way of helping the prisoners, religious and others, to bear the cross of Gutsa. The prisoners, often in a serious condition on account of the cold, lack of hygiene and wounds inflicted by torture, were denied even basic medical care. Most guards, immune to the wailing and groaning of the sick prisoners, called them a pack of liars. The fever, the backaches and the diarrhoea however were excruciatingly real.

The young nuns understood each other well and did all they could to help each other. Kinsom had been assigned to the greenhouse, which was a far heavier duty than helping in the kitchen. As soon as she returned to the cell, she told her companions of what she had seen: truck loads of new prisoners, mainly monks and nuns, a sign that the repression on the streets was growing. Dawa, the nun with the mutilated breast, was made to clean the toilets of the officials. She used the opportunity to meet other prisoners to get the latest on the political situation, the Dalai Lama and the resistance movement. Possibly as a reaction to her horrifying ordeal, Dawa convinced herself that freedom for

Tibet was near at hand. Even though her cellmates viewed her optimism with skepticism, her words did put heart in the younger inmates.

Every morning Kinsom had to collect excrement in a bag, mix it with peat and then spread the mixture on the ground. In China, human excrement was commonly used as fertilizer. And the Chinese were certainly not going to make any exception for the Tibetans. Once she had spread the mixture on the ground, she was sent to the greenhouse where the detainees grew vegetables both for the prison kitchens and the local market. A production target was fixed for each prisoner; any failure to comply meant being severely reprimanded during the political re-education sessions or, if the Chinese felt it necessary, punishment. In the course of these infamous sessions conducted in the evenings, students were expected to comment verbally and in writing on what they had learned in the morning. It was solitary confinement for those who did not answer convincingly or were simply lazy. The instructors, cadres of the Chinese Communist Party, had been sent to Tibet with the express purpose of defaming the previous regime: "We keep inviting the Dalai Lama to Lhasa and he keeps refusing," was an oft-repeated lie. "Before the Chinese came to Tibet, they used to cut off the hands and feet of prisoners. Now all that is over," the instructors would paradoxically tell an audience whose bodies bore the scars of their torture. Though Kinsom and her friends assumed a look of rapt attention, they were impervious to such indoctrination. Life in prison had taught them to be tough, and the more lies they heard the greater was their strength to resist.

Days of Moon and Wind

IV

And so the weeks and months of their prison term dragged on like a smoldering ember. One by one, Kinsom saw her friends leave. Dawa, the young mutilated nun, was the first to go. In spite of all that she had been through, she hoped to return to her convent. This was the only way she could survive, for she had no money, not even enough to go back home to her parents, living far away in the Tibetan highlands. "I will wait for you and we will all go together to see His Holiness," she told them as she left the cell. Like the others, Dawa too had cherished the dream of flight, a dream she clung to on the day of her release, as she hobbled to the door, bent, ashen-skinned and marked for life. At twenty-five, she looked like an old woman, carrying all the woes of the world on her shoulders. But she persisted in her optimism, an optimism bordering on the irrational.

Next it was Yandol's turn to leave. Kinsom was desolate. Yandol was like a sister to her, together they had experienced two years of hope and suffering. Tears welled from her eyes. When they met for the first time, she had been crying. Now as she was saying goodbye, she was crying again. How much had happened since that first meeting! She clasped her friend's face and hugged her tightly. "We shall meet up soon," said Yandol. As the door closed, Kinsom felt a great void. The next few days were hard, for wherever she looked she saw Yandol. She missed her as intensely, like a ghost limb. To forget her sadness, she took refuge in meditation, her eyes half-closed, a hum on her lips. There, in the innermost recesses of her being, she found the same strength and clarity that had enabled her to survive imprisonment. What also helped her was that it would soon be her turn to be free.

The worst, it seemed, was over when suddenly one day all the inmates in Kinsom's cell were taken to the hospital, a filthy, run down shed with antiquated equipment. Thirty prisoners were locked up in a room crammed with chairs and coal stoves. The guards were excessively polite, offering them cups of a sweet tasting drink. Kinsom could not understand this sudden change of attitude. She soon found out. The heat of the stoves and the drink had her sweating profusely, as blood rushed to her face. The others were in the same state. After an hour, a group of Chinese doctors came in, sat down, opened their briefcases and pulled out huge syringes, jabbing them in the arms of the prisoners to collect several bottles of blood. The women realized that they had been offered the drink to increase their blood supply. In view of the poor condition they were in, some of them fainted, their bodies swollen. Kinsom almost lost consciousness on her way back to the cell. She was so weak that for one whole day she was unable to move from her rickety old bed. When she tried to stand up, her legs gave way. Her face was deathly pale and the prisoners said she looked like a ghost.

A macabre farewell present indeed! Soon after, they told her that her sentence had been reduced by three months and that she would be leaving prison by the end of June. She wondered why: did they think her re-education was complete or was it because they needed the space for new prisoners? The truth was that a group of foreign observers was coming to visit Gutsa and the Chinese wanted to get rid of all those who were likely to talk too much or had visible signs of torture. Kinsom was no more than a shadow of her former self. Her instructor told her in a soft, paternalistic voice: "We are letting you leave before your time as an act of goodwill. You should be grateful."

Days of Moon and Wind

She was released on the 22nd of June, 1993. While she was filling out her discharge forms, they handed her a bill: she owed them one thousand nine hundred and eighty yuan at the rate of two yuan a day towards boarding. She said she did not have the money and was told by the authorities to borrow it from a friend. They threatened to retain her unless she paid the required amount. Kinsom then remembered that they had given her a receipt for the six hundred yuan she had on her on the day she entered prison. "You can keep that money," she told them, promising to pay the balance from whatever she got by way of begging on the streets of Lhasa. At last she was released, but not without a final word of warning: she must never speak to anyone about the following subjects: prison food, the forcible extraction of blood, the beating and torture. "If we find you taking part in any other demonstration," they threatened her while returning her personal belongings, "we will kill you." With those words of parting she heard the clanging of the prison's iron gates being pushed open.

Free at last! Kinsom took a deep breath of the dry, spring air. She found herself standing in front of Gutsa, holding a miserable little bag, penniless. But she was happy. After her terrible ordeal, she had been given a new lease of life. All those with the good fortune of leaving Gutsa alive still had to bear the marks of their stay in prison: some could not see properly due to repeated slapping, others suffered from partial deafness, limped, or remained in a state of chronic debility. Kinsom had developed urinary incontinence and was drained of all her strength after the forcible extraction of blood. But she had won. The Chinese had not succeeded in breaking her spirit. She had survived the cold, the beatings, the reeducation sessions, and the theft of her own blood! Never had she felt more Tibetan and more Buddhist in her life than when she left the prison.

Where was she to go? India was obviously the ultimate destination, the dream that she had nurtured over all these months. But she had to think things over calmly, savour her new-found freedom and get used to it like one rediscovering pleasures long forgotten. She decided to return to the convent from which she had been separated on that fateful day three years ago when all she had gone out to do was shop. She knew that they were not likely to readmit her, but she would still try. Once again, she would wear her habit, shave her head and live as before.

A truck dropped her in the hustle and bustle of Lhasa. Kinsom felt like a stranger in an unknown city. The heart of town had become unrecognizable. In 1990, three thousand single storied houses were razed to the ground[3]. The traditional quarters around the Jokhang Temple were now construction sites on which concrete buildings and commercial centres were coming up. The deafening noise of power shovels and drills could be heard over the chaotic traffic in which the new red taxis stood out prominently. Ancient monuments and sacred shrines fell victim to 'plans for urban development'. The narrow streets in which the 1989 demonstrators had taken refuge were widened into broad thoroughfares so that the riot control police could move in rapidly. Behind a semblance of modernity, Lhasa was becoming like any other Chinese city. Though tourists could still be seen, shepherded by a Chinese guide, this did not mean that there had been any real opening to the outside world. The tourists could only see what the Chinese wanted them to; many left with the idea that the political system did grant religious freedom and that Tibetans were an exotic minority of charming visionaries. If only they could see Gutsa, thought Kinsom, as she bumped into a group.

---

[3] Source: "Les rebelles de l'Himalaya", by P. Broussard (Denoel, 1996).

Days of Moon and Wind

V

The young nun realized just how weak she was, as she climbed up the last kilometres to the convent. Her legs had turned to jelly and she became breathless after every few steps. She, who had been able to carry a bag full of stones on her back, was now finding it hard to bear the weight of her own body. But the idea that she was returning home to her sisters kept her going.

She had to stop every now and then. Sitting on a rock, she contemplated the sunset in the distance. The mountain peaks, resting on a bed of fluffy clouds, gave out orange glints. Closer by, the waters of a mountain stream flowed like a flash of mercury. Apricot trees were in bloom, the scent of aromatic herbs filled the air and the singing of birds added music to this magnificent spring spectacle. Drunk with so much space and beauty, Kinsom continued her ascent slowly, conserving her energy, soaking in all that she saw around her. Gradually, the shadow of the mountains, like a dark blanket, covered the whole valley. Kinsom hurried along before the cold became unbearable.

As the flat roofs of the convent came in sight, her face lit up. This was her home, the fruit of her labour, the centre of her world. At that instant, her fatigue vanished. The trill of the birds and the sweet aroma of the junipers had a restful effect, and she felt she had reached the core of the universe. She was at one with her surroundings, a part of the primordial force of creation. Yes, it was possible to walk away from the battlefield of human existence and conquer the fear of death and suffering. She had never been more certain than in that moment of bliss, eternal and fleeting, as her mind and body merged with nature. It was not her tired heart that was pounding but that of the universe. What is religion if not to perceive the infinite in every moment? If only time would stand still! For she had experienced a moment of purity and felt exaltation of the kind she had never known before. It was as if the long night of Gutsa had never existed, as if the horror, the pain and the suffering of her country were a distant and confused memory, as if this path were heaven itself.

Night had fallen by the time Kinsom reached the convent. She knocked at the door. The cry of a bat was all she got as an answer. She kept knocking until she heard the sound of footsteps and heavy breathing. A novice opened the door. She looked fearfully at the emaciated face, the beggar's rags and the dishevelled hair of the stranger before her. Kinsom identified herself. But the novice was still nervous.

"You can't stay here," she told her. "It's too dangerous, we are being watched constantly."

Both knew that the Chinese kept those with criminal records away from the religious communities to avoid 'contamination'.

"I have nowhere to go," said Kinsom in a voice that was barely audible.

The novice stayed at the doorstep, looking at her.

"All right, come in."

The convent was a mere shadow of what it had been: a lifeless building in which footsteps echoed disturbingly. The construction work had been abandoned and a part of the roof had collapsed. The nuns lived in three crowded rooms. Kinsom learnt that after the Nobel Prize celebrations, the condition of monasteries and convents had worsened. A group of ten Chinese officials had stayed in their convent for five months. They had taken over, making life so difficult that many returned to their villages. Others had been expelled. The

Days of Moon and Wind

Chinese could reappear at any time and inspect whatever they felt like. All the novices' activities were monitored down to the minutest detail. Of the original two hundred nuns, only twenty remained.

Kinsom asked about Ani Choki, her teacher. They had not seen her since the day of her detention, but they knew that she had been interned in a labour camp near Lhasa and that after her release she had stayed on in the city, living underground. She had not returned to the convent even once. Kinsom realized how unthinking she had been in coming back. Her teacher had not returned for fear of endangering the lives of those who remained. She had acted wisely. Kinsom, on the other hand, had behaved selfishly. Her attachment to her memories had been much greater than her consideration for others. She now repented her decision.

However, Kinsom stayed on for a few days, the time needed to recover her strength. Every time she heard a noise, she would jump, thinking it might be the Chinese. Despite the fear, those few days in the convent had the sweet gentleness of a homecoming for the former prisoner, even though she knew she would soon have to leave, this time for ever. She decided not to shave her head or put on her habit. She could not stay on in Tibet, her only escape lay in fleeing to India. She would have to lie low, disguise herself as boy, as she was doing now. She decided to visit her parents one last time before undertaking the great journey. She needed to rest and she wanted badly to see them again. Had it not been for their visits, food parcels and constant presents, she may not have survived Gutsa.

The first sight she had of her village were the prayer flags blowing in the wind. Then, on a slope of a mountain lay a few houses and some tents, surrounded by grazing fields and a cedar forest. At first, her brothers and sisters failed to recognize the thin creature that Kinsom had become. But her mother let out a jubilant shout, which had relatives and neighbours all

The Mountains of the Buddha

come out to receive the prodigal daughter, the girl who had shouted slogans on behalf of them all. There was a tremendous surge of joy and solidarity in the house of these semi-nomadic peasants. Their daughter had come back, ill-treated and scarred all over, but alive. Kinsom hugged them all. Then she went to the altar and lit a small *dri* (female yak) butter lamp that she placed next to a small statue of the Buddha.

Though village life seemed the same on the surface, Kinsom soon sensed that something in the atmosphere had changed. The peasants and shepherds were restive because they had to give a part of their produce to the Chinese authorities. They had to feed the growing number of officials sent to keep a watch over the nomads. The local authorities had levied taxes on every domestic animal, a burden which proved to be ruinous for the nomadic economy. The poorest were forced into begging food from their neighbours. There was a climate of suspicion: you no longer knew whom you could trust. The Chinese, in their anxiety to keep the population on the right track, had informers everywhere.

Kinsom got to learn of the arrest of a childhood friend, who like her had become a nun. The girl's parents came to see Kinsom. They wanted to get an idea of what life was like in the Chizom labour camp, where their daughter was serving her sentence. They would be going to visit her as soon as the authorities allowed them: what would be the most useful things to take for her? Kinsom did not tell them anything about the beatings, abuse and torture. Instead, she tried to reassure them. She gave her own example: she was standing before them, hale and hearty. "Chizom is not nearly as harsh as Gutsa," she added, offering them a cup of boiling tea. The girl's parents left comforted, but Kinsom felt drained: who knows what would happen to the daughter of these poor shepherds. Their visit made her realize just how deep her wounds had gone. The reminder of what she had been through brought on an almost physical pain. Could life ever be the same again, she asked herself, or would the scars never heal? She came to realize that she would never be able to share the pain of Gutsa with anyone but those who had undergone the same suffering. Such memories could never be shared. They were a part of one's *karma* and were best left in the innermost depths of the mind.

VI

Rinsom spent the summer of 1993 with her family, reliving the pleasures of adolescence – evenings spent around a bonfire, meals in the countryside and long days herding the animals. But the thought that she had to flee was always at the back of her mind. Everything was pointing in that direction: her not being able to go back to the convent, the growing control of the Chinese over the nomads and the imprisonment of the shepherds' daughter. Across the border in Dharamsala, she would be able to continue her studies, read ancient texts and help refugees. Her life would have a purpose and she would be free to give her account of the horror of living in an occupied land. But she had to decide quickly. Winter was approaching: it was either now or next spring.

She would have liked to meet up with Yandol, her friend from Gutsa, but she did not know where to start looking. First she would have to reach Lhasa and get hold of an experienced guide, someone willing to lead fugitives like her across the mountains to Nepal. A friend of hers, in whom she had confided, told her that it would be difficult to find a decent guide though she had heard about a convent in the capital which helped those who wanted to flee by putting them in touch with trustworthy guides. The real problem was raising the money, two thousand Yuan, the equivalent of several months' salary of a government employee. Kinsom had no choice but to turn to her family for help. A delicate task indeed, as she did not want to divulge her plans to her parents. She knew that if anything went wrong, her parents would have to bear the consequences. Moreover, her father was sure to oppose her decision. This time she was staking everything she had. There was no return possible in the journey she wanted to undertake. It would be the greatest adventure of her life and she had to make her arrangements in secret.

Kinsom did not need to explain to her relatives about what she was doing. They knew that because of the social stigma attached to her, she would never be able to lead a normal life. So when word went round that she needed money, all of them — uncles, distant relatives, parents of friends in prison — rallied to the cause and gave her whatever small amounts they could. Solidarity in the highest mountains of the world is as natural as the instinct to survive. Kinsom was certain that her mother had a large part to play in mobilising the funds. But Kinsom asked no questions and the good peasant woman never once let on that she knew what her daughter was up to. Her father remained in the dark. Those who were secretly helping Kinsom out felt it was better that way.

One morning in October, Kinsom informed her parents that she was going to Lhasa the next day and would be back soon. Choked with emotion, she could barely utter a word. On the night before her departure, she was assailed by all kinds of doubts: "What if I get caught?" If that happened, the Chinese would not spare her family. "What right do I have to put their lives in danger," she asked herself. "Is my decision in keeping with the precepts of *dharma*?" For a moment she toyed with the idea of staying back in her parents' home, but that would be a dead-end. It made no sense remaining a shepherd and letting life go by when she could be doing something to help others and improve her *karma*. She had to go out and take risks. She had to face the challenge, only then could she emerge victorious. Once her mind was made, she decided she must leave as unobtrusively as possible so as to spare herself the tears of parting. However, her mother, faithful as ever to custom, insisted on accompanying her up to the pathway. Mother and daughter walked down in silence. The daughter looked at her mother and saw in her eyes trust, worry, anguish and hope. However, her mother, faithful as ever to custom, insisted on accompanying her up to the pathway. They exchanged a silent hug. The only sound was the fluttering of prayer flags in the wind.

As soon as she reached Lhasa, Kinsom headed for the convent near the Jokhang Temple, a haven of peace in the chaotic city centre. Her friend had assured her that this convent would put her in touch with a reliable guide, not someone who would run at the slighest danger. A novice opened the door and lead Kinsom through a maze of narrow corridors. They came to a small cell, bare except for a mat on the ground and a small table covered with offerings and sacred texts. After a few minutes, the lady who arranged for guides entered the room. She was old, slightly bent, thin, her face so wrinkled that she looked over a hundred. She had the fine lips of an ascetic and thick long hair. Dressed as a peasant woman, everything about her conveyed austerity. The penetrating gaze of her black eyes was unmistakable – these were eyes Kinsom would have recognized anywhere. Standing before her was her teacher, Ani Choki, the saintly rebel.

"She seemed in good health," recounted Kinsom, "although thinner than before. Her body was a like a reed after a storm."

The venerable Ani Choki was just the same as before, perhaps a little frailer, a little shorter if you looked closely. Only the brightness of her eyes revealed the intensity of her faith and the strength of her character. Spartan in her habits, she was not one to give in to effusiveness. She merely took Kinsom's hand and clasped it for a moment against her bosom. Then she burnt a couple of joss sticks, one of the refined pleasures of meditation. The gentle perfume filled the small room. Kinsom felt she had gone back to those happy times when they were rebuilding the convent. She began to speak of Gutsa. The fact that she had been forced to break her vows still tormented her. Whatever she might say to herself, the feeling that she had lost her purity would not leave her. No matter how hard she tried, it just would not go. "An act is impure only if the intention behind it is impure. You could not have done anything," Ani Choki told her. "Stop thinking about it and move ahead... Happiness is what counts, not pain."

They had no more time to talk about the past. Ani Choki was organizing an escape within the next four days, the last of the season before winter fell. Other nuns who had also been in the jails of Lhasa would be joining the expedition. But everything was still uncertain, for in circumstances such as these, nothing is ever sure. Kinsom had a few free days. Ani Choki told her to be as discreet as possible in her movements and not to speak to a soul of her imminent flight. Above all, at no cost must she try and get in touch with her cellmates from Gutsa. "They are probably being watched," she told her. Then she asked Kinsom to visit a young girl imprisoned in Drapchi, where prisoners served long terms. This girl had been arrested while demonstrating peacefully; in the eyes of the Tibetans, her behaviour was exemplary. Sandrol was twenty-one years old. She, along with thirteen other prisoners, had managed to lay their hands on a cassette recorder on which they had recorded patriotic songs and messages to their parents. The cassette was smuggled out of Drapchi and

Days of Moon and Wind

circulated all over the city. Each one of the fourteen nuns gave her name and dedicated a song to her dear ones. Theirs were vibrant, hopeful voices. One of them said[4] : "All of you outside, we thank you deeply for all your help. We will never forget it. We offer you this song..." Kinsom heard the cassette with her heart in her mouth. These songs were singing her story:

> They can beat us all they want
> We will never loose heart
> The time will come when the sun will shine.

Ani Choki had this cassette sent to India, from where it was circulated all over Europe. The fourteen nuns had, however, to pay a very heavy price for their courage and initiative.

Their prison terms were increased threefold. International opinion proved to be worthless. The case of the Drapchi singers, as they were popularly known, became yet another symbol of the Tibetan tragedy.

Kinsom had to struggle hard to overcome her fear before re-entering the gates of a prison. She was not being irrational, her fear was very real. The metallic clanging of the doors was enough to bring back her worst memories. But she managed to control herself; the hours spent in meditation had not gone in vain. The visiting room was packed with guards; Kinsom understood that there could be no exchange of information. Sandrol came in, a handcuffed skeleton, her feet bound in fetters. She had a childlike smile. Her voice did not carry the slightest trace of resentment, only a steely resolve to resist. All she could tell Kinsom was that she had spent four months in solitary confinement. After an altercation with a guard, she had been brave or mad enough to shout: "Free Tibet!". For this act of defiance, she was informed that instead of nine she would now have to serve eighteen years in prison. "When

---

[4] See "Les rebelles de l'Himlaya".

I leave, it will be the year 2010," she said laughingly. She asked Kinsom to have the news of her increased sentence conveyed to her family. At this point, the guard who had been keeping an eye on them cut short the meeting.

Eighteen years or half a lifetime behind bars for shouting a few political slogans! Kinsom was terrified. No one was better placed than her to understand what the young woman was going through. Kinsom realized just how lucky she had been to leave Gutsa... for she too had fought with the guards. As she left the prison, she vowed that not only would she convey Sandrol's message but she would do all in her power to tell her story in Nepal and India. "We'll get you out of here," had been her last words to Sandrol before leaving. In reply, she got an affectionate pout from Sandrol, very like the Tibetan greeting which consists of rubbing noses.

VII

"You'll be leaving on Wednesday," Ani Choki told her. "As far I know, there is another novice, a child and a Khampa family in the group. There may be others. You can never tell with guides."

Taking fugitives to Nepal is a risky business and requires the utmost discretion. On more than one occasion, moles had infiltrated groups and that is why a good guide kept his mouth shut. The fewer who knew the composition of the group the better it was.

Kinsom was happy. It was not the best time to cross the Himalayas; yet if all went well, within a month her dream

Days of Moon and Wind

would come true. With some luck, they would manage to avoid military patrols and storms. A woman of the mountains, she knew they had to cross the highest passes before the first snows, otherwise they would be stranded. But she had the confidence of one who had been brought up in the mountains. She knew her own limitations and all the problems that lay ahead: icy gusts of wind, freezing cold and thin air.

She carefully chose what she was going to take with her. She bought a backpack in which she put one pair of trousers, two shirts, a pull-over, woolen socks, a cap and two pairs of sports shoes. She added a thick coat, in which she kept some provisions: *tsampa*, dry meat, butter, tea and sugar.

On the first Wednesday of November, Kinsom took leave of her teacher and friend.

"So we won't see each other again?"

"If not in this life, then surely in the next," replied the old woman with a smile. They stood at the doorstep for a moment. Then she left her disciple on the street and walked back to the convent to continue her work of helping young people like Kinsom flee to the other side. Every refugee in exile was a seed, perpetuating the culture and tradition of Tibet. The Chinese might be destroying the country physically but its spirit would live on for ever, thought Ani Choki to herself on that frozen autumn night.

Her rucksack strapped to her shoulders, Kinsom walked nervously to the appointed place. At night, Lhasa gave itself up to pleasure. Young Tibetans in smoky dens got drunk on Chinese whisky and wine, much stronger than *Chang*, the traditional beer. In Karaoke bars, young prostitutes entertained soldiers with songs. Scuffles broke out at the slightest pretext. Lhasa looked like a frontier town straight out of the American Wild West or Amazonia, its streets full of violence and despair. There were people from everywhere, locals and outsiders, hustlers and prostitutes jostling each other. Though she was dressed like a boy, the young nun was still scared of being noticed. She felt that everyone was a policeman watching her. Don't they say in Tibet that even shadows work for the Chinese?

In the opaque light of a quiet street, she saw the truck — gray, without bumpers, standing like a ferocious beast. A group of people was talking in low voices in front of the cabin door. There was an old man, so thin that he seemed weightless. She could not see the face of the younger man, probably the guide. It was difficult to tell his age. His head was sunken between his shoulders. In spite of the dark, he was wearing yellow sunglasses and had hands in the pockets of his anorak. He had an abrupt way of speaking.

"Have you got the money"?, he asked her curtly.

Kinsom hesitatingly took out a wad of notes. The man did not inspire any confidence. And those crumpled notes were the hard earned money of her parents and friends, the means to make her future and fulfill her dreams.

"Come on, hand it over."

Kinsom tried to read the expression in his eyes. His face was dotted with pimples. He must be a Khampa, she said to herself, a man of the mountains, of whom it was impossible to tell whether he was honest or not. Kinsom had no other option but to give him the money. She might as well ignore the thick messy hair, stern face and brusque manner. After all, the Khampas had never really accepted Chinese domination and were the only ones to put up a resistance. Besides, there was no other guide. Kinsom quickly pressed her entire fortune into his hands. She just had enough left to survive for a couple of days in Nepal.

"Hop on."

Kinsom threw in her rucksack and clambered onto the back of the truck. Silent, miserably clad figures were huddled against each other. There was something very touching about the scared look on those coppery faces. Jumping over several

Days of Moon and Wind

passengers, Kinsom sat at the other end. As she put her rucksack on her lap, she looked up. In front of her sat a young boy whose face seemed very familiar.

"Kinsom?", the boy whispered.

Kinsom could hardly believe what she saw in the dark. This was no boy, it was Yandol, her cell mate, also dressed like a man, buried in the antelope skin jacket that her mother had given her for the journey. There was no mistaking her smile and the way her almond shaped eyes crinkled up when she laughed. Stunned, they held each other's hands tightly and let out a smothered laugh so as not attract attention. Their laughter seemed to celebrate the wonder of life. The others looked at them, discomfited; this was not the time or place for such effusiveness, they seemed to think. But how were they to understand how deep was their bond and joy at reuniting? How were they to understand the depth of pain from which they had emerged? They were friends but felt more like sisters. The bonding that comes of shared suffering is always much stronger than the ties of blood. The perils of the journey, the guide's worried face, Chinese patrols and snow storms, all seemed to fade away before the joy of this meeting. By reuniting them in this unexpected way, Ani Choki had given them a gift beyond compare. The journey was no longer an arid, solitary enterprise; they were freedom fighters walking hand in hand, with courage and determination, on the road to freedom. In one second, everything had changed.

"What has happened to Dawa?", asked Kinsom. The nun whose breast had been mutilated had not been allowed to return to her convent. With nowhere to turn to, she had for a while begged alms on the streets of Lhasa before finding work as a nursemaid with a well-to-do-family. Her stay in Gutsa had left her debilitated and she suffered from chronic anemia. Much as she wanted to accompany them, her health had forced her to give up the idea of crossing the Himalayas.

The engine roared to life. The time had come to go. The

guide helped the last passenger up: a ten-year-old child with ruddy cheeks and a running nose, wearing a jacket with practically all the buttons missing. He was crying because he did not want to leave his father, a receding shadow in the narrow street. The man had paid a fortune to the guide so that his son could go to India and study in Dharamsala.

"If they stop us, say that we are on a pilgrimage", said the guide. "And for God's sake, don't tell them you know me. Keep the child well hidden, because his presence may give rise to suspicion."

They heard the door shut and the sound of the truck move into first gear. As they drove, the wind was glacial. The passengers huddled together to keep warm. The truck passed the Norbulingka, the former Summer Palace of the Dalai Lama, before moving on to the "Road of Friendship", linking Lhasa to Kathmandu. Except for the first few kilometres, the road was untarred. From time to time, milestones appeared indicating not the altitude or the distance to Kathmandu, but the distance from Peking.

Yandol looked at the child with concern, wondering how he would be able to withstand the journey with such inadequate clothing. He was not at all prepared for the odyssey that lay ahead. He wore a jacket over a thick pullover and worn out sneakers. The young nun felt sad but she understood what had prompted the child's parents to send him away on this truck. Of all the tragedies in the Land of Snows, the exodus of children is the most heartbreaking. Hundreds of families decide every year to send their children abroad so that they can be educated in the Tibetan language and not Chinese. The separation is at times forever and the young refugees, virtual orphans, are the collective responsibility of the community in exile. In the nineties, so many children fled to India that the Chinese decided to deny jobs to those who had studied abroad and wanted to come back. They did not want an elite capable of standing up to them.

Days of Moon and Wind

What must the parents have felt when they entrusted their son to a perfect stranger to take him to Nepal? However, it was a matter not just of their son's but of their country's future. Yandol knew just what Chinese education was all about and had heard that parents did all that they could to protect their children from being indoctrinated in school. From Peking to Shanghai, the Chinese wanted students made to order, in white shirts and red kerchiefs round their necks. They knew that killing a language was the first step to destroying a culture and Tibetan was taught in schools for only one and a half hours a week. Mandarin was the language of instruction. Tibetan history had been completely distorted. As they could not understand the language of their forefathers, these children knew nothing about the roots of their country. It was precisely to avoid this that the boy's parents had decided, like so many others, to send their child to India.

The truck followed the course of the Tsang Po, a river which in the lowlands of India becomes the impressive Brahmaputra. The passengers hardly spoke. These people, normally so full of life and good humour, were in no mood for swapping the stories, jokes, tales and laughter that normally accompanied their journeys. The only sound heard was that of an occasional sigh or prayer. Comfort came not from words but from body warmth. Each traveller moved as close as possible to the other: skeleton like frames huddled together in silence.

The old man, propped against the others, seemed to know neither anxiety nor sadness. He was looking beyond the lunar landscape that they were crossing and reminiscing about the enchanted valleys, the bustling cities and the immense steppes; in short, the whole of Tibet, with all the paths and trails that he had walked. He wanted these images to be engraved forever in his memory; after all, life for him now was a trail of memories.

Kinsom tried to picture life at night in the villages they

were passing: the smell of sleeping animals, children coughing, old people groaning, dogs barking at a distance, the odours of smoke, straw and rancid butter, the vacillating flame of small lamps lighting hidden altars and the moon climbing to the heart of the sky. She thought of her family, of her father. Had he understood her decision? All he had wanted for his daughter was a simple, calm life in the village. What would he think if he saw her now in the middle of the night on a truck packed with frozen bodies. Leaving one's parents is the law of life: ultimately each one has to follow his or her own *karma*. But with each passing mile, her heart broke. She was leaving behind her parents, her city, her country. And she did not know if she would ever return to see them again. Was it cowardly to run away and leave the others to face the enemy? The thought did cross her mind but it was too late for doubts now.

The truck had to stop for a police check. With bated breath, the travelers heard the guide tell the officers that they were on their way to Mount Kailash, a place sacred to both Hindus and Buddhists. The beam of the headlights fell on the guide as he produced a crumpled piece of paper to show the soldiers: the travel permit of the pilgrims. To get this piece of paper authorizing them to travel in Tibet, the guide had paid a hefty amount. He had had to buy off a senior official and supply him with massive quantities of beer, which of course, got included in the cost of the journey.

The truck moved on. Yandol slept, her head resting on her friend's shoulder. Through the glass of the driver's cabin Kinsom could see the outline of the three men sitting in front. There was the guide and two other fugitives for whom there no was place at the back. As they went up the mountain passes, the speeding truck began to whine, painfully groaning its way up the winding road, its body creaking. The road was sometimes so narrow that the wheels turned in the air. The slightest mistake or distraction on the part of the driver, any defect in the engine or brakes, and they would fall into the abyss.

Early in the morning, as the sun's first rays shone tremulously from behind the mountain peaks, the truck was already near Shigatse, the second largest city in Tibet. The imposing Tashilumpo Monastery, seat of the Panchen Lama who was the second highest spiritual authority in Tibet, dominated the city. Plundered by the soldiers of the Red Army, it was another symbol of the Tibetan tragedy. The guide said it would be better to stay in the countryside rather than go to the city whose guest houses, restaurants and shops were teeming with informers. So they continued on until they came to a row of willows between two barley fields. As they got down from the truck, the passengers looked at each other for the first time in daylight. The morning light was pure and intense. Tibetans call light the eye of the Buddha, for it can see through the mask and reveal the true nature of things. The guide still looked like a ruffian. Each passenger wondered about the others, they were so disparate. Yet, they had been united by a common goal to live together through this extraordinary adventure. A handful of people, of various ages, carrying hardly any luggage. The women began to make tea while the child ran around the truck till he fell down, exhausted. Kinsom's robust mountain frame infused a sense of security in the others. Yandol looked more fragile though she was brave and had a strong will. She could read and write both Tibetan and Chinese, which won her the admiration of the others. The old man, somewhat aloof, kept his distance from the group. He looked like a sage out of the ancient past, a past the purity of his voice was able to recapture.

VIII

As soon as night fell, the truck set off again. The passengers had not managed to get much respite. The enormity of the journey that lay ahead made them edgy and restless. The guide had decided to go up to Tingri, the last town before the border, from where they would continue on foot. That long stretch at night proved to be very tedious. As they began their ascent to a pass 5,200 metres high, the truck moved so slowly that they could have gone faster on foot. It was bitingly cold. On several occasions, the passengers, huddled together at the back of the truck, felt they were going to fall off the mountain side any moment, especially when another vehicle came from the other side and the truck had to swerve precariously close to the edge of the precipice. As on the previous day, the guide thought it more prudent to stop in the countryside rather than the city, where soldiers, traders and truckers usually halted for a meal and some rest. They had moved out of the zones for which their permit was valid. Henceforth, any encounter with a Chinese patrol would mean the end of the journey.

It was still night when they crossed the dilapidated town of Tingri. At dawn, the outline of the mountain peaks against the skyline resembled a series of sharp teeth in which the Everest and the Cho Oyu stood out. There was one tooth missing and through the gap could be seen the blue sky of Nepal. That gap was the Nangpa Pass, located at an altitude of 5,716 metres above sea level. The road to freedom. beckoned.

The truck had to make a large detour to avoid military camps. They did not stop until they were in the heart of the countryside. A cool breeze swept across the plateau and the white crests seemed more imposing than ever. The guide asked the passengers to get down behind the hill. He then informed them that he was going to leave the truck in the city and would be back by night. Kinsom protested: "You are going to leave us alone?"

"I have to return the truck. Don't worry," replied the guide.

"Give us our money back and we will be fine."

The guide looked at her with supreme indifference, not deigning to reply. He adjusted his yellow sunglasses on his prominent nose and climbed up into the driver's cabin. He started the engine and the truck disappeared, leaving behind a cloud of smoke. Bewildered, the passengers did their best to hide their anxiety. This smacked of fraud, but what could they do? They were in the middle of nowhere, with only rocks and grass as protection against police patrols.

They set up camp as best as they could. Resting on their rucksacks, the nuns brooded. The child seemed to share the general anguish. He did not play or laugh. Like the others, he too was waiting for the guide to return; no one wanted to think of the other eventuality. The old man meditated. A little lower down near a stream, a pack of yellow and brown vultures were flying over a dead body, a normal sight in this part of the world. As the earth is very hard, Tibetans cannot bury their dead. The dead body is placed on a cliff so that it be devoured by the animals. The remaining bones are broken and crushed to dust and offered to the birds as food. In this way, everything returns to the elements and death returns to life. Perhaps the birds of prey, on that cold day in the mountains, mistook these strange shapes in the distance for dead bodies. A young eagle, with its magnificent black and bronze plumage, flew past them, letting out shrill cries, coming so close to Kinsom's head that she could feel the flapping of its wings. She was shaken by this omen of death and her abrupt start caused the dark bird to move away quickly.

The hours passed by with excruciating slowness. The guide had vanished. In spite of the outward tranquility of the group, with the exception of the old man, all of them would jump up at the slightest sound in the lunar landscape, running for cover behind mounds of earth, the only hiding place possible. But it would turn out to be just a shepherd passing by or a small herd of yaks. By afternoon, Kinsom had given up all hope of the guide's return. They might have been arrested, but the whole thing smelled fishy. All their plans for the future were crushed to pieces. What could they do? They had hardly any money left on them, certainly not enough to pay another guide. In these circumstances, they could either carry on alone or somehow return to Lhasa and start all over again. But that would mean waiting for several months, getting the money together again and giving lengthy explanations to their parents to justify their actions. Besides, winter was fast approaching ... Kinsom, still disturbed by the eagle, insisted they went ahead on their own. The old man burst out laughing, as if listening to a lunatic. She did appear to have gone mad. She tried to persuade Yandol to go with her but Yandol was not game. "It is not prudent," she said. They settled down for the night as best they could amid these stark, desolate stones, swept by the icy winds that blew across the world's highest peaks. They barely slept. As soon as day broke, Kinsom announced that she was going ahead. Yandol was torn between the desire to go with her friend and her instinct for survival. She tried to reason with Kinsom but Kinsom had already made up her mind.

"I'm going."

"*Tashi delek* (good luck)", said Yandol.

The old man smiled in disbelief. Yandol was frustrated because her friend refused to listen to her — her friend could sometimes be as stubborn as a yak. Kinsom strapped her bag to her shoulders and started walking. She had barely gone a hundred metres when she threw down her bag. After scanning the horizon, she picked up her bag and turned back. She came back not because she was afraid of going alone but because she did not have the heart to abandon her companions. Yandol received her with that unmistakable smile that dimpled her face. The old man laughed.

They spent the morning in silent fright. When the sun was at its highest, something shining in the distance caught their attention: it was the guide's truck. The fugitives hurriedly collected their belongings. But their euphoria soon gave way to suspicion: suppose it was not the guide but a truck of Chinese soldiers coming to arrest them? All of a sudden, there was panic; they started running madly in all directions. Some hid behind bushes, others behind rocks or in the hollows of the ground. The old man alone kept standing where he was, aloof. This skeleton of a man seemed to know it all. He had lived for so long and his memory went down so deep that nothing could surprise or worry him.

Thus they remained until they saw the truck in full view. Driven by the guide still wearing his enormous yellow sunglasses, it was crammed with people, not Chinese but Khampas, fugitives like them, attired in their traditional garb, their long hair blowing in the wind, dotted with turquoise, thick yak bone rings, red ribbons and old silver coins pierced in the middle. Kinsom and the others came out of their hiding places and the bewildered guide wondered what had happened to his clients. The nuns decided not to say anything about the delay. So much futile waiting, anguish and fear, all because the guide had decided to pick up some extra passengers to make a little more money. A large group like this, thought the nuns, would be more difficult to hide. However, they just had to get to Nepal as soon as possible and so they decided to trust their stars and the experience of the guide.

"We are leaving now," said the guide as the truck returned to where it had come from. He started off without waiting for the others. This man of the mountains was so dry and laconic that the group wondered whether he had a heart or just a pocket to keep his money. He was neither young nor old but could read the weather like the back of his hand. He feared the thick clouds that rose from the south. They were snow clouds. The November winds lashed the hillside but he walked tall, completely indifferent to the fate of his group, who grumbled about his "disgusting profession". The only time he condescended to speak to them was to tell them that in case they were stopped by the Chinese, they should say they were pilgrims. "And for God's sake, don't tell them that you have paid me," he repeated constantly. One had to be decidedly eccentric or mad to take such a disparate group of people across the Himalayas. Each time he looked back, the sight of the bedraggled group made his stomach churn. He doubted their capacity to withstand the rigours of a fifteen day trek. The group was too unwieldy for him to step up the pace. One strong blizzard, and most of them would perish given the way they were equipped for the journey. He could not afford the luxury of emotion. That is why he kept up a brisk pace, walking ahead like an automaton, looking downwards to avoid the wind in his face, though he knew full well that the others were having great difficulty in keeping up with him.

Ahead, the Himalayas raised their barricades; ridges and mountains etched on the skyline. As the day went by, the fugitives began to lose some of their ebullience. While walking, they tried to smear their faces with yak butter to avoid sunburn. Some member of the group would rub a little butter on the child's face or make him drink. They had adopted the little fellow, who was now wearing sunglasses too big for his face. His childish lips never let out a groan or a word of complaint.

The Khampas, like the guide, walked on effortlessly. Merchant caravans had remained in mortal fear of these

Days of Moon and Wind

ferocious warriors, who were reputed to be the best horsemen, the best hunters and the best fighters. Physically, they were taller and stronger than the rest of the Tibetans. They came from a region of eastern Tibet that was the size of the Indian state of Punjab. For centuries, no foreigner had been able to enter their territory, as these warriors had successfully put down all attempts at conquest. Against them even Chengiz Khan had not been able to do much. The Khampas were the first to take on Mao's troops; in retaliation, the Chinese called them the lap dogs of imperialism. But a Khampa never forgot what he had been taught since birth: he belonged to a race of kings.

Most of the Khampas of this group did not look like their fathers who had waged the armed struggle against the Chinese. They looked more like poor peasants, not like the rebels of yore. Only the guide had a natural sense of authority. Yandol had heard that these Khampas belonged to his village and that he had agreed to take them across without charging any money. The two friends began to revise their opinion of the guide: perhaps he was not all that greedy and money-minded after all and possessed the nobility of his race.

But he was so rude that no one dared to ask him any questions. When would they stop? Where would they sleep? In any case, he was always far ahead, never stumbling, for he knew every nook and cranny of this rocky region where not even trees dared to grow. The group behaved as if on a pilgrimage, falling behind every hundred metres. They did not really envy the travellers who, down the ages, had carried all kinds of goods to and fro on this route. But at least those travellers had animals to carry their load and escorts to repel highwaymen. Kinsom's group did not have even a pistol to face the new highwaymen – the Chinese soldiers.

IX

The trekkers would set off at dawn, walk miles on end, wade through streams and go down rocky slopes, yet the peaks seemed to be leading nowhere. After fifteen hours of non-stop trekking, they would camp near a spring or stream. To avoid dehydration at these heights, one had to drink at least six litres of water a day. At every halt, the women would prepare tea. A mixture of tea and barley flour constituted their basic diet.

They slept in the open air, curled up under their blankets. After Gutsa's frozen cells, anything was bearable and the cold air of these regions had the incomparable taste of freedom. Yandol did not fare as well. When they stopped to rest, she would put on every bit of clothing she had and draw so close to the fire that the flames would often singe the edge of her antelope skin jacket, the one her mother had given her as a parting gift. Because there was no wood, they used the yak dung they had collected on the way to keep the warmth of the fire going. The Khampas, bare-bodied, would crowd together near the fire, kneading *tsampa* and humming songs. The old man would tell stories in a soft voice, speaking of far off things and distant lands, as if in this and previous lives of his he had visited all the corners of the earth. His voice captivated even the Khampas, who otherwise kept their distance as they were wary of him, not knowing if he was a wanderer or monk, a saint or a sorcerer. Whoever he was, he seemed to have what the Tibetans call crazy wisdom. He was free.

Actually, the old man had undertaken the journey to fulfill a much cherished dream, that of meeting his grandson, a monk in a monastery of Tibetan refugees somewhere in southern India. His son had fled Tibet twenty-five years ago. The old man did not want to die before seeing his grandson, who had chosen to follow the noble path of the *dharma*. Whenever he spoke of his grandson, there was pride in his voice and a broad smile would light up his face. In the mornings, the guide had no trouble getting everybody up. The cold was so intense that in spite of stiff limbs and blisters the travellers were compelled to keep moving; they would jump and run so as not get frozen. These first ten minutes when they gathered the equipment and raised camp were critical. After that, everything depended on one's strength and one's luck.

The guide had made this trip several times before. He knew that this was just the beginning and that the real ordeal lay ahead when they reached the peaks. In the high Himalayan altitudes, winter is like a net, allowing only the fittest to pass. Everyone knew that accidents and illness would be serious and that the risks would increase with each passing day. And there was no help on these trails.

The nuns were aware of this. They had heard stories of fugitives whose frostbitten limbs had to be amputated, of others who had died of sheer exhaustion after a sleepless night. At the back of everyone's mind was the question: what about the child, would he be able to cross the passes? Could he sleep out in the open for so long? The child had a hard time keeping up with the guide. He was getting extremely tired as he walked; a grimace of pain wash writ large on his face. He had displayed great fortitude, but now he was beginning to weaken. Whenever the path became very steep, the adults took turns to carry him on their shoulders. Every now and

1. Thubten Gyatso, the Thirteenth Dalai Lama, has gone down in history as the Great XIII. He knew how to deal with Chinese expansionist designs and initiated the process of modernization. Just before his death, he had prophesied with startling clarity the disaster that was to befall his country.
© Department of Information, Dharamsala.

2. 1954: The Great Helmsman, with his dignified personality and shabby clothes, made an impression on the Dalai Lama. There was a certain empathy between the two men. Mao showed an interest in Buddhism and also spoke of his intention to help the 'fraternal people' of Tibet. The Dalai Lama believed him. Three months later when he returned to Tibet, he realized how hollow Mao's promises were. The Dalai Lama's elder brother said Mao's promises were like "honey on a knife; if you suck it, it cuts your tongue".
© Department of Information, Dharamsala.

3. *1956: The Dalai Lama, followed by the Panchen Lama, on his way to India to participate in the celebration of the two thousand five hundredth birth anniversary of the Buddha. The Chinese authorities had wanted to prevent the journey but they had to give in to pressure from the Lamas of the large monasteries, the people of Lhasa and Nehru, the then Prime Minister of India. Before he left, the Chinese gave the Dalai Lama prepared texts of the speeches he was to make and tutored him on how to answer questions from journalists.*
© Department of Information, Dharamsala.

4. *Most of the monasteries were systematically destroyed between 1959 and 1961. For years, trucks would leave for China, laden with Tibetan treasures. Thousand year old statues and images made of gold and silver were melted into ingots.*
© Department of Information, Dharamsala.

5. *Above: the Monastic University of Ganden before it was destroyed by the Chinese.*

Below: Ganden, which means 'paradise of joy', was home to 3,300 monks, who were responsible for preserving the cultural heritage of their country. Described by the Italian Tibetologist Giuseppe Tucci as 'a place out of this world', Ganden was reputed to be the most beautiful and impressive monastery of Tibet.
© *Department of Information, Dharamsala.*

6. Lama Thubten Yeshe took the greatest decision of his life when he chose to go into exile. In India, he was chosen, along with a thousand other monks, to preserve to the extent possible the religious and cultural heritage of Tibet. Later, his ability to make Buddhism accessible and attractive to Westeners lead to the establishment of a foundation whose activities spread with lightning speed all over the world.

His followers found his reincarnation in Osel Hita Torres, a child from Granada. Currently, Lama Osel (below) lives and studies in southern India in a replica of the Sera Monastery. Photo Kopan (photo of Lama Yeshe). © Javier Moro (photo of Osel).

7. Lobsang Jigme (left), State Oracle, dressed as an ancient warrior, is entering into a trance. The spirit of the protecting divinity Dorje Drakden will take possession of his body. For over 1,300 years, the leaders of Tibet have been consulting this deity on matters of state. © Department of Information, Dharamsala.

8. Just the word Gutsa sends a shiver down the spine of the Tibetans. At eight kilometres from Lhasa, the Gutsa prison is the most visible symbol of the cruelty with which the Chinese authorities have subjugated the Land of Snows. For having shouted "Long live the Dalai Lama!" and "Free Tibet!", Kinsom, nineteen, and Yandol, fifteen, were sentenced to three years in this hell.
© Department of Information, Dharamsala.

9. *The daring of the venerable Jampa Tenzin won him fame and respect in his country. During the demonstration on October 1, 1987, this forty-nine year old monk entered a police station, saving the lives of several of his compatriots detained there. As he came out of the building with serious burns all over his body, the crowds carried him on their shoulders in the streets of Lhasa. He was detained, imprisoned and later released at the express request of the Panchen Lama. In February 1992, he was found dead in his room in the Jokhang Temple, hanging from a rope. The authorities maintain it was suicide. Other sources claim that Jampa Tenzin was murdered by the police.*
© J. Ackerly/Int'l Campaign for Tibet (both photographs).

10. *The author standing between Yandol (wearing spectacles) and Kinsom.* Photo: Laura Allen.

11. *The Jokhang Temple in Lhasa – a huge, religious edifice with many chapels and altars where the most precious cult objects of the Himalayas are stored – is the spiritual centre of Tibet. Hundreds of pilgrims and tourists congregate in the temple square, which has also been the scene of numerous protest demonstrations.* © Javier Moro.

12. On the Chakpori hills, in front of the Potala Palace, stood the buildings of the Faculty of Medicine. They were razed to the ground as part of the drive to crush the 1959 rebellion. In their place are the antennas of Radio Lhasa. The highest hill has been renamed Victory Peak. © Javier Moro.

13. The Potala Palace photographed in 1997. © Javier Moro.

then, they would make him walk, not because they were tired, but because it was important for the child to move. If he did not do so, he could get frostbite. The child ran like a goat down the lower slopes. Withdrawn to begin with, he gradually opened up to the adults, laughing and speaking to them. He became the mascot of the group and even the guide, for all his sternness, grew fond of him, asking him at each halt how he was. But the child's reply always lacked enthusiasm.

As they were climbing up, it became increasingly cold and more difficult to predict the weather. A sudden wind would lower the temperature by as much as fifteen to twenty degrees. At four thousand metres, the clouds got so dense that as they walked through them they could barely see each other. Within seconds a blizzard would blow, accompanied by snow and sleet. Below in the gorge, the rumbling of rocks sliding was followed by a deep pause. Fog, snow and complete silence. Then the clouds cleared, unveiling the majestic peak of Mt. Everest. Nearby, the wings of a rook gathered the silvery light of the Himalayas. While crossing a stream, Yandol, trying to catch the pack that Kinsom threw at her from the other side, let it drop clumsily in the water. Kinsom burst out laughing as did the others although it meant wet clothes and soggy food. That happy go lucky spirit, that acceptance which is not fatalism but a deep trust in life, is typically Tibetan.

They walked the whole day till the guide stopped, sensing danger. They could not understand why he was so nervous and why he ordered them to break their file and hide wherever they could in complete silence. Everyone disappeared behind stones and rocks. "What's happening?", murmured Yandol, scared. Kinsom, used to the sounds of the mountains, had heard a distant rumble. The worried look on the guide's face made her very uneasy. There was danger ahead but what was it? An avalanche? Kinsom wondered. They often began this way, a distant rumble which finally ended in a crash.

Yandol was the first to spot the helicopter. Flying low,

it was moving towards the end of the valley in their direction. The cockpit had a red star painted on it. "Don't move!", shouted the guide. All of them – the old man, the child, the Khampas, the nuns – were petrified. Panic stricken, they huddled close to the ground, holding their breath, their hearts beating furiously. How could such a small aircraft make so much noise: it was as if the earth was trembling. The monster flew away to the other side of the valley, leaving them completely shaken. The two friends knew that being caught again meant spending the rest of their lives behind bars. The executioners of Gutsa would only be too happy to punish them for trying to meet the Dalai Lama. Once again that old feeling of terror assailed them – here in the wilderness they had forgotten the evil the world could do. This bird of ill omen was a reminder of their plight as fugitives. How much time before a patrol hunted them down?

The guide ordered them to come out of their hiding places. They strapped on their backpacks, dusted their clothes and adjusted their caps. "There are more than twenty ways to reach Nepal," said the guide. "The patrols can't keep a watch over them all. We are going to do two things: change our route and trek by night not by day."

The column set off at a blistering pace. They had to leave the trail they were following and walk through the countryside for several hours before they found another trail. A lark, a swift and some vultures mournfully flapped their wings, as they flew past them. While crossing a low mountain pass, they came across a *chorten*, a mound of heavy stones on top of which are poles with strips of cloth hanging. Inside, there is also a small shrine in which to make offerings. The long strips of cloth fluttering in the wind bring good luck to travellers crossing a pass for the first time. Sacred inscriptions are engraved on the stones of the shrine. Whenever they had the opportunity, the nuns would take off their backpacks and pray for a few minutes next to these prayer flags, which may have been left behind by other fugitives wanting to flee Tibet. These multicoloured banners with prayers stamped on them are a distinctive feature of Buddhist countries in the Himalayas. They can be found everywhere, in houses, temples, remote caves and mountain passes. According to popular belief, the wind that makes them flutter carries the blessing of the printed prayers to the four corners of the universe. The Tibetans call them wind horses because they look like the mane of a galloping steed.

During the day, the travellers barely spoke to each other. At these heights, air is a precious commodity, so they limited their speech to what was strictly necessary; otherwise it made more sense to keep quiet. At a canyon bend, the guide pointed to a buldered slope across the stream where five silver blue-gray animals were moving up. All of them watched the animals climb till they reached the snow line. There they vanished, gobbled up by the clouds that covered the mountain slope above them. They were *bharals*, the blue sheep of the Himalayas. The Himalayan peaks shone in the east, bathed in a halo of sunlight. The sun broke out incandescent in a cloudless sky — pale and warm to the south over India, cold and dark over Tibet.

They saw eagles, foxes, bucks and gazelles but the king of these mountains is undoubtedly the yak, a shaggy black bovine with closely set horns, often preceded by the cool tinkling of bells. The sound of the bells told them that humans were not far. Very soon, a man and his wife came down the path in full Tibetan dress: the man in a blanket, a belted coat and baggy pants tucked into red wool boots tied around the calf and the woman in a striped apron and black clothes. The guide reassured his group: these shepherds had nothing to do with the Chinese. Shepherds usually brought valuable information about the weather. It was better on the other side, they told the guide. The fugitives had yet to cross the Nangpa Pass, which had seemed so close from Tingri.

Days of Moon and Wind

The child, his face burnt by the sun, his clothes almost in rags, greedily drank the *dri* milk that the shepherds offered him. Weighing more than half a tonne, yaks and *dris* are shaggy beasts that make an attractive sight with their flat noses. Yaks can be ill-tempered and stubborn but they have many qualities the most important of which is their ability to live in high altitudes. They are only found at altitudes above 3,500 metres; lower than that they cannot withstand the atmospheric pressure and the heat. In this part of the world, the yak is a very useful animal indeed. Its meat is rich, its milk creamy and its wool used to make clothes, coats and rope. From yak leather are made bags, tents and canoes. The yak is a fiery beast. Kinsom remembered that her father had to extract several litres of blood to quell the ardour of their yak. The old man chipped in, telling them how in the past Tibetans derived great amusement by offering yaks to people they did not like, especially the Chinese. The story of a Chinese rider being unseated by a wild yak gave rise to much hilarity.

X

They reached a glacier. The terrain was irregular and hard. Even Kinsom, the strongest of the lot, was showing signs of exhaustion. Each ice hummock broke her rhythm. Every joint and muscle in her body was creaking. Yandol, trailing behind, was too weak to say anything. Her feet were hurting terribly and she would soon have to change her shoes for the pair she was wearing was

The Mountains of the Buddha

worn out. Sturdy shoes are the most precious commodity in these heights where just to keep walking is an acrobatic feat. The travellers were constantly slipping and falling, and it took them all their strength to heave themselves up again. The snow and frost on the rocks made the ascent even more difficult. To make matters worse, some of the Khampas began to suffer from snow blindness, causing a burning sensation in the cornea of the eye. This ailment occurs unexpectedly and there is no cure other than waiting for it to go. When they set up camp, the Khampas, who felt as if they had sand in their eyes, huddled around the fire and blew desperately into each others' eyes. Yandol applied tea leaf poultices; they got some relief but not for long. In the days that followed, these valiant warriors, eyes covered with cloth, stumbled and groaned behind the nuns who lead the way with them following like a pack of blind men. The guide chose to ignore them, irritated that they had not taken any precautions.

The journey began to take its toll on the members of the group. While crossing the glacier, Kinsom noticed a few drops of blood on the snow. She saw that the child's feet were bleeding: his sports shoes were completely worn out and the soles of his feet had cuts from the frozen crust of the snow. In spite of the pain and the beginnings of a limp, he did not utter a word. Like a good Tibetan he must have felt that the salvation of the group had to take precedence over his own destiny. Mountains are merciless, his only hope lay in his strong instinct for survival. Not wanting to stop in such an open area, the guide made them climb to a higher spot, sheltered by rocks. They had reached the southern most extremity of the plateau. From here began another world, that of the mountain passes. The terrain was far more hostile, but it was the only way they could get to the valleys of Nepal. The guide told them they had one more difficult week ahead before they reached the border.

Kinsom doubted whether the child could hold out; she

Days of Moon and Wind

wondered how they were going to cope. The Khampas carried him uncomplainingly on their shoulders through difficult stretches but they were worn out, half-blinded and stiff with cold. In spite of her natural optimism, Kinsom could not help feeling that something tragic was going to happen. There was only one thing to do: appeal to the gods and pray that winter give them a few days of good weather.

That night they sat up with the child; his feet were bleeding and his toes had turned blue, the first sign of frostbite. While the Khampas carried him on their shoulders, the child showed no signs of insecurity or exhaustion. But the cold, the silent enemy of the mountains, was getting the better of him. Yandol melted a little snow in a pan. That however was of little help because the water turned back to ice in few seconds, making it impossible for her to clean his wounds. After massaging his feet, Kinsom covered his shoes with a leather sheath — an old shepherd ploy to avoid slipping and keep one's feet dry. It never once struck Kinsom that she herself might need the sheath, as she had only one extra pair of shoes left. Seated around a weak fire, they stamped their feet on the ground to keep themselves warm, shared their rations of dried meat and drank boiling tea. Their backpacks were empty; they were wearing everything they had. They lay down on a bed of stones, set in the frost, curling up under their blankets. Yandol held on tightly to Kinsom's hand with her purplish fingers. The real cold of the high mountains brings silence and a blizzard put an end to their hushed conversations. There was a sudden drop in temperature; the frozen air infiltrated their blankets and deprived them of their sleep. They huddled together, shivering, and spent the night listening to the howling wind lash against rocky peaks.

Fortunately, the next day the sky was clear, which meant they could cross the pass. Chinese patrols were once again the guide's main worry. From this point onwards, no matter what trail they took, they would have to skirt several check posts on the way to the Nepali border. The guide thought it more prudent to travel by night along routes previously used by smugglers. The attitude of the Chinese perplexed him. Not a week went by without a group of refugees risking their lives in an attempt to flee Tibet. But very few were detained or imprisoned. The world's largest nation seemed to be doing a poor job of controlling its border. Perhaps they thought the Himalayas would do their dirty work for them. Or could it just be that they found it more convenient to allow the opponents of the regime to escape?

After walking the whole day, the group climbed a steep cornice. Like the night before, this one too was dark, windy and glacial. The guide ordered them to keep quiet. Even a murmur can get amplified in the high mountains. Half a kilometre below was a check post. From where they were, the fugitives could barely see the lights in the barracks but they could hear the echo of laughter, doors slamming and music. The nuns groped their way in the dark, feeling the rock walls. The path became narrower: on one side the wall, on the other, the abyss. The guide lead this strange procession, holding the hand of a Khampa. Then came the child, the old man, with the two nuns right at the end, looking like delirious teenagers. From below they could hear voices, crockery rattling, and the nasal twang of a Chinese song being played on a badly tuned radio set.

The old man slipped on a stone. He stumbled and found his feet dangling in the air, as he clutched onto his backpack wedged between two rocks. Kinsom hurried to help him up. The reverberation of the falling stones had them paralyzed with fear. This was the first time since the Lhasa check post that the Chinese seemed so near. They stood rooted to the spot, silently praying that the soldiers had not heard. The old man looked ashamed and bowed his head before the others, as if to beg pardon. Had the Chinese found them out, he would

Days of Moon and Wind

never have been able to forgive himself. Just the thought of it made him feel uneasy.

The cold was relentless and forced them to move on. All of them knew that a moment's respite had cost many a traveller his or her life. To stay still in these heights is synonymous with death. That night, the guide, scared by the presence of the Chinese, decided to get as far away as possible. It seemed that he would never stop and when, late at night, he finally did stop, he chose a slope shielded from the wind. To avoid chilblain and mitigate the impact of the cold, the nuns kept rubbing themselves and moving: they changed their socks, had a bite and set up camp in no time. They forced the child to move; his spirit was willing but his poor body needed help; he bobbed up and down like a disjointed puppet. Once again they spent the night curled up under their blankets. As they stared at the sky, they heard the wind howl. It was hard to tell which was worse: Chinese soldiers or bad weather. In any case, what did it matter? So near the stars, this disparate group of fugitives pinned their faith on the Buddha of Infinite Compassion, eternal protector of Tibet. What else could they do?

4
THE YEAR OF THE EARTH PIG

I

In early 1954, at the time the Chinese were trying to disarm the Khampas and confiscate their land and animals, these nomads, who comprised the bulk of the population of eastern Tibet, retreated to the mountains, ready to fight.[1] The Khampa rebels asked Lhasa for help but their appeal fell on deaf ears, as life in the capital continued at its own pace. In any case, the young Dalai Lama, who wanted to avoid a blood bath, was working to reach a compromise with the Chinese. The Khampas thought the God King was conceding far too much to the invader. Not only had he dispensed with both his Prime Ministers, but he had also accepted an invitation to Peking. In the eyes of the rebels, Tenzin Gyatso was playing into Mao's hands. Like many Tibetans, they were of the opinion that the God King was stepping into the lion's den and would end up a captive of the Chinese. As soon as they learnt the Dalai Lama would be traveling across their territory, they hatched a plot to carry him off to the mountains and keep him hostage there. The Chinese got the wind of this plan and lined thousands of soldiers along the route on which their precious hostage was to pass.

The highway constructed in Khampa territory was what had sparked off one of the longest and most ferocious resistance movements ever, even though in the outside world

---

[1] For an account of the Khampa's fight against the Chinese, see "Cavaliers of Kham: The Secret War in Tibet", by Michel Peissel (Little & Brown, 1972)

The Mountains of the Buddha

little was known of it. The highway was a marvel of Chinese engineering: thirteen hundred kilometres long, at an average height of four thousand metres, spanning fourteen mountain ranges and seven wide rivers. The Chinese had reckoned with everything save the Khampas. And between Chinese and Khampas, there could be no meeting ground. Till today, Khampa nomads live by the wisdom and laws of their forefathers — simple, straightforward in keeping with nature and the struggle for survival. Before the construction of the highway, the ancestral customs of these tribes, living in small yak wool tents, had not been touched by the Chinese invasion. They had continued to live as in the past, bellicose, independent and rebellious. Had not the Dalai Lama said of the Khampas that their most precious possession was their gun? Born on horseback, only the strongest survived the endless struggle they had to wage against the cold and the wind, the wolves and the bears with whom they shared grazing lands around secluded lakes fed by glaciers. For them, the gun meant hope and survival. They recognized no authority; their only political ties were those of blood.

The presence of the Chinese in the region caused widespread resentment. Public meetings organized by the Chinese in which the Khampas were asked to denounce serf owners proved to be a complete fiasco. The Chinese were to discover that in spite of the feudal appearance of Tibetan society, there was no class hatred of the kind that existed in China. Tibet had no discontented peasantry or proletariat, crucial for the development of Communism. Tibetan society, with the exception of the Khampas, did support several thousand poorly paid monks who devoted their lives to the quest for enlightenment. To this extent, it could be called a feudal society. But the Tibetans were an essentially democratic people: it could not be otherwise, given the harsh natural terrain and the temporizing nature of the Buddhist faith. As early as the seventh century,

The Year of the Earth Pig

the death penalty had been abolished. Punishment for murder was that the murderer had to compensate the family of the person he had murdered; offenders were rarely imprisoned unless they were hardened criminals. Lhasa had no large prison. The monasteries owned and lived on vast tracts of land, tilled by the peasants, who like the Khampas, believed in spirits. Influenced by the superstitions of Bon, the original religion of Tibet, they would go into group trances. They were often deep in the debt of monasteries or *gyalpos*, local lords and petty kings, who refused to step out of their house without a servant holding a parasol over their head. Touring government officials, their retinue and animals were provided hospitality by these peasants. Though such inequalities did exist, the notion of caste or social prejudice was virtually non-existent. In the absence of a monetary economy, differences in wealth were not very significant. The rich were restricted to a handful of lords and priors, willingly accepted by the people because of their religiosity. In Tibet, half the population that lived on the land owned something, a much higher proportion than in any other country of Asia.[2] This section was the only one obliged to pay taxes to the state. Since taxes were linked to property and paid in kind rather than cash, the Chinese assumed that all Tibetan peasants were serfs. In reality, they had nothing in common with the serfs of the Middle Ages in the West. They were free to dispose of their lands, their money and their person. And they were certainly not ready to accept a Marxist revolution, especially one their traditional enemy, the Chinese, were trying to impose on them.

The key to understanding Tibet is Buddhism, a philosophy of peace. Because of their belief in the law of *Karma*, rich and poor alike learnt to accept life with equanimity and a certain sense of resignation. Social mobility was difficult

---

[2] Source: "Cavaliers of Kham: the Secret War in Tibet" by Michel Peissel (Little Brown, 1972).

though not impossible. A soldier could receive a title and land in recognition of his valour and both were hereditary. Children were admitted to monasteries regardless of their social class; their progress depended solely on their merit. The highest positions both in monastic and national life were often occupied by children of humble parents, as is the case of the present Dalai Lama.

Perhaps what distinguishes Tibet from other countries is the extent to which Buddhism has permeated every aspect of life. It is much more than just the performance of rituals associated with certain days of the week or birth, marriage and death ceremonies — it is a way of life. Tibetans, conservative as a society and tolerant as individuals, have always placed spiritual concerns above material ones. Tibetan culture has never held material well-being as an ideal. The Chinese thought socialism to be the panacea for all ills; for the Tibetans, freedom meant release from the inevitable cycle of suffering caused by birth, old age, disease and death. It was this detachment that fascinated Western visitors, who for the most part were of the opinion that Tibet was a land of peace and harmony. Alexandra David-Neel, one of the rare women to travel across Tibet in the early twentieth century, wrote that though she saw many beggars, no one died of hunger. Men and women were ever ready to rejoice in the pleasures of life, and there was laughter in the air. Unlike in other feudal systems, here ultimate authority lay in the hands of the incarnation of a Buddha, one who had been revered for hundreds of years. Officials could be corrupt, but at the highest level, people had full confidence that justice would be done. A leader with the kind of rigorous religious training the Dalai Lama received could never become a despot or a tyrant. Tenzin Gyatso, the Dalai Lama recalls.[3] "We were happy. Desire breeds discontent; happiness comes from peace

---

[3] Source: "Freedom in Exile", by the Dalai Lama.

The Year of the Earth Pig

of mind. For many Tibetans, life was hard, but they were not victims of desire. In the simplicity and poverty of our mountains, we found more mental peace than in many cities of the world."

It was this mental peace that the Chinese sought to destroy. Aggressive tactics were used to arouse the masses. Beggars were told they would be shot as reactionaries if they refused to denounce the rich. Chinese soldiers would publicly humiliate landowners before the villagers. These crude methods failed to make any impression. The Tibetan resistance to change infuriated the Chinese, who shed all semblance of legality to impose their writ. Landowners and members of the upper classes from Kham were detained and those who opposed the reforms – collectivization and redistribution of land – shot. This marked the beginning of a reign of terror during which the Chinese committed the worst kind of atrocities: mass murder, child deportation and public torture.

In August 1954, while an armed rebellion broke out in Khampa territory, Tenzin Gyatso was being accorded a warm welcome in Peking. The young sovereign had been very apprehensive before meeting Mao, but when they actually came face to face, his fear vanished. "Physically, he was extraordinary," recounted the Dalai Lama. "He looked like a real peasant. He was wearing a shabby jacket, threadbare at the cuffs and collar." The young Tibetan too made a good impression on the old revolutionary. At official banquets, Mao always made him sit at his side and on occasion even insisted on serving him food. During the interminable dinners, Mao would hold forth on the art of governance. He even conceded that Buddhism was a good religion and that the Buddha was sincerely concerned about the people. The Great Helmsman expressed his admiration for the Tibetan people and his desire to help them catch up with the time they had lost on account of several centuries of isolation. Tenzin Gyatso openly acknowledged that Tibet had much progress to make. "On that point we had no disagreement," said the Dalai Lama. "We shared a common principle."

The Dalai Lama willingly admitted that corruption had undermined all levels of the Tibetan hierarchy. There were monks who spent more time on amassing wealth and influence than spiritual realization. Sometimes, the search for a reincarnation was conducted somewhat arbitrarily in order to favour a powerful aristocratic family. But no society was completely free of corruption, argued the Dalai Lama, though firmly convinced of the need for radical political reform to modernize his country.

One day, Mao confessed that he had initially intended to rule Tibet directly from Peking. But the conciliatory attitude of the God King had made him change his mind. He had now decided to set up a new committee, comprising four Tibetan and one Chinese group to govern the land of snows. This was good news for the Dalai Lama; by winning Mao's trust, he seemed to have achieved his purpose of limiting the absolute authority of the Chinese. This minor victory confirmed his belief that some sort of settlement with the invader was possible. For the young man, steeped in the principles of non-violence since his earliest childhood, this journey was fully justified even though it had been the subject of sharp criticism in his own country.

II

Alas, on his return to Lhasa, the Dalai Lama realized how worthless Mao's promises were! The news from the Khampa region was extremely distressing. A village chief had been dragged around like a cur with a chain around his neck for having tried to flee. In another village, fifty babies had been snatched away from their mothers and sent to China to be educated there. Parents who dared to protest were drowned in the river. A girl of twelve was made to shoot her father, accused of being anti-patriotic. In another village, some people were gunned down for having set the bad example of making religious offerings. In Takster, the village where he was born, he had great difficulty in meeting one of his cousins. When he asked him if people were happy, the cousin answered with tears in his eyes: "We are very happy and prosperous under the Communist Party and Chairman Mao Tse-tung". This was enough for the Dalai Lama to understand all the fear and anguish those words must have contained.

At the end of his journey, the Dalai Lama, confronted with violence, hatred, and lies felt the bitter taste of deceit. He was overcome by a sense of frustration and helplessness: there was nothing he could do to help his people or fulfill the divine task assigned to him by his reincarnation. As the Boddhisatva, which literally means the Wise One, it was his mission on earth to stay and help others. Like Judaism and Christianity, Mahayana Buddhism as practiced in Tibet emphasizes that spiritual perfection sought only for the self is limited. This is

The Mountains of the Buddha

how the ideal of the Bodhisatva developed. A Bodhisatva is one who rather than enter the glorious peace of eternal *nirvana* chooses to return to earth in a human form to comfort and guide all suffering beings on the path to supreme realization. In this way, Buddhism in Tibet has responded to the human need for a divine guide, a concept that does not exist in the Hinayana or early Buddhism.

Tenzin Gyatso was deeply disturbed. A magazine photograph showing severed heads confirmed his worst fears about the atrocities being committed by the Chinese. The caption read: "Reactionary Criminals". From that moment onwards, he had absolutely no reason to doubt the horrors people were speaking of. This and the fact that the new committee — Mao's way of appeasing the Tibetan demand for autonomy — was a complete eyewash made him wonder if there was any hope for the future at all. News from the east spoke of terror and death. The Khampas had declared war. From their hiding places, they would attack the invading army in a display of remarkable courage. They were fighting to defend their home, their faith and their race. Mounted on horseback, these fearless warriors, brandishing sabres and guns, fell furiously on the long columns of Chinese trucks. Not a single garrison on the highway passed unscathed. Desperate, these wild riders of Tibet followed on the trail of their great ancestors. They were joined by the monks from Kham, attired in their crimson habit. These monks had pulled out the arms kept in the monastery and used by their predecessors in times when monasteries were often at war with each other. Along with the arms, they also took the sacred relics whose power guaranteed a long life and provided holy immunity.

Fifty thousand nomads left their women, children and flocks to meet the enemy. They managed to overpower most of the Chinese detachments and gain control over the highway. For the invaders, the situation was critical: in the face of such resistance, they ran the risk of losing their newly

The Year of the Earth Pig

acquired territories. But as calm prevailed in Lhasa, the West received no news of the Khampa war. This was an unequal war: the roar of Chinese planes over buildings, the din of walls crashing and wood being smashed into a thousand pieces against the occasional crack of a shotgun aimed at the steel birds on their way to bombard the monasteries of Kham. The Chinese did manage to wrest a few cities and villages where the wives and children of rebels as well as the monks were executed and tortured. The campaign against religion was intensified. Priors and Abbots were tied to horse tails and dragged before the petrified children, women and elders, who had to stay back. Mass executions took place and blood curdling forms of torture were practiced. Monks wrapped in petrol-soaked woolen robes were set on fire as Chinese soldiers would look on jeeringly and ask these human torches what had become of their Buddha.

As news of the brutal repression reached Tenzin Gyatso, he sent a letter of protest to Mao, but weeks passed by without a reply. He wrote another letter, which too went unanswered. The Chinese General stationed in Lhasa did promise to take some action against such brutality, but nothing happened. The situation was desperate. The news of the atrocities sparked off further revolt. After the Khampas, it was the turn of the Goloks from Amdo to raise their arms, followed by the Sherpas from Kansu. Then there was trouble in Turkistan with the Muslim Uigurs deciding once again to revolt against the "motherland". The Dalai Lama's worst fears were being confirmed. There he was, barely 23 years old, helpless in the face of the growing violence.

For the Chinese leaders, these developments posed a serious challenge to their supremacy over the high plateaus. Mao acknowledged that his old dream of dominating Central Asia could collapse at any moment. The 1956 popular rising in Hungary came as a warning to the Chinese of the risk they ran in the territories they had annexed. Reports from Kham revealed that the air raids had not been able to weaken the resistance of the guerrillas. Every time the Chinese captured a village, they only encountered children and old people: everyone else had fled to the mountains. The Khampas naïvely believed that victory was at hand; soon their country would be free and they would rebuild the great Tibet of their forefathers. They returned to Lhasa and appealed to the Dalai Lama — the centre of their universe and the embodiment of the values they were fighting for — to let Central Tibet join their crusade. One word from the Dalai Lama was all that was needed for the whole country to rise against the Chinese.

Tenzin Gyatso knew this. Though he admired the guerrillas, he was convinced that to encourage violence would be madness. The Chinese may have suffered a few reverses but they were by far the more powerful. He had been to Peking, he had seen China, he had measured the strength of the adversary. If one word from him could incite the whole of Tibet to revolt, one word from Mao could raze it to the ground.

III

It was at this point that the God King received an invitation from India to attend the twenty-five hundredth birth anniversary of the Buddha. For the Dalai Lama, it was like a breath of fresh air, a sign that the outside world was beginning to understand: "I have no words to describe the feeling of political isolation that exists in Tibet," he declared. In New Delhi, Prime Minister Nehru took a whole afternoon off to let his guest discover the splendour of the Mughal Gardens in the Presidential Palace, riding on an elephant.

The Year of the Earth Pig

It was also a time for confidences. The Dalai Lama spoke of the horror his country was going through and of his own personal dilemma. On the one hand, the Khampas were asking him to join the rebellion; on the other, the Chinese were insisting he dispatch his soldiers to fight against the insurgents. He had opposed this, though he had also officially condemned the rebels. The situation was developing in a way that seemed to preclude any role for him. His failure to prevent his people from taking recourse to violence and the acknowledgement that his efforts for peace had been a fiasco made him wonder whether it would not be more advisable for him to seek political asylum in India from where, with the help of the Indian people, he would be in a better position to secure the freedom of his country through peaceful means. But Nehru turned a deaf ear to this appeal for help. He advised him to return to his country and try the path of negotiation to avoid the worst. The Indian Prime Minister did not want any trouble with his powerful Chinese neighbour with whom he felt a close affinity. As soon as he learnt of the Dalai Lama's intentions, Chou En-lai, Chinese foreign minister and a friend of Nehru's, rushed to the Indian capital to persuade Tenzin Gyatso to return to Lhasa. The Chinese could not bear the idea of losing the "sacred incarnation", the man who had proved to be their trump card in gaining control over Central Tibet. Though they had tried hard to glorify the Panchen Lama, the fact was that the Dalai Lama remained the undisputed leader of all Tibetans. Chou En-lai reiterated to the Dalai Lama his government's determination to withdraw its troops from Tibet and postpone reforms until 1962.

Once again, Tenzin Gyatso was faced with a conflict. His family members were of the unanimous opinion that he should seek exile. And this time even his ministers, skeptical of Chou En-lai's promises, gave him similar advice.

While in Delhi, he went to pay homage to a man who had fought unto death to preserve the spirit of India and mankind, a true believer of peace and harmony among peoples. "If only I had the privilege of meeting him in this life!", thought the

Tibetan. Standing before the marble mausoleum of Mahatma Gandhi, Tenzin Gyatso wondered what advice Gandhi would have given him had he been alive. The Mahatma would have surely spared no effort to launch a peaceful campaign for the liberation of Tibet. "At that moment, I felt very close to him, I felt his advice would have been to always follow the path of peace. Today, as then, my faith in the doctrine of non-violence that Gandhi preached and practiced is unshakable. At his mausoleum, I took the firm decision of following his example, regardless of all the difficulties that I would have to face. I was more convinced than ever that I would never encourage or participate in any act of violence."[4] He had got his answer: he had to return to his people and, without any trace of hatred or weakness, confront the Chinese oppressor. This was his mission, however hopeless it might seem.

IV

In 1957, the Khampas realized that to incite the people to a general revolt, they would need the backing of the sovereign. Opposing the Dalai Lama and his cabinet was a dangerous plan, but they saw it as the only way to free Tibet[5].

The vastness of the plateau and the rugged nature of the terrain gave the Khampas an edge; they were able to check

---

[4] As reported in the Dalai Lama's autobiography.
[5] Source: "Cavaliers of Kham: The Secret War in Tibet" by Michel Peissel (Little & Brown, 1972).

The Year of the Earth Pig

the advance of the Chinese soldiers in spite of the Chinese being far greater in number and better equipped. Even after seven years of occupation, the Chinese only controlled small parts of the highlands. It was easy for them to reduce a monastery to ruins, but they could do nothing to wipe out these horsemen constantly on the move. Fearing only air raids, the Khampas moved freely all over the territory. They were better adapted to the climate and had a long martial tradition. Fighting came as naturally to them as breathing. At the end of 1957, eighty thousand Khampa warriors began their conquest of the Loka region, which they thought was a stepping stone to Central Tibet. In a short space of time, they neutralized all the Chinese strongholds. Next, they managed the astonishing feat of taking over the whole of south-eastern Tibet.

The Communists had to acknowledge that their initial offensive to put down the rebellion had ended in a fiasco. They had tried propaganda, they had bombarded three hundred cities and monasteries of Kham, but they had failed to intimidate these men who were determined to free their country. For the third time, the Chinese asked the Dalai Lama to order the Tibetan troops to fight against the rebels. Tenzin Gyatso squarely refused to do so; the Tibetan troops, he said, would probably desert and join the guerrillas. As the Khampa rebellion spread to Central Tibet, the Dalai Lama felt he was being cornered. He admired the Khampas, he could understand their thirst for justice and freedom, but he knew that openly siding with them only meant provoking the invaders and adding fuel to the fire of repression. On the other hand, if he went into exile, the Chinese would be free to unleash their wrath against the people. He was well and truly trapped.

In December 1958, the guerrillas gained access to Lhasa from the south-east. The number of fighters infiltrating the capital was swelling by the day. Many of them came in broad daylight, armed to the teeth, harassing passersby.

Seven years of occupation had made little difference to life in Lhasa. It was a carefree world in which the refinement of the West blended curiously with the traditional pomp of an ancient society. A feudal theocracy co-existed in apparent harmony with the most dogmatic Communist party in the world. Together, they constituted the elite of the capital from where they ran the country. In exchange for their loyalty, the regime maintained their privileges. The capital's gentry enjoyed nothing more than a good game of tennis. In affluent homes, young couples attired in their traditional best gaily swayed to the music of records purchased in Hong Kong. With his silky voice and broad sideburns, Dundu-La was a household name, the Elvis Presley of Tibet, as writer and explorer Michel Peissel described him. Men and women enjoyed the good life and romantic intrigues. Many Tibetans blithely continued in the belief that theirs was a charmed land that not even time could touch. Any one who respected the law and performed all the rituals would be granted divine protection.

Unfortunately, the government and aristocracy of Lhasa completely disregarded what was happening around them. When the Chinese came, they believed they could merge their old lifestyle with militant socialism. So, the women took up humanitarian causes: they did voluntary work in the newly built schools and hospitals. They enjoyed the thrill of modern gadgets, an exciting novelty for them. But Lhasa also had its share of cardinals who ruled over large monasteries. Most of them were men of great integrity even though they lived in the gilded apartments of their predecessors. But there were also those who wanted nothing more than to escape the rigours of the monastic life.

The Lhasa elite could take pity on Chinese soldiers suffering from altitude sickness, but they could not see the trouble brewing on their own streets. Due to the repression in the east, a growing number of women and old people were fleeing to the capital. By early 1959, more than fifteen

The Year of the Earth Pig

thousand families were camping on the outskirts of Lhasa at the foot of the Potala, as thousands of young monks from Kham sought refuge in the schools of the great monasteries of Drepung, Sera and Ganden. With the infiltration of the Khampa guerrillas, tension mounted in the holy city. The Chinese armed civilians and raised barricades. The army raided the houses of those suspected of giving shelter to the rebels. In the daytime, corpses of captured warriors were displayed in the streets for everyone to see. The Chinese feared an imminent uprising. At the Norbulingka Palace, a war of attrition was being waged. With each passing day, the anger of the Chinese officers who went to meet the Dalai Lama grew, as he refused to accede to their demands, in accordance with the teachings of his masters. The generals accused the Tibetan government of complicity with the Khampa rebels while the latter thought that it was colluding with the invaders. Tenzin Gyatso was in a desperate situation.

After a group of Khampas dislodged a garrison of three thousand soldiers stationed forty kilometres from Lhasa, the rebels made a last appeal to the Dalai Lama to join them. Tenzin Gyatso turned it down, reiterating his distaste for violence. He begged the Khampas to return to their homes and make peace with the Chinese. His exact words were, "I admire the valour of the Khampas, but their actions are causing great harm to all those who are trying to find a way of co-existing with the Chinese." The Khampas, exasperated and convinced that the Chinese had brainwashed the God King, refused to wait any more. They had decided to take the reigns of power in their own hands.

On the first of March in the year of the Earth Pig, that is 1959, the Dalai Lama went to the Jokhang to attend the annual prayer festival, after which he would be taking his final exams for a doctorate in metaphysics. While the ceremony was still going on, two Chinese officials asked to see him. Nervously, they requested the Dalai Lama to choose a date on which it would be convenient for him to attend a Chinese opera that a general of the army was intending to stage at the military headquarters on the outskirts of Lhasa. Tenzin Gyatso accepted, but said he would decide on the date only after finishing his examinations. Disappointed, the two men left.

The next day, Ocean of Wisdom debated logic and metaphysics before hundreds of monks. He had spent hours practicing first with students of his own level and later with more erudite Lamas. After answering all the trickiest questions with ease, the jury unanimously awarded him the degree of Doctor of Buddhist Studies.

On the fifth of March, he left the Jokhang to return to the Norbulingka Palace. It was for the last time that this thousand-year-old civilization would display its pomp and pageantry. The horses moved proudly, as if they knew their bridles were made of gold. Behind the God King's palanquin came the members of the Lhasa government and nobility, richly attired in their silken clothes. They were followed by eminent Abbots and Lamas, some dignified and ascetic, others looking more like prosperous merchants in spite of their high spiritual attainment. At the end of the procession were thousands of Tibetans.

Five days later, the Chinese sent another message to the Dalai Lama, urging him to fix a date when he could attend the opera. The Dalai Lama chose the tenth of March. But a day before, his chief of security conveyed to him another message from the Chinese General. His Holiness was requested to reach the headquarters without his habitual escort. Only two unarmed guards could accompany him. Furthermore, he was to keep his visit a secret. That was enough to spread the rumour that the opera was a trap and that the Precious Protector would be taken hostage. Thousands of Tibetans marched from all sides to the Norbulinkga Palace. A huge crowd of angry men and women started congregating outside the palace walls. The inhabitants of Lhasa had decided to do all they could to protect their God King.

The Year of the Earth Pig

On the morning of the tenth of March, the Jewel Park was surrounded by thousands of people. The Khampas, seeking to take advantage of this spontaneous outburst and hoping to force the Dalai Lama to declare his opposition to the Chinese, took charge of the feverish crowd.

Tenzin Gyatso, sensing the mood of the people and wanting to protect them, sent a message to the Chinese, communicating his inability to attend the opera. Immediately after, when he told the crowd he was not going, they were jubilant.

But not a soul budged.

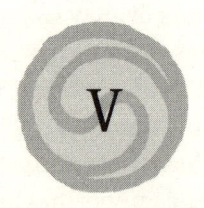

V

There was little the Dalai Lama could do to avert the tragedy about to be enacted. The Chinese wanted the Tibetan Government to disperse the crowd, or else they would do it themselves. Any which way, it meant destruction and death. The Dalai Lama tried to play for time. He wrote to the Chinese generals, begging them to be patient. His next task was to try and pacify the leaders of the insurgent crowd. But all his efforts failed. People in the streets were already branding whatever arms they could, even if they were just kitchen knives. Barricades were put up all over the city. This was becoming a full-fledged battle. A group of hotheads calling itself the Committee for the Liberation of Tibet marched to the Potala. Before a crowd of thirty thousand people, the members of the Committee claimed to have set up a new government of which they were the leaders and rejected the seventeen point agreement signed in Peking. They declared war on China and ordered the occupation forces to evacuate the capital. Thus, in front of his eyes, the Dalai Lama saw his nine years of striving for a peaceful settlement with the invader go up in smoke.

Scores of trucks loaded with men and munitions arrived at the Chinese army headquarters. The soldiers mounted heavy machine guns and canons on strategic spots, all pointing to the Norbulingka. As always in his moments of crises, Tenzin Gyatso consulted the Oracle. "Stay," the Oracle told him. "try and keep up the dialogue with the Chinese." For the first time in his life, the Monarch doubted the Oracle's answer. Had not his tutors told him that when in despair even the Gods lied?

The following days were marked by total confusion. For the crowds, the much awaited moment of jubilation had come at last. Tibet had united again, a unity it had lost in the centuries of discord and factionalism that followed the reign of Songtsen Gampo, the unifier of the country. The Tibetans had come together not to fight against the privileges of the aristocracy but the tyranny of Communist China's imperialism. Much to the delight of the rebellious crowds, seventy officers of the Dalai Lama's guard publicly associated themselves with the Liberation Committee, declaring that henceforth they would not take orders either from Chinese officials or Tibetan ministers.

On the morning of the eleventh of March, one of the military quarters of the Tibetan army opened its doors and soldiers started distributing arms to the crowds. The rebels raised barricades in the northern part of the city, blocking the road leading to the airport, where the Chinese had amassed tanks and machine guns. The Dalai Lama convened a meeting of the rebel leaders, which was attended by seventy chiefs and high officials. He pleaded with them to remove their barricades and put an end to their military activities. But his call went

The Year of the Earth Pig

unheeded. The rebel chiefs replied that irrespective of his advice, they had made up their minds to press for a complete Chinese withdrawal from Tibet. The Dalai Lama wrote later that, "The cause of events filed me with great despair. I had the impression that we were heading toward disaster."

On the sixteenth of March the Chinese general sent a letter to the Dalai Lama. They were going to attack the Norbulingka Palace and wished to know his exact whereabouts in order to avoid bombing that portion of the building. Were the Chinese really concerned about his life or was it a ploy to get at their target? There could not have been a more ambiguous promise of protection. The ministers and members of the Kashag, the Dalai Lama's cabinet, were of the unanimous opinion that the time had come for the sovereign to escape. The Oracle too changed his advice: "Go!" he told him, "Leave this very night!". On a sheet of paper he scrawled instructions for the flight. Forty years later it transpired that the real oracle in this case had been the CIA. Without the knowledge of the Dalai Lama, the CIA, which was also aiding the Khampas, had told the Oracle what to say. This operation had been personally supervised by Alan Dulles, the then Director of the American agency. At the very moment the Oracle was speaking, two mortar shells fell on the Jewel Park, as if to give further weight to his words. Time was running out; it was now a question of life and death.

As night approached, the young Monarch withdrew to his apartments. He removed his monk's habit and dressed in the clothes and leather hat typical of the Khampas. It was strange that he, who had so long opposed the violence of these warriors, should now be dressed like one. He entered his sanctuary for the last time. Some monks were saying prayers in the feeble light of yak butter lamps. Though they noticed his presence, not one of them looked up, not even when he placed a white silk scarf on the altar, a traditional farewell custom. The monks knew how to keep quiet. One of them played the cymbals while another blew an oboe, producing a plaintive moan. Its vibrations had a tranquilizing effect on Tenzin Gyatso. Seated on a meditation cushion, he opened a sacred book and started reading a passage in which the Buddha exhorts one of his disciples not to lose courage. Then he closed the book. For the last time, he looked at this place which had given him so much peace in his moments of uncertainty, blessed it and slowly withdrew.

The escape was planned in the utmost secrecy. Both the Chinese and the people of Lhasa were completely in the dark about the impending flight. The escape was organized by the Khampas, supposedly in consultation with the CIA. A rebel captain of the God King's personal guard was assigned to accompany the Dalai Lama till the main gate of the Norbulingka Palace. Carrying a gun on his shoulder, the sovereign looked like an ordinary soldier. To further disguise himself, he had removed his spectacles. The captain told the crowds thronging the palace gates that they were carrying out a routine inspection and so the Dalai Lama left unnoticed.

It was a clear, starry night. The lights from the Chinese headquarters glittered in the distance. On the lookout for enemy patrols, the small group advanced stealthily. At ten o'clock, after crossing the Kyichu river, the Dalai Lama joined his mother, brother and sister, who were waiting for him there, in disguise like him. The three main Khampa chiefs and a young CIA agent were also present. In a brief and solemn ceremony, they exchanged silk scarves. The rebels had, at last, gotten what they wanted: the God King was in their midst. Then began the trek across the mountains. Though his body was fleeing, the Dalai Lama's thoughts remained in Lhasa. He wondered what would become of his people. When they reached a pass 4,800 metres high, the God King stopped to look back. This was the last time he would be seeing Lhasa. The old city, extending across the valley, seemed as serene as ever. He barely had enough time to say a prayer before

The Year of the Earth Pig

going on with the journey. They had to hurry. That very night, the CIA agent sent a radio message to Okinawa to say that the operation was under way. The message was then relayed to Washington, where Dulles, head of the CIA, immediately informed President Eisenhower. Tibet was lost, but the Dalai Lama was safe.

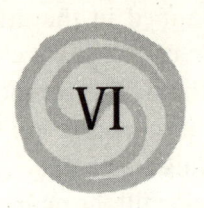

VI

In the early hours of the nineteenth of March 1959, as the God King's caravan advanced slowly over the mountains, the occupation troops fired their guns at the Norbulingka Palace. The thundering of mortar and canons in the dark had the inhabitants of Lhasa jump out of their beds. Convinced that the Dalai Lama was in mortal danger, men and women, young and old, rushed out onto the streets with whatever arms they had, without stopping to think just how powerful the enemy was. Years of occupation had revived the old warrior like spirit of the people. When the battle broke out, many harbored the naïve hope that the outside world would finally react and do something about the sorry plight of Tibet. But this did not happen. The CIA limited itself to covert assistance to the Khampas. The North Americans were not ready to jump into another Korea or Vietnam. On direct orders from Nehru, the news of the Lhasa rising was blacked out in New Delhi. The Indian Prime Minister did not want to do anything to jeopardize his policy of friendship with China.

The Mountains of the Buddha

In spite of Nehru's efforts to prevent the world from knowing, the truth filtered through gradually thanks to the courage and persistence of an old English missionary, George Patterson[6]. Patterson knew Tibet like the back of his hand and was a friend of the Khampas. From the Indian border town of Kalimpong, he dispatched articles to the Daily Telegraph in London, in which he wrote about the resistance of these incredible mountain warriors on horseback. By Friday, the 21st of March, the streets of Lhasa were strewn with corpses and Patterson's reports got front page coverage. He wrote about the Chinese bombardment of the Summer Palace and the massacre of hundreds of civilians. In the heap of bodies lying under the rubble, the soldiers searched feverishly for the mortal remains of the Dalai Lama. Till the very end, the high command simply refused to believe that he had escaped. They had to destroy this living symbol of the country they wanted to wipe off the map. In retaliation to the attack on the summer palace, the Khampa guerrillas, who had taken refuge in the medical school on the Chakpori hill, fired at the Chinese. The Chinese razed the building. On the same day, they gunned down all the civilians out on the streets of the city and came down viciously on those demonstrating in front of the official cars.

On Saturday afternoon, a pitched battle took place in the city centre. Chinese and Tibetans exchanged fire from the rooftops while below a frenzied crowd ran down the streets, hurling Molotov cocktails at buildings fortified by the Chinese. Columns of smoke were rising from all directions, as houses went up in flames. The massive stone walls of the Jokhang temple withstood the constant fire of the Chinese artillery until, finally, a shell smashed its golden dome, exploding in the chapels where women and children had taken refuge. By the morning of the twenty-second of March, the Tibetans in

---

[6] As reported by Michel Peissel in "Cavaliers of Kham: The Secret War in Tibet".

The Year of the Earth Pig

the valley, the Summer Palace and the Potala knew they were fighting a hopeless battle. Two days of intensive bombardment left a heap of bodies against the holy walls. Gradually, the firing in the heart of the city died down and monasteries, surrounded by tanks on all sides, capitulated one after another.

At a distance of four kilometres from Lhasa, the Monastic University of Sera resembled a fortified city sprawling over a hillside on top of which towered gigantic statues of the Buddha sculpted in rock. Inside was a maze of small narrow streets joining multicoloured buildings of different shapes and sizes that housed nearly four thousand monks. In sharp contrast to the dark cells whose walls had been blackened by incense fumes, the facades of the temple were painted in dazzling colours: crimson, yellow, emerald green, marine blue, gold and silver. Buddha images filled walls twenty metres high and visitors had to look up to see the serenely smiling face of the Enlightened One. In this ancient landmark of Tibetan culture, imbued with centuries of deep spirituality, Lama Thubten Yeshe had spent nineteen of his twenty-five years: "It was a marvelous place, so sacred... It was a seat of learning and we had a lot to study, in particular some of the finer points of Buddhist philosophy, such as the nature of reality, emptiness and the doctrine of the middle path. My needs were looked after by the religious community. I did not desire very much. It was very peaceful and I was convinced that I would spend my whole life there."[7]

But destiny-or was it *karma*?– had decided otherwise. While the firing was going on and bombs were being hurled nearby, Thubten Yeshe was compelled to leave what had been his home since the time his parents had left him there in the care of a monk who was his uncle. Like many other monks,

---

[7] Quoted in "Reincarnation", by Vicki Mackenzie (Time Books International, New Delhi, 1992)

he decided to flee with a group of companions. "I realized I had to go", he recounted later. "I had no choice: it was either leaving Tibet or renouncing the spiritual life and prayer. I knew intuitively that Lhasa and the monastery were finished forever. I remember how depressed I was those days; it was very difficult for me to hold back my tears. My friends said we would return, but in my heart of hearts I knew no one would ever return. It was awful to have to say goodbye. I had the time to go to Tolung, the nearby village in which my family lived. My parents were peasants. My sister begged me not to go and said I could hide in her house till the storm blew over. But I knew I had to go. I did not dare say goodbye to my mother. It would have broken her heart."

Thus, Lama Yeshe and his friends took off their monk's robes to dress as peasants and flee across the Himalayas, following the same trail that the Dalai Lama had taken a few days earlier. For the first time in his life, he had to face adversity and beg for food. At the rate monks were fleeing, there would soon be no hermits left in Tibet. Tibetan hermeticism had been forced open; its main treasure, the teachings of Mahayana Buddhism, till then the preserve of a chosen few, began to be disseminated across the world. One of the people who played a major role in spreading Tibetan Buddhism was this young Lama from Sera, whose reincarnation would be discovered years later by his disciples in a village of Andalusia in southern Spain.

VII

The Dalai Lama's caravan was making its way slowly through snowstorms and blizzards when they heard the news of the massacre on the radio. Tenzin Gyatso was heartbroken. He had seen it coming, yet he had been unable to prevent it. The party halted at the place where the Dalai Lama announced the formation of his own Government. But there was no time to waste. The scouts had signalled Chinese troop movement near the border. An advance party of Khampas had already left for India to seek political asylum for the God King. If their request was turned down, they would either have to hide in the Loka region or ask for refuge in Bhutan.

Four days later, Ocean of Wisdom, exhausted and sick, reached the last village of Tibet. There, under rains, he learned that the Indian Government had accepted his asylum petition. In spite of his wanting to play it safe in his relations with China, Nehru could not ignore the wave of sympathy that existed in India for Tibet. When he stood up in Parliament to announce the arrival of the Dalai Lama in India, the whole hall broke out in thunderous applause.

On the morning of 31 March 1959, after bidding a tearful farewell to his Khampa escort which was going back to continue the struggle, Tenzin Gyatso was helped onto the rump of a black *dzo*, (a cross between a cow and a yak). It was on this humble mount, suffering from acute dysentery and in deep pain, that the God King left the land of his birth. He was twenty-four years old and he was going into exile.

On hearing of the Dalai Lama's escape, Mao uttered a sentence that for many years was to baffle all Tibetans in exile: "In that case, we have lost the battle." The news from Lhasa was humiliating. Even after nine years, China had not managed to dominate what it thought was a "country of feeble monks". Furthermore, how would they explain the absence of the Dalai Lama at the People's National Congress after all the propaganda they had done about his visit? The Chinese were furious. The army clamped down on Tibet and political repression of the most brutal kind was unleashed in the country. It was exactly as the Dalai Lama had predicted.

In Lhasa, ten thousand people, about one-fourth of the population of the city, were detained and imprisoned. No one was spared: men, women and children, rich and poor, were put behind bars. Some were sent off to re-education camps, others were publicly humiliated and executed, still others were forced to work as slaves near Lhasa. Curfew was imposed. The houses of rebels and their sympathizers were looted. The spoils were divided into three categories. The most valuable objects — jewelry, silver, gold and religious antiques — were sent to China. Furniture and carpets went to the Chinese army officers and civil servants. Finally, day to day objects such as watches and clothes were sold to the revolutionary workers. Then, announcements were made over loudspeakers telling the poor that local committees would be distributing the wealth of those who had exploited them. When they reached there, what the beggars found was a mound of broken chairs, empty chests, dirty clothes and if they were lucky, a pot or a pan. It was the same story in the countryside. The Chinese kept the farmers' animals, money and equipment whereas the poor got the same kind of worthless objects as were distributed in the cities.

This plundering marked the beginning of a well thought out policy aimed at destroying the six thousand monasteries and temples of Tibet. In the late sixties, when the Chinese

The Year of the Earth Pig

realized they had gone too far, they conveniently shifted the blame on the Gang of Four and the Cultural Revolution. But the fact remains that most of the monasteries were razed between 1959 and 1961. It was a systematic destruction. Ninety-seven trucks, each one weighing three tonnes, were required to carry off to China the treasures of the Sera Monastery. In order to avoid detection, the trucks would leave in the dead of night. Ancient monastic libraries were converted into storehouses and meeting rooms. The holy scriptures were used as fuel, fertilizer or wrapping paper in Chinese shops.

For many years, convoys continued to leave for the motherland, loaded with treasures from Tibet. Antique shops in Tokyo and Hong Kong abounded in priceless Tibetan objets d'art. However, gold and silver statues and images, some of which were more than a thousand years old, were melted into ingots in the Peking mint.

All the streets and parks of Lhasa that had names referring to Tibetan culture or religion were renamed. The new names – the Great Leap Ahead, Freedom Avenue, Happiness Street and Dawn Street – had something cruelly ironical about them. The hill on which had stood the most famous medical school of the region was now called Victory Peak and the gardens of Norbulingka, the People's Park. Lhasa was a city drained of life. For the world, the Chinese mounted a relentless propaganda campaign. They underplayed the extent of the revolt, saying it was the handiwork of serf owners and the upper classes. The crusade to defend the poor and oppressed Tibetans, claimed Peking, fully justified military control over the country. In reality, the hapless Tibetans were forced into working as peons and becoming "revolutionaries"; they were made to denounce the enemies of the people and punish them accordingly. They had no choice but to do as they were told. If they did not, they themselves became victims of "re-education". Never before had such a savage class war been waged: workers were pitted against bosses, peasants against landowners, monks against Abbots, students against teachers and children against parents. In comparison to what was happening, the excesses committed against the Khampas seemed mild. Public hangings, decapitation, organ removal, crucifixion, dismemberment and lynching inevitably followed the re-education or *thamzing* sessions.

In the year that followed the rebellion, thousands of Tibetans perished in these re-education sessions, which were nothing more than summary trials; many more were amputated. Monks who followed Tantricism were forced at gunpoint to break their vows of chastity and publicly copulate with nuns in front of the entrance of the Jokhang. As a result of the *thamzing* sessions, not only were the Tibetans in mortal fear of the Chinese but they also came to distrust one another. Old friends could no longer talk to each other and parents had to watch what they said in front of their children.

However, it was the clergy that had to face the worst of the Chinese ire: two years after the rebellion, only thirty of the ten thousand monks at the Drepung Monastery — one of the largest in the world — were left. The Chinese knew that the clergy constituted the most cohesive and potentially dangerous group. After plundering the monasteries, they launched a vicious disinformation campaign against the monks in which they accused them of having committed crimes of the worst kind. Ignorant of Buddhist practices, the Chinese came up with novel forms of punishment. Monks who had developed esoteric singing techniques, enabling them to intonate three notes at the same time, were made to undergo *thamzing* for possessing bourgeois voices. Seven months after the Lhasa rebellion, thousands of monks were sent to the first labour camp in Tibet, located a few kilometres east of the capital. Others were sent up to the north to work in borax mines. The Communists had wanted to keep them alive, but nearly all the monks died in the first few years itself, unable to withstand the rigours of the camps: twelve hours of hard

The Year of the Earth Pig

labour every day on a starvation diet, with no medical care to speak of and hardly any clothing to brave the cold. Only a handful of monks were left to look after the ruins of the Sera and Ganden monasteries that had been the pillars of Tibetan culture. What the Chinese did not realize however was that by attacking the monasteries, they had attacked each and every family of Tibet, as it was the custom for each family to send at least one son to a nearby monastery; and by attacking the Gods, they had insulted the entire nation. Not even the Panchen Lama, the most prominent collabourator of the regime, could find it within him to continue defending the revolution. He gradually distanced himself from the official line and began to support the demands of his people. Life under the People's Liberation Army was harsh. To make matters worse, China was faced with widespread famine on account of the utter failure of its Great Leap Forward policy whereby the peasantry was made to bear the entire burden of modernization. As if that was not enough, the break with the Soviet Union had deprived China of vital wheat supplies. This happened as a result of China's expansionist designs.

In the middle of the twentieth century, a great and powerful nation was trying to wipe out an entire race, its religion and people. The world, evidently, did not care. But when Chinese territorial claims extended to countries beyond Tibet, then problems arose. The Chinese declared that all Tibetan speaking regions of Central Asia were an integral part of China. By virtue of this reasoning, thirty thousand square kilometres of Russian soil and forty thousand square kilometres of Indian and Nepali soil belonged to them. The Soviets reacted violently. They suspended all cooperation with their former ally, called back their technicians and stopped the export of spare parts, arms and, worse still, food grains. The Chinese decided to make up the shortfall with crops from Tibet. Consequently, the Tibetans were left to starve, their diet reduced by two-thirds. Tens of thousands died in the famine.

There were stories of fathers feeding their dying sons their own blood mixed with water and *tsampa* . Many would eat the scraps the Chinese threw at the pigs. Others ate mice, cats, dogs and insects. Prison conditions were awful. But it was absolutely forbidden to speak of the hearses that left the prison each day, piled with dead bodies of starving prisoners.

The Panchen Lama, who was in Peking in his capacity as Chairman of the Preparatory Committee for the Autonomy of Tibet — a responsibility he had accepted at the time of dissolution of the Tibetan government which had gone into exile — denounced the situation. The Chinese army surrounded his monastery Tashi Lumpo, the only one they left untouched, and detained the four thousand monks there. Accused of having taken part in the Lhasa rebellion even though there was no proof of it, many monks and Priors were put through barbaric *thamzing* sessions and then shot dead. Others including Lamas and respected scholars, fearing a similar or worse fate, chose to take their own lives. Those who remained were deported to labour camps. The destruction of this monastery and the brutal way in which the monks had been treated caused deep distress to the Panchen Lama. He wrote a strong letter to Mao, condemning what had happened — the chaos, the starvation and the abuse. He also asked for the restoration of all the religious monuments destroyed. Mao assured him that they would seriously consider the points he had raised. What actually happened was that he was forced to relinquish his post and the old monks of Tashi Lumpo were publicly mistreated. But the Panchen Lama did not budge from his stand and, faithful to tradition, repeatedly declared that the Dalai Lama was the real leader of Tibet. The Panchen Lama had met his spiritual father only once in Lhasa when both were teenagers. Fourteen and seventeen years old, they were puppets in the hands of the Chinese. The Dalai Lama had managed to escape from the clutches of the invaders. The Panchen Lama had not.

The Year of the Earth Pig

The Chinese were furious; this change of attitude was the last thing they had expected from one whom they had always considered a collabourator. They gave him one last chance to mend his ways. He was told that he had to denounce the Dalai Lama in public during the Annual Prayer Festival, permitted that year for this express purpose. But the Panchen Lama had other ideas. In front of a crowd of ten thousand, from a pulpit on the southern side of the Jokhang temple, the Panchen Lama asked for greater freedom of religion for his people. When the time came for him to denounce the Dalai Lama as a reactionary, he stopped to pause and look at the crowd: "I must pronounce my firm belief that Tibet will soon regain her independence and that His Holiness the Dalai Lama will return to the Lion Throne. Long live His Holiness the Dalai Lama!". The collaborator had redeemed himself in the eyes of his people. But for the Chinese the ally had become a traitor. Stunned by this open act of defiance, the Chinese immediately put him under arrest. A few days later, he was made to stand trial for crimes against the people. He was pulled from his chair and made to bow while cadres, springing from their seats, began to slap, punch and kick him. The spectacle of seeing one of Tibet's highest Lamas beaten in this way deeply disturbed the Tibetan delegates. After the trial, the Panchen Lama, his parents and retinue were handcuffed and taken away in trucks to an unknown destination. The Panchen Lama was twenty-seven years old at the time. Nothing was heard of him for the next fourteen years.

VIII

On the other side of the mountains, the Dalai Lama was discovering the free world. However, things were not quite as he had hoped they would be. His long conversation with Nehru had left the young monarch disillusioned. It was clear that Indian diplomacy would never support Tibet against China, a neighbour too dangerous to be provoked. The Indian Prime Minister was ready to extend hospitality to the Dalai Lama provided the latter confined himself to his religious duties and refrained from any political activity or propaganda in favour of independence for Tibet. However, Nehru assured him of all humanitarian aid possible.

In keeping with Nehru's wishes, Ocean of Wisdom remained silent for two months. But the horrifying accounts of the havoc wrought by the Chinese as told by refugees who crossed the Himalayas in their thousands compelled him to break his silence and publicly condemn the Chinese. He issued an appeal to the International Commission of Jurists to investigate the atrocities the refugees spoke of. The Commission, comprising eminent legal experts, also decided to look into the question of Tibet's sovereignty. In its report, China was found guilty of having committed the worst possible crime against humanity: genocide, i.e., "the attempt to destroy in totality or partially a national, ethnic, racial or religious group as such". The report concluded that Tibet had been a sovereign and independent state before the invasion. Heartened by the findings of the Commission, the Dalai Lama attempted to raise the question of Tibet in the United Nations. Unfortunately, in the political climate of the Cold War, there was not one member of consequence willing to sponsor the cause of a country lost somewhere between heaven and earth. In world politics Tibet meant nothing. Once again everyone deserted Tibet.

The Dalai Lama soon realized that politics had little to do with faith and idealism, even less justice. He would never give up the demand for the freedom of his people. But he learnt that things happened in their own time and that he had to wait. Some day in his lifetime truth and justice would prevail. The tragic plight of his people continued nonetheless to torment him. There was nothing he could do for his compatriots back home, but there was plenty he could do to help the refugees. The first batch of refugees were men; then came entire families. Clad in their woolens and fur boots, they made an odd sight in a country where temperatures often soar beyond forty. They were tired, ill and hungry, with nothing but a few religious relics to call their own. They spoke of their journey across the Himalayas: of storms, frost, avalanches, and fugitives bombed by the Chinese; of their companions who had died of cold and of despair. Out of the four thousand refugees who left Tibet in June 1959 only twenty-five made it to India.

However, arriving in a friendly country did not mean the end of the ordeal for the survivors. It just assumed another face. The refugees were taken to two camps, Missamari and Buxa Duar, the latter being an old British prison, located near Bhutan, which consisted of thirty sheds spread over three densely covered hills. Lama Yeshe, who had survived the bitter cold of the month long journey across the Himalayas, said: "It was a great shock. I thought I had returned to the same hell."

In spite of the terrible conditions, these camps did represent a major effort on the part of the Indian Government.

In consultation with the Opposition, it was to decided to set up a rescue committee to provide food and medicine and channelize international aid. But there was no way of dealing with the oppressive heat, lack of immunity and unfamiliar food very different from the Tibetan staple of barely, butter and meat. All these took their toll. Lama Yeshe hated the Indian way of cooking rice and lentils. He could not stand the smell and felt sick for months on end. Many died of dysentery, tuberculosis, influenza and malnutrition. Others died of nostalgia, as they yearned to return to their homeland and continue the struggle. Amidst all the wailing in the camp, the lone voice of a monk, dressed in the clothes given by the Indian government, could be heard reciting a sutra. "It was our duty to tell the refugees that it would not be easy to return. Our stay in India was going to be a long one. We had to be mentally and physically prepared for it," said the Dalai Lama.

After being subjected to health and security checks by the Indian border police, monks, guerrillas and entire families waited in barracks to be sent to build roads in northern India for which they would receive a meager wage. This was part of a plan drawn up by the Dalai Lama and Nehru to stop the growing number of camp deaths and make the Tibetans feel that they were not living off Indian charity. But when the God King actually went to visit the site, his heart sank. How would his compatriots be able to withstand this foul smelling, mosquito laden air? And it was dangerous work with accidents occurring frequently. Somehow, Tenzin Gyatso managed to conceal his dismay. He kept telling his people not to lose heart, for some day they would surely return to their country.

It was on this trip that he realized that something had to be done for the children. Making them work on the roadways was condemning them to a life of brutality and poverty. They had to be cared for, fed, clothed and educated – they were, after all, the future of Tibet. Nehru understood the problem at once and was quick to provide help. As concerned about the little ones as his guest, he ordered the setting up of a Department of Tibet in the Ministry of Education within twenty-four hours. He agreed to the Dalai Lama's proposal of providing schools where the children could learn English — an international language and one of the official languages of India. The idea was to give them a well-rounded education, to teach them about the modern world — history, philosophy, science and technology — and give them, at the same time, a traditional Tibetan education. In 1966, seven thousand children were released from road construction work.

Ancient texts and holy writings were retrieved from the roadway workers, many of whom were monks who had managed to smuggle them out of the country. These texts were kept at the Buxa Duar camp where one thousand five hundred monks worked devotedly to preserve the teachings of Tibetan Buddhism. This community of scholars was the brainchild of the Dalai Lama, who, anxious to keep alive the religion and culture of his country, convinced the Indian Government to give it a subsidy. With stone and ink, the scholars began composing lithographs for two hundred volumes of sacred teachings — a fraction of the treasures of this millenary civilization. Thanks to their monastic discipline, they were able to pick up the thread of their existence. They resumed their studies and took on the task of saving what they could from oblivion. One of the scholars was Lama Yeshe. His friends recalled that he often reached late for the morning debate. He could never wake up on time because he stayed up the whole night, studying a subject whose utility no one could understand. Lama Yeshe was learning English. He did so with a passion, though his masters and friends opined it to be a waste of time; he would do better to study Hindi, they said. Fortunately, Lama Yeshe paid no heed to their advice and in time became one of the rare bridges between Tibetan Buddhism and Western culture.

The harsh conditions at Buxa Duar claimed many lives. After the morning prayer session, two to three hundred men would line up and wait their turn until they were attended to by the only health assistant available at the camp. Tuberculosis spread rapidly, as the Tibetans had not been immunized against such diseases. "We put up with all these hardships because we knew that the religious tradition of Tibet depended on us," said Lama Yeshe.

IX

It was in Dharamsala, an old British cantonment on the slopes of the Himalayas, at a day's journey from Delhi, that the Dalai Lama gave shape to his vision of Tibetan-society-in-exile. On April 29, 1960, the Dalai Lama arrived at the place chosen by the Indian Government as his permanent residence. On his way, he crossed some of the most beautiful landscapes in India, bright green fields dotted with trees and flowers. The Kashmir Cottage had been restored to welcome His Holiness, his mother, both his sisters, his brother-in-law, his master of the robes, the Chancellor and a group of secretaries and translators. Life was very different from that in Tibet. When it rained, buckets were placed next to the God King's bed to collect the water that fell from the leaking roof. He derived much pleasure from the simple things of life: long walks in the mountains, snow ball fights in winter, ping pong and badminton in the evenings. He had as pets a fawn and two Golden Apsos from Lhasa.

Ocean of Wisdom discovered he enjoyed simplicity. He was relieved to do away with most of the old protocol that had surrounded him since childhood. He hated formality. It was his wish to interact freely with his people and in Dharamsala he was able to do so, released from the rigid etiquette of the past. "My new circumstances allowed me to change things. To this extent, becoming a refugee was quite useful. It brought me much closer to reality," said the Dalai Lama.

Tenzin Gyatso used the money raised from the sale of the gold and silver that in 1950 the members of his government had taken out of the Potala and transported on yaks to safe-keeping to set up the Dalai Lama's Charity Fund in order to boost the cultural reconstruction of Tibet. He and his advisors were determined to keep alive that part of their culture which could help them face the present. While all forms of pomp and ceremony were discarded immediately, things like theatre, opera, literature, medicine, religion and trades that could help the refugees earn a living — painting, bronze work, architecture, woodwork, carpet weaving — received ample encouragement. Prime Minister Nehru kept his promise of providing all the humanitarian aid possible. Thanks to the generosity of the Indian government, twenty colonies were set up, accommodating as many as a hundred thousand refugees. The agricultural cooperatives prospered, leading to the resurgence of several monasteries. For the Tibetans, one was of special significance. It was the replica of the Monastic University of Sera near Lhasa. A great of deal of effort had gone into the construction of the central temple of the new university. An entire jungle had to be cleared for it to be built on a headland, surrounded by fields on all sides. Thirty years later, the monastery became the home of four thousand monks. Like the flame of an oil lamp that refuses to be snuffed out by the wind, they continue to keep alive the memory of Buddhism and Tibet.

X

In the meantime, most Tibetan villagers had taken to arms. Led by the Khampas, they ambushed and attacked Chinese military posts and convoys. Towards the end of 1961, the rebel chiefs decided to shift their headquarters to the Mustang region from where it would be easier to receive arms and ammunition from abroad. Starting from Nepal, this region juts into western Tibet like an elevated wedge. The kingdom of Mustang was a pocket of Tibetan language and culture. Though it belonged officially to Nepal, it was administered by a Tibetan king whose sympathies lay with the rebels. Their new headquarters made it much easier for the Khampas to plan and coordinate their resistance. It became commonplace to find these curiously dressed warriors roaming the streets of the Nepali capital, Kathmandu. There, they would meet their allies, Taiwanese and CIA agents. After the breakdown in Sino-Soviet relations, they once again began to intervene in Tibetan affairs, though in the utmost secrecy.

The Khampas set up a permanent base in the kingdom of Mustang, convinced that sooner or later foreign countries would play an active part in their war of liberation. They did not seem to realize that the great powers were not interested. George Patterson, the old missionary who had done so much to inform the British public of the Khampa struggle during the 1959 rebellion, went into Tibet, this time with a team of cameramen who filmed a Chinese convoy being attacked by the guerrillas. For the world, he hoped his film would be proof of an unknown struggle taking place in a far off land. In return for his labour, he was arrested by the Nepali authorities, in whose eyes he had committed a "major crime". This was proof that no one wanted to know. Patterson had managed to capture the Khampas as proud soldiers, well versed in warfare. Some of their raids met with unexpected success. In 1966, a group of horsemen ambushed a Chinese convoy and recovered extremely valuable documents from the body of the general in charge of the western command of the Chinese army, who was travelling with the convoy. It was a windfall both for the Tibetans and the CIA. One of the documents bore proof of the fact that eighty-seven thousand Tibetans had died in the 1959 rebellion, which the Chinese had consistently attempted to pass off as a "minor revolt". They also got precious information about Chinese plans that were going to cause an upheaval both in China and Tibet. Mao was determined to put an end to all internal dissent. Thus began the Great Proletarian Cultural Revolution, a period of collective madness, destruction and murder.

Though the Cultural Revolution unleashed a reign of terror in China, this was nothing in comparison to the suffering inflicted on Tibet. Mao's Red Guards decided to make a sport of the Land of Snows. In July 1966, a small group of Red Guards arrived in Lhasa to spark off the revolution. By the end of the month, they had shown just how brutal they could be. They had burst into the holy temple of Jokhang and indulged in an orgy of profanation, destroying its priceless treasures. For days on end, these fanatics had gone on the rampage, burning holy scriptures, decapitating Buddha statues and tearing up paintings. A part of the temple was destroyed; the remaining rooms were converted into a slaughterhouse for pigs and the chapels, later renamed Guesthouse No. 5, served as their headquarters. The few remaining monasteries came under relentless attack. Three years after the Cultural Revolution had begun, Tibet was reduced to a mound of ruins. The persecution of individuals had been just the first act in this gory drama which was to culminate in the wiping out of an entire civilization. The cultural heritage of Tibet had to give way to the thoughts of Chairman Mao. For sometime, it had become mandatory for all passersby to carry his Red Book. Chinese soldiers would stop people on the streets and force them to recite the thoughts of the Great Helmsman. Anyone incapable of doing so was taken to the nearest police station. The Apsos, a Lhasa breed of dogs, became special targets of the Red Guards, who viewed them as relics of the old society. And the Tibetans, who had been taught since childhood to protect all sentient beings, were given orders to kill them. Golden Lhasa Apsos became a dying breed, beaten, lynched and poisoned, victims of human madness.

Forcible collectivization was taking place in the countryside. Many peasants, initially pleased to see the old order crumble, later felt cheated, as the Chinese took all they had. They were compelled to hand over their livestock, implements and equipment to the authorities in exchange for a compensation that was never made. Collectivization also caused an upheaval in the life of the nomads, who had to give a part of their earnings to the authorities. In the communes, movement was restricted from the house to the field and back. Even to gather firewood from the nearby forests, permission was required. Worse still, in a religious country like Tibet, all references to religion were proscribed in attempt to completely obliterate the existence of Buddhism. The Red Guards ordered people to express disgust for the old society and "corrupt monks". Senior Lamas and officials were singled out for a particularly cruel form of punishment: made to wear to caps with donkey ears, they were paraded through Lhasa while being lashed by the Red Guards.

The Cultural Revolution lasted seven years. As the power struggle intensified, so did the atrocities. *Thamzing* sessions were followed by public beatings and rape. In the winter of

1967, for instance, a gang of revolutionaries carried off a group of nomad women, stripped them naked, handcuffed them and left them for six hours in freezing water. Suicide became a common occurrence. Rather than fall into the hands of the Chinese, the Tibetans preferred jumping from a cliff or drowning themselves in a river, despite the strong stigma that Buddhism attaches to suicide.

In the face of such brutality, the Tibetan response was to take to the mountains, some to flee to India, others to join the rebels. In 1968, "wind horses" fluttered all over Tibet, as rebels lay in wait to ambush the enemy. For the Tibetans, who have been punished to the point of being exterminated, these quiet deeds of heroism — episodes of a long, untold saga — and the figure of the Dalai Lama have come to symbolize the same thing: hope. It is to this hope that they cling, a hope that lies deep in their hearts, a place where the Chinese can never reach.

5
THE REALM OF THE GODS

I

The generation born in the early seventies had experienced the mindless brutality of the Cultural Revolution. Kinsom still remembers clearly how some young Red Guards in uniform forced her mother to hand over to them her prayer wheels, sacred scarves and yak butter lamps, which they burnt in a bonfire. Her mother somehow managed to keep a few sacred images and buried them at the foot of a tree. From time to time, she would take them out and look at them with reverence. Kinsom, a child then, did not realize that her mother was risking her life each time she did so. She also remembers the anguish on her father's face the day he had to give almost all his cattle to the Communist authorities as part of their collectivization drive. The Red Guards took cultural fanaticism to absurd heights: even singing traditional songs became a punishable offence. Her father got to learn of the new order when he was arrested for whistling a popular tune. He was thrashed by the Red Guards, who wanted to make him understand that the only language permissible was revolutionary newspeak. Expressions such as "please" and "thank you" were prohibited as was the ancient Tibetan custom of greeting one another by sticking out one's tongue and clicking it as a mark of affection. Kinsom recalls that her father had to cut his hair before going to the cattle market to avoid the ignominy of having his head shaven by Mao's cubs in the middle of the road.

The more populous was the area, the greater was the repression. Yandol was brought up in Tolung, a large town, situated at an hour's distance from Lhasa. Her uncles had been monks. As a child, she had seen them being executed, a sight that haunts her till this day. Her parents were pious people. Like the others, they had suffered because of the ban on religion. At the height of the repression, simply moving one's lips was an offence; one was immediately accused of being a counter revolutionary and punished with a torturous session of *thamzing*. Saying prayers and lighting lamps were banned. Perhaps it was these restrictions that drew Yandol to religion. As they say, forbidden fruit is always sweeter. The terror however could not stop Tibetans from praying in the privacy of their homes. As the repression intensified, people felt even more deeply the need to hold onto what was theirs. Like in other Tibetan families, Kinsom and Yandol were secretly taught by their parents how to meditate and read the scriptures. They kept in touch with the monks, who, though forbidden from wearing their habits, persisted in their faith. Some of these monks committed to memory sacred texts thought to have been burnt. In the land of snows, the spirit waged a desperate battle to survive, thus, sowing the seeds of religion in the generations to come.

To combat the cold of the high mountains, Kinsom and Yandol took refuge in the memories of their childhood. Every morning when they woke up, they hardly knew whether they were dead or alive. Still, each campsite, each bed of stones left behind gave these travellers on the roof the world the feeling of taking one more step on the road to freedom. The guide's impatience spurred them on, though at times his abrupt manner could be hurtful. The man just kept pushing them harder. If they lagged behind or made too much noise, he could be downright insulting. He knew that danger lurked in every corner and that one small error could prove fatal for them all. Kinsom and Yandol began to realize that behind his gruff exterior and bad temper he was, more or less, a good-hearted man.

They had been on the trail for only two weeks, yet it seemed like an eternity since they left Lhasa. The journey was endless. Each passing day brought new fears and worries — storms, the border police or simply coping with the cold. A cloudless day could suddenly turn into snow or a hail storm and the shivering travellers would be plunged into darkness. Then, as if by magic, the clouds would lift and the sun would smile down again. While following the trail between two towering mountains, they would often cross a canyon in the steep black rocky faces of which the lacerating cold of winter seemed to have been buried forever.

Everybody was worried about the child. He was still walking, but for how long? The child himself maintained a stoic silence, pretending to ignore the seriousness of his condition. The old man with the faraway look kept a good pace. So light was he that he seemed to fly and he never tired. He was a man in a hurry. Death held no fear for him, but he had to fulfill his dream before he died. To be blessed by his grandson and die, he could not ask for more. It would compensate for a lifetime of pain in a country where history had taken a tragic turn. For him, this journey was a means to be freed from the cycle of suffering and the agony of separation. Once they recovered from their snow blindness, the Khampas proved to be so resilient that it seemed they could go on crossing mountains all their lives. Though not on horseback, they carried their daggers, sheathed in magnificent silver cases. They and the Amdo Goloks were the only people allowed to carry arms by the Chinese Government. The official justification was that nomads needed to defend themselves and their flocks from wild beasts. But the truth is that the Chinese never succeeded in disarming them, though they had tried to do so on more than one occasion.

Every time they had to cross a frozen stream — an icy tongue between two peaks — there was always a Khampa ready to carry the child. At these heights, water flowed in all directions. It sprang from the bowels of the earth — cracks and shadowy rocks — to feed the great rivers of Asia: the Mekong, the Ganges, the Indus, the Brahmaputra and the Yellow River. On the other side of the Himalayas, thousands of millions of peasants depended on the waters of these streams to irrigate their lands. The two thousand turquoise lakes on the high plateaus of Tibet constitute the main water reservoir of Central Asia.

The guide would follow the course of the stream, looking for narrow passes and clearings. In some places, there were so many streams and these were so wide that the trek became a painful obstacle race. To avoid wetting their feet, they tried to place big stones in the shallowest parts of the stream, which would immediately get covered by a fine layer of slippery frost. Then they would throw some sand on top and jump from stone to stone. Kinsom had slipped so often that she was completely drenched. Each time they found a little warmth, another stream would appear, flowing fast and wild.

At night, the nuns, wrapped in their blankets, would remove their socks to dry them next to the fire, The socks gradually dried out as their supply of yak dung got exhausted. They would then begin to massage their feet. These young girls faced adversity with the serenity of mature women. They were following in the footsteps of their ancestors, who used to set out on long pilgrimages from one end of the country to the other, encountering the same problems in conditions that were sometimes far more difficult. These journeys took at least three years and represented a complete break from home and family. The pilgrims did not know whether they would come back alive, but to die on a pilgrimage was a guarantee of a better rebirth. In the past, people travelled to purify themselves; today, they were fleeing the enemy.

In addition to the cold, there was the problem of diminishing food supplies. The nuns had run out of butter and salt; they could have asked the others for some, as from the

The Realm of the Gods

very outset everyone had shown them great consideration. But they preferred to do without — young Tibetan women are proud of their independence. Besides, the nuns knew the respect in which the Tibetans held their clergy. For them, monks and nuns were the custodians of their heritage, the spirit of their land. Kinsom and Yandol, therefore, willingly endured the pangs of hunger rather than do anything that would lower the dignity of the clergy.

"Don't stop so often, keep moving!", said the guide. That morning Kinsom and Yandol ate their last ration of dried meat. They looked at each other in silence, slowly chewing the few morsels left, trying to squeeze out of them the last bit of juice. Then they got up, picked up their gear and started walking. Though their stomachs were growling, they kept walking, not letting on that they were without food.

II

The day began splendidly; the sun shone brightly in the crisp, frozen air. The coolness brought tears to their eyes, tears which soothed their sunburnt cheeks. The old man used the sleeve of his jacket to dry his face; for over seventy years, he had not shed a single tear. The trail they were following was the highest and the last. From the distance, it looked like a V cut in the sky. As the path got steeper, a strong north wind began to blow, bringing snow and dust that blinded them. They moved ahead on all

The Mountains of the Buddha

fours, heads sunken in, face covered with ski masks, concentrating on the track so as to move ahead without losing their way and keep their grip on the ground. One false step and they would fall and roll down more than half a kilometre. Every now and then, they had to stop, breathless, their lungs at bursting point. At these heights, they felt the effect of the rarefied air much more. Even the guide slackened his pace, stopping to catch his breath. The trails were shorter and the climb more painful. Great weariness fell upon the column of fugitives, numbing them and slowing their movements. It was as if they were walking in their sleep. Each obstacle on the trail brought out symptoms of altitude sickness. They were too dazed to notice their hearts beating frantically to compensate for the lack of oxygen. Kinsom could hear a whirring sound in her ears; Yandol felt sick and had a headache. There came a time when she felt she could no longer hold out. "Leave me here," she said. "I'll catch up." Her lips were cut, her eyes bloodshot, her mouth opening and closing like a goldfish. But her friend Kinsom would not allow her to give in to fatigue. "We cannot stop," she told her, pulling her up by her belt and pushing her on. They knew that if the storm got worse, they would die, their lungs choked with melted snow flakes.

Suddenly, they noticed that the child was missing. Every one including the guide had thought he was with somebody else. It was only when they stopped together that they realized he was not with them. The guide asked one of the Khampas to go back with him on the trail they had so labouriously climbed. They treaded cautiously: one fall and they would come rolling down to the bottom of the slope. In spite of the blizzard, it did not take them long to find his childish figure concealed between the rocks. His lips were a pale blue, his skin, eyebrows and ski mask covered with frost. Immobile, he lay in a foetal position. He must have fallen and rolled down. Lacking the strength to get up, he lay there, resigned to his fate, waiting to die. He could not even cry. His breathing was

The Realm of the Gods

laboured, his hands and feet numb. The Khampa picked him up and with the help of the guide positioned him on his back. They started walking slowly. The guide vigorously rubbed the child's body, feet and hands to restore his blood circulation and keep him alive. The child kept sleeping, his head resting on the Khampa's neck. Looking at his beatific smile, one would think he had experienced *Nirvana* rather than a deadly blizzard. When they returned, the Khampa, worn out, placed the child on the ground. But the young fellow could not walk, unable to keep his balance. The nuns gave him tea and insisted that he move, but the child looked at them helplessly, as if begging forgiveness for his debility. Everyone knew that to keep carrying the boy was harmful for him, for if he did not move, he would get frostbite. But they had no choice. So a third Khampa took him on his shoulders and then a fourth while the others stopped whenever they could to massage his hands and feet. Though they lost time, the halts were necessary to try and make the child move and breathe properly. The wind blew for several hours and at one point of time it seemed as if Yandol too was going to faint. She lagged behind the rest, ashamed that the group had to slow down because of her. When the wind finally abated, she asked for a halt, but the guide refused. He feared another sudden blast of wind, worse than before. Travellers had often been forced to halt for three or four days, waiting for the wind to subside. So the guide had no choice but to order them to keep moving. Yandol, crestfallen and breathless, obeyed mechanically. When pushed to the limits of their endurance, Tibetans manage to find an almost superhuman strength – call it what you may, the instinct to survive, the ability to overcome adversity, or simply the strength of their faith.

    The complete stillness of the snow-covered passes they crossed filled them with awe. When they finally reached the highest one, the exhausted travellers stopped to pause. The child got off the Khampa's back and managed to walk a couple of steps. He too was quiet, overcome by the altitude, the weariness, the grandeur and the beauty. The distant, howling wind was like music in this sublime landscape where glaciers shone in the golden light of evening and eternal snow speckled the majestic mountains nearby. Further away, springs gushed, their waters flowing down like silver needles, covering the sides of the massif. Mountains ascended into the skyline. Much lower down, below the tree line, was a world inhabited by humans.

When the wind had ceased to blow, the women moved forward to the side of the mountain and looked below. They forgot their hunger and their fatigue. Through the dark haze of night, they could almost see below them valleys covered with dense vegetation, villages inhabited by families and children rushing around, mangers in which animals huddled together to keep warm. Below, there was Nepal.

They took their time savouring the sublime beauty of the moment, one that may never come again. It was moments such as these that Kinsom and Yandol had dreamed of in prison, that had given them the strength to withstand life in the dungeons of Gutsa. At this time, guards would be opening cell doors for prisoners to empty the lavatory bucket. There would be those suffering quietly the torture they had undergone during the day, others crying in pain. The nuns thought of their friends, Ani Choki, the Drapchi singers and their own families. Kinsom thought of her father returning with his flock; of her mother preparing *thukpa*, a noodle soup with vegetables; her brothers and sisters playing in the last light of the day. The other travellers, it seemed, were immersed in similar thoughts, as if the beauty of the moment allowed them to see with the eyes of the heart. They had reached a milestone in their journey, and felt the urge to look back. They reviewed the journey and with it, their lives. From this balcony that gave onto the world, it seemed as if the worst had been left behind. They had staked their all to escape, and the gamble appeared to be paying off. There was a mood of elation with the feeling of being free and independent.

The guide warned them that it was too early to rejoice. Many perils still lurked ahead. The wind could start blowing again at any time and leave them trapped in the high mountains. Then there were the problems of cold and dehydration to be dealt with. They had no water to drink, for there was no way to melt the snow. "We have to go down a little and look for a place to camp," he informed them. Though he was breathing heavily, he strapped on his rucksack and set off alone with firm, decisive steps. The child, who had recovered some strength, said he would walk. But he had difficulty in moving, slowing down the entire column.

III

They came to a glacier among moraines that looked like statues sculpted by the gods. Staying on their feet was no less than an acrobatic feat. They slipped and stumbled, only to fall again. The child insisted on walking alone. Strangely enough, he had the least difficulty in keeping his balance, perhaps because he was the shortest of them all. The strong winds that blew in these parts made the guide fear an avalanche. He ordered them to walk in pin drop silence; even the slightest sound could cause these precarious snow masses to fall. One afternoon, as they were setting up camp, tired and thirsty, they heard a dull thud that turned into a crash. The child, scared stiff, clung onto the guide's jacket. The old man peered into the distance and pointed to a spot near the trail they had covered the day before: ice floes like huge walls of frost were dangling loosely. They came crashing down, detaching huge blocks the size of a house that seemed to be coming straight at them. Kinsom and Yandol, frightened out of their wits, thought it was the end of the world. The avalanche brought on a minor snow storm. At last, the deafening noise died down, the snow cloud cleared away slowly and peace returned.

After the fright, they were hungry and thirsty. They had no wood or yak dung to boil the snow, so they tried sucking it but it froze on their tongues. No one had any food left. Kinsom felt giddy and Yandol was so weak that all she could think of was sleep. They quietly accepted the meager portion of *tsampa* the old man offered them. He smiled as if to say that he had triumphed by giving away his last meal. The lighter they travel, the happier Tibetans are.

The frosty landscape and vast expanses of rock seemed to stretch interminably. There was a marked difference in level, which lead them to hope that they would soon come across fields, roads and perhaps other human beings. They were approaching the Solo Khumbu, the land of the Sherpas, the most well known mountain tribe of the Himalayas.

Though the forty thousand Sherpas constitute a very small part of the Nepali population, they shot into prominence the world over with the arrival of the first Western mountaineering expeditions that came to conquer the peaks of the Himalayas in the twenties and the thirties. These courageous and sturdy peasants, who know the mountains like the back of their hand, became porters for mountaineering teams. So good were they at their job that in the West the word "Sherpa" has come to mean guide and porter. The most well known Sherpa is undoubtedly Tensing Norgay, the guide of the New Zealander

The Realm of the Gods

Edmund Hillary. Together they were the first to reach the summit of the Everest in 1953, after five abortive attempts. Unlike the rest of the Nepalis who are Hindus, the Sherpas are Buddhists like the Tibetans and have their own customs. They believe in the legend of the Yeti, the abominable snowman, a legend that has become famous all over the world with several expeditions going out in search of this legendary creature. However, till date, all that has come to light are some amazing foot-prints, thirty centimetres wide and fifteen centimetres broad, giving rise to the theory that, at best, Yetis were a species of primitive humanoids of which a few members may have survived. Their habitat is supposed to be the cloud forests of the myriad Himalayan canyons, which are exceptionally inhospitable to man. There are still some who believe that the existence of the Yeti is not a mere fable. For a long time, Tibetans and Sherpas have been convinced about its existence. Many have sworn to have seen one while crossing the mountains. Should one encounter a Yeti, the best course of action to escape from its clutches, they tell you, is to run in the direction of the wind, because the Yeti's long hair covers its eyes, forcing it to give up the chase.

They had been walking for over three hours. When they saw the guide frown, the group began to worry. He pointed below to a flat terrace on which little dots could be seen: it looked like a camp. "They might be smugglers or bandits," he said. Not all Tibetans were seeking exile. There were some who could come and go as they pleased. And when they travelled, they were well-equipped, well fed and well-armed. They attacked groups of refugees, stripping them of all their belongings. But the guide was not worried, for he had a Khampa escort.

IV

That day at four o'clock in the afternoon, Jordi Risa, a Spanish doctor, came out of his tent to discuss with the Sherpa guide the best way to continue the climb. Their base camp was located at an altitude of five thousand metres. While he was talking to the Sherpa, the Spanish doctor suddenly saw a row of dots coming down the mountain.

"We were astonished," said Jordi, a middle aged man with white hair and an athletic build. "Even the Sherpas were perplexed. We all wondered who they could be and what they were doing there. Perhaps they were smugglers." A few days earlier, a group of Tibetans, clad in hats, fur boots and leather jackets, had approached the camp site. Already reeking of *chang,* they asked for whisky. The doctor offered them tea instead. Next they demanded a tent to sleep in. As they were armed with knives and looked like medieval bandits, the doctor told the sherpas to put up a tent for them. They were still not satisfied: they wanted one tent per person. Jordi refused flatly, saying this was all that they would get. There was a heated exchange of words and the noise woke up the other mountaineers, who came out of their tents to see what was happening. Seeing that they were outnumbered, the intruders beat a hasty retreat. An hour later, Jordi received a radio message from another camp: "Watch out, a group of Tibetans is going by." "We are taking another route," he answered. They had to take this precaution to keep a safe distance from the highwaymen.

The Realm of the Gods

Ang Kami, the Sherpa leading the expedition, watched them come down through his binoculars. Though it was hard to make out who they were, he guessed that they were refugees. It was difficult to tell how long they would take to reach the camp site. The column followed the edge of a glacier, then went up a small rocky mound, came down again, went up, came down... In the distance, towered the Cho Oyu, the Everest and the Lhotse, the majestic trio, so grand that they seemed unreal. Jordi and Ang Kami lit a small fire to help the refugees get their bearings. The doctor thought it would take them a couple of hours to reach. But even after nightfall, there was no sign of them, further proof of how easy it was to misjudge distances in this vast Himalayan space. On the following day, the doctor rose as usual at seven and went out to check the weather. As Ang Kami had predicted, the sky was absolutely clear. A light snowfall the night before had left three inches of snow on the tents. There was still no trace of the refugees. When the glaciers were flooded with light, the doctor scanned the mountains to look for them. He saw them at last: the little dots were now more like a swarm tenaciously moving ahead. It was towards afternoon that the refugees finally arrived at the camp. At close quarters, they looked like a group of beggars. Jordi said, "The first one to come appeared to be the guide. He was wearing yellow sunglasses and ordinary shoes. The rest followed, wearing nothing more than jackets, shirts and sports shoes, as if they were going for a stroll on the streets of Barcelona". They, the mountaineers, were wearing special boots made from very sophisticated materials, silk tights, double wool socks, thermal underwear, jerseys, feather quilted anoraks, and they still felt cold. "The refugees had been sleeping on the ground at sub-zero temperatures. That they managed to survive such conditions is nothing short of a miracle." It was almost three weeks since they had been on the trail. Though the doctor did not know this, he guessed as much, looking at their pitiable physical state. Practically all of them had some kind of injury. The Khampas had burnt eyes. "Those who did wear sunglasses had burnt eyelashes because of the glare. There was a child traveling alone and his condition was terrible. He was far more exhausted than the adults. All of them were dying of thirst." After giving them something to drink, Jordi examined them thoroughly. The child's toes had turned black, there was every chance of him developing an infection as necrosis had set in. The doctor examined his frozen toes to see if they could be saved. He did not hold out much hope. All he could do for the time being was to clean the wounds. The feet of the women were red, swollen and covered with blisters and chilblains; however, there was no sign of frostbite.

The doctor gave them rice, tea and something to wear. While he was tending to their wounds with the help of the Sherpas, Yandol, curious as ever, decided to take a look around the camp. She discovered about a dozen ardent mountaineers staying in the tents, on an expedition organized by Ang Kami to Cho Oyu, the seventh highest peak in the world. Besides the Spaniards, there were Italians and French, all of them mad about mountaineering and, as Yandol learned, ever ready to strike a good bargain. One of them was very taken with her antelope skin jacket. She took it off, a little sad at having to part with her last remembrance of home. But she needed the money for her stay in Nepal. Freedom, she thought, was well worth a coat. The jacket turned out to be too small for the mountaineer. So Yandol was as penniless as before. In a way she was glad, for she still had her second skin.

The meeting with the Sherpas and the foreigners raised everyone's spirits. They had had a good meal, plenty to drink and a whole day's rest. They were relaxed both physically and mentally, free from the tension of having to deal with extreme situations and the unknown. When evening came, a song sprang from the old man's lips. He seemed to be singing the

The Realm of the Gods

ballad to himself, one that went back to times when the towns and valleys had still not lost their names. For centuries, new born babes had been rocked to sleep with this lullaby. Every fibre of the old man's body swayed to the melody. In spite of his years, he could not stop his heart from trembling. As if in a dream, he relived those magical moments, timeless and full of wonder. His words were like a balm to a weary mother earth, frightened by the call of night. As he sang, he knew his destiny and that of the earth were one. He wondered what was the purpose of living longer when all life, no matter how long or short, would ultimately dissolve. What was the purpose of wisdom when the only thing that mattered — and he could see this very clearly — was to to accept this dissolution? Behind him, the purple peaks shone. The old man confessed to Kinsom and Yandol that the last thing he would like to hear before dying was this song, which reminded him of his mother. He would be able to say goodbye to his old friend and the only family he knew — solitude. And then this vagabond, old and wise, would sleep the sleep of a child. The mountains were slowly turning the colour of ash.

For the first time since they had left Lhasa, the guide looked contented. The smell of burning wood, the dancing flames of the fire, the comforting presence of foreigners, the salty thick tea, the spell of the old man's voice, warm like sap, inviting one to dream, the general sense of well being — all of this had perhaps lifted the mood of the guide. Kinsom was surprised to find him talking to the porters. He was actually smiling! And she had thought that he was physically incapable of stretching his lips and showing his teeth in a smile. This fierce man was behaving just like one of them. He responded to the Sherpas' generosity with the characteristic good humor of the men of the mountains. All human beings, thought the nuns, carried the seeds of a Buddha within them.

The Mountains of the Buddha

V

"When things get rough, the Sherpas' first thought is to look after you," said the Spanish doctor. And so they did all they could to help their Tibetan cousins. These simple men behave with serene wisdom and are sincere in their desire to help others. The mountains have taught them that without solidarity, surival is impossible in the high altitudes. Resentment and antagonism can have tragic consequences in the isolation of the peaks. They have no secrets, envy or greed for money and could not understand why some foreigners behaved the way they do. A little while earlier, a Japanese expedition, in its anxiety to scale a peak, had refused to come to the rescue of a rival team, resulting in the death of a mountaineer. Like good Buddhists, the Sherpas consider performing one's duty more important than success or reward. Their belief in *karma* makes them tolerant and reluctant to gamble, as they know that bad deeds will be duly punished.

The Spanish doctor felt a deep affection for the Sherpas. This and his love for the mountains had brought him to Nepal several times. His meeting with Ang Kami, a serious, mild mannered man, youthful in appearance, was not entirely accidental. They had got to know each other through their respective wives, both of whom come from Catalonia. The Sherpa's wife, Victoria Subirana, was a teacher. She had married him only to get a visa so that she could stay on in Nepal. At twenty-nine, she had given up her job, her fiance, a comfortable, steady life in the Spanish town of Gerona to set up a school for the poorest and most deprived children of Kathmandu. Her fight against poverty in Nepal had given her life a sense of purpose. The school had been running for several months when one fine day she found the police at her doorstep. She was told they were going to deport her because she was working on a student visa. But for Victoria the idea of leaving the school was unbearable. She had moved heaven and earth to raise funds for the school and so many people were now involved in it. So she finally accepted the suggestion of one of her friends, a Lama close to the Sherpa community, to marry a Sherpa and get her papers in order. But that was not the end of the story. Even after their "marriage", Victoria and Ang Kami stayed together and grew to love each other. What had started out as a marriage of convenience turned into a real life romance. They had a son; after some time, they adopted a Sherpa girl as their daughter. Victoria Subirana became Vicky Sherpa, her school, an exemplary institution, and her husband Ang Kami, the owner of a travel agency which organizes expeditions for Europeans.

Before leaving, Ang Kami advised the guide to make a detour eastwards in order to avoid the main check posts. The refugees were a source of wealth for the police, who would return them to the Chinese for a price. Recently, a skirmish had taken place between the police and a group of fugitives who refused to pay extortion money. Ang Kami knew that every month between thirty to a hundred and fifty clandestine immigrants were sent back to Tibet in spite of the repeated protests by the representatives of the United Nations High Commission for Refugees in the region.

The nuns had heard similar stories in Lhasa but chose to ignore them. They were counting on their luck and hoped they would escape the clutches of the police in the same way as they had survived the journey. Still, while collecting their belongings and saying goodbye to the Sherpas and mountaineers, they began to feel afraid. The wheel of life was still in spin and anything could happen. There was an old Tibetan song that said: "Tomorrow or the next life, who knows which will come first?" In the twinkling of an eye, they could lose the security, camaraderie and comfort of the mountaineers' tents to be locked up in a Nepali police station and handed over to the Chinese border police, perhaps to the same guards who had been listening to the radio a few nights ago. A fate worse than death. All of a sudden, an awful thought crossed Yandol's mind. Perhaps the Chinese were playing cat and mouse with them. If the mountains did not get them, the Nepali police would and it would be back into a Chinese jail.

Ang Kami told them about the incident with the Tibetan bandits. They had since moved westwards, he warned them. The white men had succeeded in overawing the bandits, but it was unlikely that they would be intimidated by a group of poor refugees, who ran the risk of losing even their underclothes. The guide, fully alive to the dangers of the situation, assumed once again his habitual dour expression. They were restrained in their farewell, as the fear of what lay ahead was uppermost in their minds. With hands folded in gratitude, they took their leave, put their knapsacks on their backs and left the camp.

Watching them go like ants filing down the mountain, the Spanish doctor noticed that, in spite of the bandage on his foot, the child was still limping. The night before, he had found the child crying, clutching onto something. He thought it was the pain but he was wrong. It was not his hands, feet or the exhaustion that were making this Tibetan child cry. The doctor asked Ang Kami to act as the interpreter. The child was homesick. He was remembering his family in Tibet; he was missing his parents. In his hands he held a little bell, the one on the collar of his horse, which he had wrapped in paper so that its tingling could not be heard. The doctor thought how tough it was that parents should send away their children on such a perilous journey to an unknown destination. It just

The Realm of the Gods

showed how desparate they were. The open wounds of Tibet were there for all to see.

The image of the refugees walking, uncertain of what lay ahead, kept coming before his eyes for many days. The mountains, thought the doctor, were like an open book. They told him that on the other side, there was something that would never die: a tireless spirit of resistance, faith and the wanderlust of the Tibetan soul. For one brief moment, he had seen the beauty of a way of life that could vanish forever. What could be done against an enemy intent on destroying the very existence of a people, isolated for centuries from the modern world? For how long could the Tibetans hold out before they lost their culture and religion and submitted to the uniformity, mediocrity and competitiveness imposed on them by an alien civilization? The doctor turned away and went back into his tent.

VI

Above and below was a maze of valleys. As the refugees continued their descent, rocky slopes gave way to damp meadows. Coming down the slope reduced the strain on their knees. Below were neatly cultivated terraces, cut in perfect steps that hugged the contours of the hillside. They were enchanted by the gentleness of this landscape, so different from what they had left behind. The guide looked for a trail that would lead them to the interior.

All of a sudden, he told them to stop. He had spied a group of people. He could see them clearly as they crossed a clearing in the woods. They could be anybody: Tibetan smugglers, Nepali policemen or the Chinese. The group was in a no man's land: only the strongest could survive here. The guide lead his group to a spot behind the rocks and decided to wait for night before going any further.

As the sky filled with stars, he ordered them to move ahead. They walked to a point near a village, close to the Chinese border in a heavily patrolled area. The guide did not know which was worse, running into the bandits or the policemen. Because of their distinctive features, it was easy to recognize the Tibetans, who were easy prey. The police knew that they often carried with them money and valuables.

The air smelt of pine trees, rhododendrons and berries. From a far, the village houses appeared deserted. Only a solitary bulb shone from what must have been the police post. The refugees hid behind trees. After going past the village, they felt euphoric. They were in Nepal, walking at last on a road – even though bumpy and full of pot holes – instead of slipping and stumbling between rocks and slopes as they had for the past three weeks. Fear and exhaustion were now a distant memory. Only the guide refused to smile and take it easy.

Through the mist of dawn appeared a green and brown landscape. There was the wonderful smell of earth and grass, the fragrance of life itself. On the terraces, like sculpted steps on the dark mountain crust, they saw farmers ploughing their fields with the old, women and children sowing barley seeds. The stillness of the morning was broken by the crowing of roosters. Further down, there was a woman angrily shouting at her buffalo, which was ambling among the pine trees. As they approached another village, the sound of a gigantic trumpet and rows of multicoloured wind horses fluttering in the breeze greeted them, a reminder that they were in a

The Realm of the Gods

country which shared a common religion and customs. From the peaks down to the valley blew a wind, carrying with it prayers and blessings that traveled across fields and mountains. Over and over again, far and wide, down streams and brooks, in barley stalks, in the ruffled hair of children playing, in the horns of oxen, in small towns, in their empty, narrow streets where stray dogs slept, and in the golden domes of temples, their murmur could be heard.

They had been walking throughout the day on empty stomachs when the guide decided to halt in a small wood. Leaving his group behind, he went to a nearby town in search of food and a place to stay for the night. Men were returning home from the fields, carrying their tools on their backs; women were chatting on their doorsteps, enjoying the cool evening air. A street vendor was watching over his wares: fruit, cigarettes, matches and biscuits. The sight of food made Kinsom and Yandol dizzy. The child and the Khampas stared longingly at his cart. The old man seemed far away, unaffected by hunger. He was contemplating the scenery below: rocks bathed in golden light, small, sparkling streams running between trees and birds humming. He seemed happy and at peace.

As night fell, the guide came back with some comforting news. He had rented a house in which they could sleep and recover. The house was far off, so he asked them to hurry. The group started walking again. The fatigue of their ordeal in the high mountains was evident in all they did. They had to force themselves to move. Their lips and skin were chapped, their hair, long and unkept and their cheeks, sunken in. The guide hoped that a good meal and a day's rest would make them look somewhat more respectable. They had to look decent if they were to board the bus to Kathmandu without arousing suspicion.

It was a farmhouse, bigger than the usual village houses. They were met by a middle-aged woman. She was alone, the guide explained to them, her husband and children had gone to work on the fields in the neighbouring valley. The woman did not seem in the least concerned at the travellers' scraggly appearance. It was quite common in these parts, though even she had never seen such an undernourished lot.

The guide asked everyone to contribute for the roof and meal. Kinsom and Yandol's first reaction was one of joy: they were safe at last. Then the dangers of the past few days began to sink in. Anything could have happened to them at anytime, but they had not even come across bandits. The aroma of vegetable stew cooking on a bed of burning coal reminded them of their home and family. The farmhouse was a haven of peace that gave them a sense of homecoming. Propped up against the adobe walls, they decided to stretch out on the mats and fell into a deep sleep, enveloped by the thick kitchen smoke. The child and the old man too were nodding. The guide and the Khampas were sitting at the entrance outside; their whispers sounded like bees buzzing.

By the time the food was ready, even the group outside had fallen asleep. As the farmer's wife placed bowls of soup in front of them, they slowly emerged from their stupor. They ate in silence, like Buddhist monks, concentrating on every morsel and savouring it. The food provided much needed warmth and sustenance. The woman kept generously refilling their bowls till there was nothing left in the pan. Then she left, telling them she would be seeing them in morning, and the refugees went back to sleep.

They were rudely woken up by the sound of violent banging. They thought it was an explosion. They had been in such deep sleep that it took them a few minutes to gather their wits. Four shouting Nepali policemen entered the house, after kicking the door open. The obliging farmer's wife had denounced them to the police. A preposterous idea crossed Kinsom's mind: was the guide acting in connivance with the woman? After all, it was he who had lead them here.

The Realm of the Gods

In one split second, their world came crashing down. Their dreams of freedom and a new life lay shattered. That the guide could be an accomplice of this woman and rob them of their last possession made them sick. Was there no salvation possible?

The old man remained impassive. He wore his usual smile and his gaze was as clear as ever. In all this violence, his serenity appeared insolent. One of the Khampas got up, flashing his dagger menacingly. In reply, the policemen pulled their revolvers out from their belts. The guide told the Khampa to sit down and started a long negotiation with the policemen, who were badly shaved and dressed in shabby uniforms. Every now and then, they would point to the refugees, indicating that the group follow them to the police station. The guide did not seem in the least nervous and asked the others to stay put.

Yandol, who had heard about Tibetan women being raped at checkposts, was terrified. Kinsom did her best to pacify her friend: dressed as they were, no one would be able to guess that they were women. Kinsom was more worried about being sent back to Tibet. They hardly had any money left to bribe the police and the Chinese were known to give a handsome reward for each refugee returned.

The guide went out with the policemen, ordering the group not to leave the house. So began a torturous round of negotiations. The way their moods kept changing, no agreement seemed in sight. The guide used all his powers of pursuasion to lower the price the refugees would have to pay for their freedom. From time to time, he would come back inside the dingy house, sit down among the bags, coats and scraps of food strewn all over and ask them: "Do you have any jewelery, anything of value we can give them?" The answer was always no and the guide would go out again to deal with the police party. At last, the guide returned, with a grin on his face: "Six hundred yuan, they want six hundred yuan. That includes the journey to Kathmandu. And they'll escort us there."

The Khampas protested over the price. Furious, they took out their daggers again. "This is the law of the border: if they raid you, you pay. The choice is yours: either you pay or you go back to Tibet." There was an uncomfortable silence. The oldest Khampa finally spoke: "They want all our money. But what is there to guarantee they won't hand us over later?"

"I give you my word that will not happen."

"And if we are detained by other policemen, with what will we pay them off? "

"Nobody is going to detain you, because they are coming with us to Kathmandu. The deal is that they will personally see us to a representative of the UNHCR or the Government of His Holiness."

The refugees rummaged in their belongings, taking out whatever little money they had left, hidden in the folds of their clothes. The nuns were now penniless. The guide handed over a thick wad of notes to the policemen. Dirty, exhausted, without any money and completely defenseless, the refugees trudged down to the town of Jiri from where buses left daily for the capital. There were mortally afraid. They had nothing but the clothes on their backs. "What will we do if they ask for more money?", wondered Kinsom. Their fate depended on the whims of these policemen. In the distance, they saw a small town, with brick houses and dilapidated buildings. Outside was the police post.

The Realm of the Gods

VII

The refugees were taken to a bare room and detained as they had been in Tibet. They were no longer the same people, free to follow their destiny. Once again they had become hostages, carrying a price on their heads. They were miserable. And to think they were so near their goal. The guide talked to the policemen; for the refugees, the night was excruciatingly long. Unlike in the mountains, where their fate depended on their courage and strength, here they were at the mercy of the authorities.

They were bone tired, yet within the four walls of that grimy room, through the barred windows of which shone a pale moon, no one got a moment's rest. Twenty years of Chinese occupation had taught them how arbitrary the men in uniform could be. They were terrified. They had given away everything they had and they could still be handed over to the Chinese at any time. Some of them had their doubts about the guide. The Khampas said they would cut him into small pieces bits if he had betrayed them. A poor consolation indeed!

In that sweaty room, the hours passed by in anguish and despair. For the first time since leaving Lhasa, the refugees talked to each other about themselves, their lives, their fears. Kinsom and Yandol told them about the demonstrations, the hell of Gutsa and their decision to leave. The child spoke of his family and how they prayed every night for the return of the Dalai Lama, as that would bring back peace. He told them about his school, where he was looked down upon because he spoke in Tibetan, and about the raid at night when they took his uncle away.

A young gentle-eyed Khampa with a deep voice said two bombs had exploded in the heart of Lhasa a few months ago. There were entire provinces where the Chinese dared not go. He told them about the Tiger Dragons, a group that operated clandestinely. Listening to him, it seemed that the Tibetan will to fight the invader was still as fierce as ever. But the oldest Khampa thought otherwise. "The young are not interested in fighting the Chinese," he said. "All they dream of is replacing their horses with cars and motorcycles." There were a few pockets of resistance left, but for him, the heroic armed struggle of the horsemen from Kham had ended twenty years ago.

He recalled perfectly that day of 1974, on which ten thousand Nepali soldiers reached the Mustang base and forced the Khampas to lay down their arms. The soldiers had been sent by the King of Nepal under Mao's threat of military reprisals if the guerilla base, the nerve centre of Tibetan resistance, was not destroyed. A little earlier, the Khampas had received a terrible blow, as they learnt that the CIA had withdrawn its support to them. It was part of the price that the North Americans had to pay for a reconciliation with Mao's China.

At first, the Khampas refused to surrender to the Nepali troops. "How can we surrender before the Nepalis when we refused to do so before the Chinese?", said the leader of the guerillas. But after an emissary brought him a recorded message from the Dalai Lama, his attitude changed. The Dalai Lama said it was senseless to continue such an unequal struggle at a time when both Nepal and the United States were withdrawing their support. And it made even less sense to fight against Nepal, a country that had offered them assistance and hospitality. The Tibetan struggle needed a long term approach. So, the old Khampa recounted, the guerrilla leader got up and said to his soldiers: "I will never lay down my arms. But I cannot go against the orders of the Dalai Lama." A few days later, they found his body: he had slit his throat with his dagger. Two other officials followed suit. The fiery guerrillas chose to take their lives rather than disobey the Dalai Lama, which would have been worse than suicide. Deserted by everyone, the Khampas were forced to give up their struggle, though even till this day, guerrilla activity continues sporadically in the interior of Tibet.

Should their struggle be violent or non-violent? This was the eternal debate that raged in Tibetan resistance circles and even in the police station the discussion inevitably turned to this question. The youngest of the Khampas considered the Dalai Lama naïve. The old Tibetan, however, was of the view that the Dalai Lama was a wise man whose actions transcended immediate history. The old man who never lost his smile had spent several years in a labour camp, accused of participating in the 1970 revolt that had spread to sixty of the seventy-one districts in Tibet. He had seen his companions fall like flies; he himself had been tortured even more brutally than the nuns. He, who had lost everything his work, his freedom and his wife, a victim of the famine that followed the Cultural Revolution was convinced of the futility of an armed combat against a far more powerful enemy. "This can only bring more suffering," he said.

The old man was released in 1972. At the time, life had become increasingly insecure. His first concern was for his son: he had to help him flee to India. The son had left in exactly the same way as the little fellow twenty years later: he had been sent off by his father to seek exile, all alone, with a group of refugees. Now the old man was making the journey to meet with his loved ones.

The old man told them of an astonishing event that took place in those dark years of Tibetan history: the Dalai Lama's brother had actually visited Tibet, accompanied by eight dignitaries of the government-in-exile. The visit was the result of a rapprochement between the Chinese leader Deng Ziao Ping – concerned at China's deteriorating international image and the frequent revolts in Tibet – and the man Peking hated most, the Dalai Lama, who was the only leader capable of uniting all Tibetans. Tibet supposedly constituted one-fourth of the Chinese territory and the Chinese needed the Dalai Lama to pacify the people. For this reason, Deng Ziao Ping offered him the possibility of returning to Tibet. Tenzin Gyatso was pragmatic enough to realize that the only hope for his country lay in some kind of compromise with China, so he did not reject the proposal outright. However, first he wanted that fact-finding missions be allowed to visit Tibet in order to make an assessment of the situation prevailing there and re-establish contact between the exiles and their compatriots back home. He further asked that such missions be given full freedom to travel and talk with the people. Strangely enough, the Chinese acceded to his request.

The delegation, headed by the Dalai Lama's brother, spent four months in Tibet and travelled to many villages. The Chinese had warned the Tibetans to be discrete. However, said the old man, as soon as people came to know that the procession was passing by, they hurried to pull out their prayer wheels, sacred scarves and rosaries that they had kept hidden all those years, their eyes full of tears. Everywhere they went, the exiles were welcomed by delirious crowds. Much to the horror of the Chinese, the numbers kept swelling with thousands of children and young people begging for the Dalai Lama's photograph and blessings. At times, it was so moving that even the official Chinese guides had tears in their eyes. In Lhasa, hundreds of thousands of people flocked to the streets to greet the envoys of their spiritual leader, flouting the order that forbade them to assemble in groups. The delegation returned to India, taking back with it hundreds of metres of film, thousands of hours of recording and a vast

The Realm of the Gods

amount of information. In addition, there were six thousand letters written by Tibetans to their families in exile, the first mail to leave Tibet after twenty years. One of them was a letter from the the old man who never lost his smile to his son settled in India. "I did not know which address to put," the old man told the nuns and the Khampas, who were listening, spellbound. "All I wrote was his name and India. A few months later, I got a reply from my son. He wrote to me that he lived with his family in an agricultural colony in southern India and that a grandson had been born to me."

VIII

Though things were somewhat better in the early eighties as compared to the previous years — the ban on wearing traditional clothes had been lifted and a certain degree of freedom had been granted in respect to religion and trade — the Dalai Lama's envoys could clearly see that their old culture had been practically wiped out. Worse still, they learned of the years of hunger, the public executions, the imprisonment of innocents and the death of thousands of monks and nuns in concentration camps. It was a horrifying tale, corroborated by photographs of monasteries and convents that had been reduced to rubble. The Chinese put all the blame on the Band of Four, that is Mao's widow and the extremists who had unleashed the Cultural Revolution. The Chinese talked of progress and the newly set up factories.

But all the envoys could see there were poorly paid Tibetans, performing menial tasks. There was electricity, but only in the Chinese quarters. There were roads, vehicles and trucks but only for the army and for Chinese officials. There were consumer goods but beyond the reach of Tibetans. There were modern hospitals, but they practiced inhuman policies: whenever Chinese patients needed blood, Tibetan 'volunteers' were called in. Life in the countryside became far worse than before. The Cultural Revolution put an end to the traditional herbal medicine villagers had been using for centuries without providing any substitute.

As they travelled across the country, the envoys noticed vast tracts of land transformed into deserts. There were no bears, eagles, geese, wild yaks, stags or gazelles to be seen. During their four months, all they came across was a lone rabbit and some marmots. The Tibetans told them how the Chinese liked to hunt. Riding on motorcycles fitted with sidecars, they would drive very close to a flock of deer, machine-gun the hapless animals, throw the carcasses in jeeps and speed away. When the envoys reached the Kham region, where dense forests had once covered the hills, they could hardly recognize it. For the last thirty years, the Chinese had been felling trees ruthlessly without bothering to plant any new ones. They had set about destroying Tibet's natural resources with the same savage determination as they had shown in trying to destroy its culture.

In order to spare his people further reprisals, the Dalai Lama refrained from making public the devastating findings of the first fact-finding team, preferring to wait for the reports of the subsequent missions. There were nine such teams sent to Tibet. Each time, the Chinese imposed a very strict code on the people. They were not supposed to smile, cry, shake hands, offer scarves or invite the visitors to their homes. The Chinese tried to doctor their responses: they were given pamphlets containing the 'correct answers' to likely questions.

The Tibetans refused to be cowed. In spite of all the threats, people were, it seemed, more emotional with the arrival of each new delegation. Crowds prostrated themselves on the road to try and stop the procession from moving ahead. Young children between ten and twelve offered the envoys flowers, saying, "May the sun of the Buddha's teachings rise again". When the second mission saw what remained of the Ganden Monastery — Ganden means paradise of joy and thirty-two years earlier the Italian Tibetologist Giuseppe Tucci had called it "a place out of this world" — the atmosphere was electric. Seven thousand people were standing on the surrounding hills. They had been driven there by Tibetan truckers, who later had to suffer the consequences of their action. Nothing had prepared the envoys for what they saw. The immense monastery where the Dalai Lama had spent a night on his way to China and where he had had premonitory visions had been wiped off the face of the earth. All that remained were a few ghostly walls, a poignant reminder of what it had been. They were immediately surrounded by young and old alike, who clutched onto their jackets. With tears in their eyes, they asked when the God King would return. Those behind tried to console them but they too broke into sobs. Pointing to the hill they said, "There stood our Ganden. Look what they've done to it!" In the midst of the barely visible remnants of Ganden, the envoys of Tenzin Gyatso addressed the crowd while thousands of Tibetan voices clamoured for freedom. The next day, the envoys were greeted in front of the Jokhang with shouts of : "Long live the Dalai Lama!"

This was too much for the Chinese. In a complete volte face, the authorities clamped down. The envoys were not allowed to leave their rooms; they had no choice but to go back.

While in Peking, they had been able to meet the Panchen Lama, taken for dead by many. But the statements of Wei

Jinsheng, one of the most well known dissidents and a cell mate of the religious leader, revealed he was still alive. To escape from the horrors of the prison, the Panchen Lama had tried to commit suicide on several occasions. He was released subsequently but only after the Chinese had forced him to publicly declare his loyalty for the regime. This implied that he was willing to collabourate with the party leadership, though no one knew to what extent. When the Dalai Lama's envoys came to see him, he showed them the torture scars on his body. He said that his real allegiance was to his people and that he was willing to work as a mediator between the Chinese and the Tibetans in exile, a task to which he devoted himself until the day he died.

The third delegation, headed by the Dalai Lama's brother, had been asked to collect information on education in Tibet. Though the team did report a slight improvement in educational standards, the fact remained that more than seventy per cent of the population was still illiterate. The Tibetan language was considered a drawback, a relic of the past, and few children could speak their mother tongue correctly. A foreign ideology had been imposed on all levels of teaching.

The three delegations sat together to draw up a joint report on the the thirty years since the Chinese invasion of Tibet[8]. Their conclusions were as follows: one million two hundred thousand Tibetans, i.e., one-fifth of the population, had died of starvation or mistreatment; six thousand two hundred and fifty-four monasteries and convents had been destroyed, their treasures sold or melted into ingots or coins; sixty per cent of their ancient literary texts had been burnt; the province of Amdo had become the largest *gulag* in the world, which could take in ten million prisoners; one out of every ten Tibetans had been sent to jail and a hundred thousand were in labour camps.

---

[8] As told in the Dalai Lama's autobiography.

A two thousand year old civilization was on the verge of extinction. Hu Yao Bang, tipped to be Deng Ziao Ping's successor at the time, summed up the situation well in an interview that he gave to a Hong Kong based newspaper: "This is nothing but colonialism". Upset at the way the extreme left had treated Tibetans like second class citizens in their own country, Hu, the then General Secretary of the Party, replaced the orthodox elements by those whose approach was more moderate and pragmatic. He also drew up a plan for the improvement of living standards and social conditions, giving the Tibetans greater freedom and opportunity. Hu promised that the Tibetan economy would reach its pre-1959 levels within a period of three years. These promises were too good to be true.

The first effect of the new measures was that all sections of Tibetan society, young and old, urban and rural, workers and intellectuals, nomads and peasants, began practicing their religion again. For the children born and brought up during the long night of the Cultural Revolution, like Kinsom and Yandol, Hu Yao Bang's policies meant a new dawn. Once again the faithful could be seen prostrating themselves in front of all the old places of worship or rather their ruins, as most of them had been destroyed. They would touch the ground with their forehead, knees and hands, which symbolized the five evils – hatred, desire, ignorance, pride and envy – that they wished to rid themselves of and transform into the five virtues. Monks and nuns in crimson-coloured habits came back to the temples. Yak butter lamps burned in front of statues of Buddhist gods from which the dust had been removed after they had been taken out of their hiding places. The Jokhang was re-opened and permission given to rebuild some monasteries. Convents began to take in novices, though there was a restriction on the number they could admit. The largest monastery in the world, Drepung, in which the child Tenzin Gyatso had been received with great pomp and ceremony by over ten thousand monks on his way to Lhasa before his enthronement, had been given permission to take in four hundred and fifty novices. But they were no more the great centres of learning they had been in the past. It is true that Hu Yao Bang's initiatives did ease the situation somewhat; there was less repression and daily life was not so harsh. Most importantly, religious and nationalist sentiments could be expressed freely, something no one could reverse. The ultra-conservatives accused Hu Yao Bang of going too far in his policy of granting religious freedom. This was one of the reasons that lead to his resignation; he was perceived as being too soft on Tibet.

After 1983, no one believed any more in the promises made by the Chinese. That year Peking tightened the screws on Tibet, flooding the country with a massive influx of Chinese. This was a time-tested method that the Chinese had used in other regions to put down minority opposition. In Manchuria, there were just two to three million Manchurians in a land colonized by seventy-five million Chinese. In Turkistan (called Xinjiang by the Chinese) more than half the population are the descendants of Chinese colonizers and in Inner Mongolia there are only two million Mongolians for nine million Chinese. The same fate was reserved for Tibet. A dual strategy of Chinese immigration and birth control for the Tibetans was put into practice. "Soon, my compatriots became a tourist attraction in their own country," said the Dalai Lama, reacting to this policy.

The delegations that had been sent to Tibet failed to bring the God King back to his country. The conditions imposed by Peking were unacceptable: the administration of the territory was not negotiable and the Dalai Lama would have to live in Peking instead of Tibet. What mattered for the leader of the Tibetans was not his own future but that of his six million compatriots. The God King continued to work for an open dialogue with the Chinese but Peking chose to maintain a stony silence. Forty years after the 'peaceful liberation of Tibet', the aim of the conservative Chinese leaders remained unchanged: to eliminate what remained of the traditions and culture of the Land of Snows.

IX

Huddled together in a dingy room of the Jiri police post, the drowsy refugees felt they were back in the truck in which they had left Lhasa. Sitting there, they wondered whether they were free or not. The guide had assured them they had nothing to fear but they did not fully trust him. Not having a single rupee in their pockets worried Kinsom and Yandol, who asked for permission to go out. As the bus for Kathmandu was leaving at noon, they had time to spare. The guide talked to the policemen, who did not raise any objections: after all, they had already got their money. The nuns put on their caps, raised the collar of their jackets and began walking to the centre of the town, backs hunched to hide the fact that they were women.

When they reached there, they found it was a market day. After the stillness of the mountains and the fatigue of a sleepless night, the commotion was bewildering. Villagers thronged the stalls that sold everything from vegetables to medicines, breathing the exhaust fumes of motorcycles whizzing past. It was an explosion of life.

The nuns moved towards a clothes stall that belonged to

a young Sherpa. Using sign language, Yandol explained to him that she wanted to sell her antelope skin jacket. "I'm not going to need it anymore," she thought to herself. The cold at night was far more bearable than in the high altitudes. The Sherpa tried on the jacket. A few onlookers burst out laughing when they saw him in it. The sleeves were a little short, but otherwise it fitted him well. After some quick bargaining, they struck a deal. With the four hundred rupees they got, the friends bought bananas, oranges, biscuits and tea, which they shared with their fellow travellers on returning to the police post.

At two o'clock in the afternoon, a horn blared to announce the departure of the bus leaving for Kathmandu. Painted in garish colours, the bus had enormous wheels. The doors did not close properly and the dirty, broken windowpanes could be neither opened nor closed. At the back of the bus was a small ladder to climb up to the roof, on which luggage, animals and passengers vied for space. The engine roared to life amidst loud cries and shouts, reverberating across the square.

The Tibetan refugees were the first to board the bus, escorted by the policemen, who sat at the back. Leaning on each other, the policemen slept throughout the journey. The liquor bottles they bought with the money they had got from the Tibetans peeped out of the pockets of their dishevelled uniforms. Neither the loud roar of the engine nor the thick smoke that came in through the windows could disturb their slumber. It was a glorious afternoon. Each curve of the winding road revealed Nepal in all its magnificence. Kinsom and Yandol leaned out of the window. Flocks of vermillon birds flitted above fir trees. Willows and lillies dotted the road, too narrow for two vehicles to pass at the same time. Women and goats walked alongside porters and men on horseback. The mountains had been left far behind, yet they still seemed so close. From time to time, the passengers could make out

The Realm of the Gods

a rope and wood bridge suspended precariously over a chasm. The smell of humid wood, dung, earth and trees filtered into the bus. The damp fragrance of wild flowers alternated with the nauseating smell of exhaust smoke emitted by vehicles coming from the opposite direction, constantly reminding the travellers that they were moving between two worlds.

The driver raced his roaring machine in the middle of the narrow road, oblivious to the smaller vehicles, which were invariably forced to swerve into a ditch to make way for the king of the road. The only time he would slow down was when a vehicle of the same size – a bus or truck – came from the other side. Then at the last moment, he would blow his horn loudly and press the brakes hard, making the bus tilt dangerously to one side of the road. The Tibetans, unused to such driving, were terrified. The policemen, on the other hand, continued to sleep off their hangover without turning a hair.

The mountain road began to take its toll: the nuns were feeling sick. When they turned behind, they saw that they not the only ones. The child was green in the face. A few Khampas had crowded around a half-opened window, desparately trying to find an opening to vomit from. These dauntless refugees, could withstand everything – high altitudes, bitter cold, snow, icy winds – but not the antics of a crazy bus driver. Yandol, completely nauseated, made her way through bundles tied with rope and baskets of live hens, to the driver's seat and begged him to stop. The driver nodded his head as if to say he would, but kept going till he reached a small town. There drove past many shops before he finally drew up in front of a wayside restaurant selling sweets and soft drinks. The Tibetans stumbled out of the bus. Looking at them, the owner immediately pointed to the cloakrooms and they rushed to relieve their churning stomachs. Kinsom and Yandol forgot that they were dressed as men. They entered the ladies room, making the other passengers stare.

When they came out, they were accosted by several people, who blocked their passage. Among them was one of the policemen escorting them. A swarthy, well built man came close to Yandol and molested her. The man tried to touch her breast. Yandol began to shout and to struggle. Kinsom, the sturdier of the two, jumped into the fray. At that moment, the child came out of the toilet, still green in the face. When he saw what was happening, he shouted for help. He began to pull at the men's clothes and beat them with amazing grit and determination. The nuns had never thought that a child so fragile was capable of so much courage. The men, furious, beat him, trying to get him out of their way. At last, the guide came along with the head police constable. When order was finally restored and the racket subsided, the head constable told the guide in a voice full of reproach: "You didn't tell us there were women in your group." The guide stared hard at them and said: "So what, they've paid, haven't they? What difference does it make whether they are men or women?" But the constable would not listen. This could have meant the end of the journey.

When the nuns tried to board the bus, the policeman refused to let them get on. He said "protecting" women was more expensive, so they would have to pay more. "Those policemen were real rogues," Kinsom recalled. The guide did his utmost to defend the nuns. Tired of waiting, the driver dared to blow his horn only to be shouted at by the policemen. Though she was loath to do so, Yandol finally pulled out a hundred rupee note from her pocket and gave it to the head constable. The journey continued.

However, this incident shook the nuns' confidence. They were filled with the same kind of fear they experienced before leaving Lhasa. These drunken policemen behaved so unreasonably that they did not know what to expect next. In jail, they had been mentally prepared to be badly treated. But this assault had taken them completely by surprise. The fact of being so vulnerable depressed them, though the scenery outside helped them restore their peace of mind. Flowers springing out of crevices in large rocks along the road; shining streams; a sudden glimpse of slopes bathed in the mountain light; peaks now dark, now glowing — all this beauty made them forget the world of men.

"Had we been monks, this would not have happened to us," said Yandol after a long silence. "They would not have dared to pick a quarrel with us and we would not have had to defend ourselves." Kinsom laughingly nodded in agreement. "In my next life, I'd like to born a man," Yandol confessed. "Me too," said her friend, "but as a monk..."

X

The next day, they reached the filthy, noisy, crowded, and wonderful city of Kathmandu. Glued to their windows, the nuns looked in wonder at the permanent spectacle offered by the city. Its one million inhabitants seemed to live on the streets where they spat, bathed, defecated, prayed and slept. Women sat stitching and spinning at their doorstep or window sill; some sold vegetables and tools on the temple steps. Magnificent temples with golden domes stood next to garbage dumps, beautifully carved balconies in wood overlooked clogged, uncovered drains of narrow streets. There were squares flanked by extraordinary monuments and markets overflowing with fruits of all colours. Everywhere, a teeming mass of humanity jostled for space, taking in the exhaust fumes and dust. Since times immerorial, Kathmandu has opened its doors to all: the rich and the poor, the wise and the mad — a city where one could live alone without feeling lonely.

Kathmandu was full of tourists, very different from those who had come in the seventies. Heroine and cocaine can still be bought easily on the streets but it is not drugs but the natural beauty and religion of Nepal that attract the young Western tourist of today. The hippies of the seventies have given way to the ecologists and mystics of the nineties. There are over a hundred travel agencies, run mainly by the Sherpas, which specialize in treks and adventure tourism to cater to the needs of these tourists. But how many of them could guess, as they insouciantly strolled down the streets of Kathmandu, that there were other travellers who had risked their lives to get here. Could they understand the frightened gestures of the child or the bemused expression of the Khampas?

The Tibetans were taken by the policemen to the Darbar Square Police Station, a white, colonial building in the heart of the old city, surrounded by some of the most beautiful Hindu and Buddhist temples. At the entrance, a godman, his body smeared with ash, was stroking his penis with a stick in front of an astonished group of tourists, who were laughing and throwing coins into his bowl.

Once again, the Tibetans found themselves locked up in a large hall, being questioned by policemen in gray uniforms. This was a routine affair, but they were nonetheless scared, as they had been through other kinds of interrogation. Freedom was so near, yet their were petrified lest it be snatched away from them forever. Their fears were not misplaced. More than one refugee had been taken back from this building to a Chinese border post, in spite of the repeated protests of diplomatic legations and humanitarian organizations. The refugees had learned that it did not take more than a second for things to go wrong.

The Realm of the Gods

Their fear did not leave them till the time that two protection officers from the UNHCR came in search of them a few hours later. As soon as they learnt that they were safe at last, a heady feeling of jubilation came over them.

In the Darbar Square facing the Royal Palace, it was the time to say goodbye. The child, the nuns and the old man were being taken to the official reception centre. The Khampas were going up to Mustang, where some members of their family had settled down after the surrender. They wanted to start a new life, to do what they knew best: engage in the cattle trade and perhaps the arms trade. They bowed to the nuns, grateful to them for the exemplary faith and perseverance they had shown during the journey. As they embraced the child, their eyes glittered with emotion. They left in silence, forlorn, to an uncertain destiny.

Kinsom and Yandol could not keep back their tears as they bid farewell to the guide. With this man, of whom they had been wary till the very end, they had shared fear, disappointment and joy. Because of him, they had reached this far, so near their gods. Because of men like him, the flame of Tibet continued to shine in the world. Shyly, they folded their hands to convey to him their heartfelt gratitude. The guide's hard exterior finally cracked. His eyes crinkled, the corners of his mouth turned upwards and a few lines appeared on his cheeks. As a parting gift, he gave the nuns a smile. Then he put on his yellow sunglasses and disappeared in the crowd.

Born of Tibetan parents, Nurse Tsering Lhamo was inured to seeing refugees arrive from Tibet in a terrible state. The closer it got to winter the worse was their condition. Tsering Lhamo was forty years old. Her eyes gleamed with intelligence and she spoke several languages fluently. In charge of the infirmary at the Tibetan Refugee Centre, all her life she had wanted to do something to help her people. For she herself had left her parents behind in 1959 to come to Nepal, with nothing but the clothes on her back. She had never been able to forget this. Neither did she want to. As soon as she reached the infirmary, she would find a long line of undernourished refugees, ailing from severe gastric problems, sunburn or frightening injuries received during the journey. She would set about her business: some had broken collar bones after a thrashing from the Nepali police, others had open purulent fractures. That day, there were a few nuns who had been raped by mountain guides and a group of half-frozen children. Every morning she came to the Reception Centre, located behind the Swayambu Buddhist Temple, one of Nepal's best known symbols. It is said that here the Buddha preached amidst the monkeys and the pine trees. She would examine, clean, cut, disinfect and treat thousands of wounds — the living, bleeding tale of an exile that has lasted for almost forty years.

The nurse examined Kinsom, Yandol, the old man and the child. Then, after vaccinating them, she treated their wounds with iodine and gave them vitamin pills. A health assistant cut their entangled locks and nails. The nurse kept back the child to examine him further. As she soon as she removed the bandage the Spanish doctor had put, there was an unbearable stench. The foot was badly infected. It had to be operated. She told the child that the doctors might be able to do something about the infection, but said they would probably have to amputate the toes of his right foot. She wanted to prepare him for this so that after the operation, he did not wake up to the nasty shock of finding his toes missing.

The nuns said goodbye to the little hero, who had withstood the cold and the dangers of the journey without uttering a word of complaint. He had been the chivalrous knight who had rushed to their defence, a model of discretion and courage. "We will see each other in Dharamasala," Yandol told him as they parted. The child stood alone, a sad look in his eyes. He was not going to be alone for long. But to him it seemed as if he was breaking his last links with Lhasa and his family. That broke his little heart far more than the pain in his feet.

The nuns were put up in brick huts. Inside were many rickety, old beds. Plastic sheets hung from the windows and the only other furniture were a couple of hooks on the wall to hang one's clothes and bags. There were other refugees — families, monks and children — who had come by other incredible routes. All of them had a card with their photo on it. They would keep taking it out of their bags, as if to ensure that it was real, and look at it with pride. It was the only document they had to prove their identity. Stamped with the Lion Seal, the card symbolized a Tibet they had never known, a Tibet that was now welcoming them. It bore the signature of the Government of His Holiness the Dalai Lama. It was a dream.

Lying down near the open door, Kinsom and Yandol could see green hills and the Swayambu Temple. A sense of security so comforting that it seemed unreal enveloped them. As they savoured the joy of overcoming the Himalayan ordeal, the bad moments of the journey faded away. Gradually, they became aware of their freedom. One day, they decided to go to the market. With the money they had got from the jacket sold to the Sherpa trader, they bought six metres of crimson cloth and two woolen shawls of the same colour. They rushed back to the Reception Centre, removed their trousers, shirts and jerseys and dressed themselves in their habits once again. At last, they had returned home.

6
WHEN HORSEMEN GALLOP ON WHEELS

I

Two thousand kilometres away from Kathmandu, in the upper reaches of Dharamsala, where traditional Tibet has taken roots, a solitary monk, a rosary of thick wooden beads in his hand, walks around the gardens of his residence. It early morning. Falcons, crows and vultures soar over the treetops while the monk continues his walk. This has been his morning routine, since that day in 1960 when this place was chosen as his residence. Walking helps to meditate. Tenzin Gyatso, the fourteenth Dalai Lama, finds this time he spends in the open the best moment of his day.

An hour earlier at dawn when all is silent, he has prayed for peace in the world to the ringing of small, sacred bells. He does not pray to any God. He is in a state of pure meditation from where he reaches a different level of consciousness. He thinks once again of his mission as a Boddhisatva — to dedicate this life and the lives to come to the alleviation of suffering and the awakening of all mankind through action and meditation. As morning progresses, nature unfurls itself. Greenfinches and sparrows flit from tree to tree and his thoughts tend to stray, as he remembers the long road that had brought him here.

This man, who at the age of fifteen had already experienced the relentless brutality of politics and imperialism as well as the futility of armed struggle, has become a living symbol of his times. The twentieth century has seen the triumph of science and great inventions, but it has also been a century of genocide and exile. Millions of people — Europeans,

Indians, Chinese, Russians, Africans — have been forced to sever their ties with the land of their birth. Never before in the history of mankind have so many races been uprooted.

This man, who had lost his land, was now forced to helplessly watch the slow agony of his people. He had seen his loved ones die — a brother, a sister, his mother and his tutors. Other friends and monks had perished in Tibet in dreadful conditions. The news of the recent death of the Panchen Lama affected him deeply. Of late, they had often spoken to each other on the telephone. Their conversations had convinced him that, in his heart of hearts, the Panchen Lama had remained loyal to his religion and country. After releasing him from prison, the Chinese used him as a puppet. But he had never stopped opposing them and did so till the very end. In one of the last speeches he made in Peking, he boldly declared that Tibet had paid a terrible price for the progress the Chinese claimed to have brought about. Two days later, he died of a heart attack in the Tashi Lumpo Monastery. He was fifty-three years old. Many Tibetans thought that he had been poisoned by the Chinese. Yet others believed that his was a symbolic death, a deliberate act of a genuine spiritual master. "Had I fallen into the hands of the Chinese, I do not think I could have been as brave as he," said Tenzin Gyatso, removing once and for all the doubts about the loyalty of his spiritual son.

There were so many times the Dalai Lama could have lost hope, so many times he could have allowed depression or sadness to drag him down, but this never happened. His training helped him discover an inner strength with which he continues to strive tirelessly to preserve the memory of his land.

Tenzin Gyatso is the beacon guiding his people through the long night of Chinese occupation. In India, he is looking after a hundred and thirty thousand refugees of which thirteen thousand are living in monasteries, studying and protecting their tradition. The orphanage built for the children of the first

When Horsemen Gallop on Wheels

batch of refugees has grown into a network of children's villages all over India, which take care of more than thirty thousand children. The diaspora has grown in numbers but it has been able to transmit the faith, the scriptures and the legends of Tibet as well as the stories of its Dalai and Panchen Lamas, nomadic warriors, political monks and wise hermits. Tenzin Gyatso has instilled in his companions in exile the sense of purpose required to protect the soul of Tibet. He knows that the enemy will withdraw some day, for when a people struggle for their existence, they can only emerge victorious, that the love for freedom inherent in each and every human being will finally prevail. It is merely a question of time. Even the Chinese cannot live forever without freedom.

For the time being however, his people are being martyrized and Tenzin Gyatso never spares an occasion to condemn this. Winning the Nobel Prize has helped him in his task. He himself craves for no honours but the Nobel Prize has provided him a platform from where he can be heard. At the same time, he continues to try and find a compromise with the invaders. However, each time he initiates a dialogue with Peking about the future of his country, he is immediately accused of wanting to re-establish the old feudal system. In the beginning, he underestimated the impact of the Chinese Government's propaganda, which consistently portrayed the invasion as the liberation of an enslaved society. It was only after the Cultural Revolution and the Tiananmen Square massacre that the world recognized how hypocritical and cruel the Communist Chinese were.

A six-year-old child, Gendun Chockyi Nyina, recognized by the Dalai Lama as the reincarnation of the Panchen Lama, was the victim of the Chinese regime's most recent act of barbarism. When the Lamas announced their discovery, the Chinese authorities were incensed. They had wanted a reincarnation of their choice, whom they could indoctrinate and present as an alternative political figure to the Dalai

Lama. One day, the child and his parents, a poor couple who raised yaks, were flown out of Tibet under strict security and given the same treatment that is reserved for all political prisoners considered dangerous. In spite of strong international protest, till date no one knows what has become of them. Using bribes and threats, the Chinese government forced a group of clergymen to substitute him with another child, who was subsequently enthroned as the Panchen Lama in the Jokhang Temple. Thus, the Chinese have the dubious distinction of keeping the youngest political prisoner in the world.

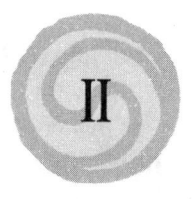

II

At six o'clock in the morning, the Dalai Lama walks back from the garden to his residence. Outside his study is a bird house, built in a manner to drive away the greedy ones. Chattering birds draw near their protector, who scatters seeds for them. That day, however, the protection of the bird house proved to be inadequate. The Dalai Lama uses an old air gun to frighten the cats away. Then, he returns to his prayer room and prostrates before the altar. He seats himself on an ochre-yellow cushion and enters into meditation: "As we gradually plumb our inner depths, there is the feeling that peace exists within us. All of us have this deep desire, though very often it is masked, hidden," he never tires of saying.

Tenzin Gyatso often meditates on death. He knows the best way to die is to completely detach oneself from everything — within and without — so that at that crucial moment one is free of desire and attachment. His meditation on death is a constant reminder to him of how tenuous the thread of all existence is and this is what gives meaning to every second of life. Motionless, back straight, legs crossed, breathing light, he seems to have reached Nirvana, for Nirvana is not a place like the earth or sky, but a state of mind that can be attained here and now in the midst of life's agitation.

What do human beings seek? Tenzin Gyatso travels often and each time he journeys, he sees people rushing frantically from one place to another and he wonders if they really know where they are going to. In his public audiences, he talks with people from all walks of life, people who seem to have everything they need to be happy, and yet feel dissatisfied. He sees them tense, fearful, constantly competing with each other. It seems as if they have lost contact with their innermost self, the most joyful and fruitful part of their being. They are struggling on the surface of the sea whereas peace lies far below in its depths. They have lost their peace of mind. If human beings are not at peace with themselves, how can there be peace among nations? If man cannot heal himself, how can he dream of setting the world right?

When the Dalai Lama went to Spain, he met a Catholic monk, near Montserrat, with whom he discussed Christian faith and Buddhist philosophy. A genuine spiritual master, Father Basili lived the life of a hermit, having withdrawn himself from the world like an oriental sage, living on bread and water alone. Though the two could exchange only a few words in English, it was enough for Tenzin Gyatso to realize that he was in the presence of an exceptional being, a man of faith. When the monk was asked to reveal the contents of their discussion, he simply said: "Love".

Love is also at the heart of Ocean of Wisdom's meditation. Without love or compassion, there can be no joy. And love is born only when the mind is at peace. Material comfort is not enough to attain happiness; spiritual development has to accompany it. Such is the Dalai Lama's firm belief. .

Serenity, love, compassion and tolerance — an unusual discourse for a Head of State, who looks and lives likes a humble villager. In whichever city or country he goes and to whosoever he speaks, be they kings, presidents, mayors, or religious leaders, he never shows hatred for his enemies. Not a word of resentment or condemnation has been uttered by him or the greats Lamas and Abbots who have lost everything in exile, often the victims of the worst kind of violence. The Abbot of the Namgyal Monastery, imprisoned in 1959 and subsequently kept in a concentration camp for twenty years, told him about the great risk he ran while in prison. Intrigued, the Dalai Lama asked him what was that danger. His answer was extraordinary: he had been afraid of losing his compassion for the Chinese. Men such as these are living examples of the true meaning of religion.

III

On the day when the iron bird flies,
When horsemen gallop on wheels
The people of Bodh shall travel across the world like ants,
And Dharma shall arrive on the red man's continent.

When this prediction was made centuries ago, no one understood it. Today, steel birds carrying bombs have flown over Tibet; the horsemen on wheels are the Chinese soldiers, riding on tanks and trucks. And the people of Bodh are scattered in the four corners of the earth, taking Dharma or the Buddhist law, to foreign lands.

Much of the prophecy has, thus, come true; the rest is being fulfilled. In his travels, Tenzin Gyatso has witnessed the spread of Buddhism. Today, there are over five hundred Buddhist centres flourishing in the West. It is worthwhile noting that the Lamas who best succeeded in spreading Buddhism were not the most erudite ones but men with a strong personality, capable of relating to Westerners, who are more sensitive to the Master's charisma than his saintly qualities. One such monk was a humble Lama from Sera. A refugee at the Buxa Duar camp, he struck up a curious friendship with a Russian princess, which lead to the establishment of a Buddhist organization that extended across the world with lightening speed.

Lama Yeshe could never forget that extraordinary day he encountered the dazzling Russian princess Zina Rachesvsky. "How can one get peace and enlightenment?", she demanded the minute she arrived at the doorstep of the Darjeeling monastery where the monk was in retreat. Never had a foreigner ever asked for enlightenment in this way, as if looking for a bulb in a shop.

Zina Rachesvsky had lead a far more tormented existence than the Lama from Sera. Daughter of a Russian prince who had fled at the time of the Revolution, and of a rich North American heiress, Zina had been brought up in Hollywood and became a spoil teenager, then an insecure and deeply unhappy adult. When she met Lama Yeshe, she was tired of living. An overdose of drugs, alcohol, money, late nights and sex had taken a toll on her body. Lama Yeshe and his companions taught her all the things she had longed to know. "She was unhappy with everything," remembered the Tibetan Lama. "She said her life was empty. In comparison, I had nothing

— no country, no home, no money, no possessions, no family, and yet I had everything because I was happy. Zina and other Westerners were suffering from the same problem: they did not understand their own selves and their inner life. They were incapable of realizing their own potential for happiness. Zina thought happiness came from outside, but that is not how things are, happiness comes from within[9]."

Zina started to find meaning in her life. After nine months of training, she declared to the Lamas that she wanted to become a nun. Lama Yeshe agreed. Although he did not realize it at the time, her involvement with them would ultimately help spread Buddhism to the West. As time went by, Zina used a part of her inheritance to buy land on top of a hill near Kathmandu. Gradually, a monastery came up, and took the name of Kopan. The atmosphere here could not have been more unlike the austerity of the Sera Monastery. The first to come were a group of hippies, who had experimented with all kinds of Eastern philosophies. Some of them had followed a guru. It was a disparate group: a few were tired of drugs, others were really trying to find an answer to the mystery of existence and yet others were vagabonds on the lookout for new experiences. Lama Yeshe kept an open mind. He devoted all his energies to convey the sacred teachings to anyone who cared to know. He never asked his followers to renounce their own culture. He said of Westerners: "They were intellectually well prepared but lacked direct experience of the teachings, which can only be achieved through meditation. It is only through inner experience that one's intellect can help one in one's daily life." Lama Yeshe and Zina Rachesvsky had absolutely nothing in common, yet together they set up a foundation to spread Buddhism in the world. Lama Yeshe said: "She was convinced that Tibetan Buddhism had something very precious to offer

---

[9] Quoted in "Reincarnation", by Vicki Mackenzie.

When Horsemen Gallop on Wheels

to Westerners. It was the essence of Buddhism that she wanted to convey to them, not its external form. The essence has interested men and women through the ages, as it deals with human nature, suffering and joy. And this essence ought to be linked to Western science, philosophy and psychology. Otherwise, there can be no connection. Westerners are unaware of the tremendous joy that can be attained through the mind." Lama Yeshe tried to show his disciples the immense potential of their inner world. He had his own inimitable style, very different from the dry, medieval interpretation of Tibetan Buddhism in its strictest form. Because of this, wherever Lama Yeshe traveled, the number of people who came to listen to him grew.

Anyone who knew the spoilt child from Hollywood would have been amazed at the incredible things she did. She lived in a cave in the Himalayas and recited as part of her spiritual duties three million six hundred thousand mantras. In the beginning, she found the solitude and the isolation of the mountains unbearable. Afraid, she spent most of her time writing her diary. But slowly her fears began to recede and she felt happy in her retreat. She could sit still for hours on end in meditation. She was a transformed person. When she came back from her retreat in the mountains, her friends found her radiant, her face glowing with a serenity and calm they had never seen before. Soon without anybody telling her to, she returned to the mountains to be with herself. But her life was marked by tragedy. The dazzling North American beauty who became an ascetic died suddenly at the age of forty-two. The reason of her death was never specified; some say it was liver infection, others heart failure. She left at the best moment of her life, having found a much longed for peace of mind in a mountain cave.

Lama Yeshe continued his teaching in Kopan, instructing hundreds of Western disciples. He later set up the Foundation for the Preservation of the Mahayana Tradition and opened another monastery in the Solo Khumbu and an international retreat centre in the hills of Dharamsala. He became a tireless traveller. As soon as his students returned to their own countries, they would invite him to come and help them in the establishment of new centres of learning and retreat, open to all who wish to meditate, study Buddhism or simply get away from the tumult of the world. A publishing house brings out basic texts on Tibetan Buddhism.

In the mid-seventies, during the course of his numerous journeys, Lama Yeshe visited the island of Ibiza, in the Mediterranean Sea. He was awaited by a large number of people, many of whom were hippies. Lured by the call of the East, they were all looking for meaning in their lives. "He had the knack of being able to extract the essence of Buddhist philosophy – things that make us happy or sad, the meaning of life... – and explain it in such a way that it became comprehensible and attractive to Westerners," said Paco Hita, one of his first Spanish disciples, a shy, friendly man with deep blue eyes. "Knowing him was a revelation," said his companion, Maria Torres, dark haired, attractive and intelligent. "For the first time in my life, I got clear cut answers to all the questions I had been asking myself: Why are we born? Why do we die? Why do some people have a comfortable life and others a hellish one? But Lama Yeshe was not just a communication genius, he was a good man. He was a true friend, full of laughter, very intelligent, very sensitive. Though a monk, he has an extremely open mind. He was a rebel – he never wore the crimson habit."

His Spanish disciples suggested to Lama Yeshe that he set up a centre in Spain for people of all religions. After a long search, they finally chose a site in the village of Bubion, in the mountains near Granada. The place looked like the Himalayas, with spectacular views and crisp, pristine air. For six years, this group of friends gave freely both of their time and money to build the meditation centre with an access road.

When Horsemen Gallop on Wheels

It was a huge effort, but they did it wholeheartedly, pushed on by the strength of their faith.

Their efforts did not go unrewarded. Lama Yeshe announced unexpectedly that he would be coming accompanied by none other than the Dalai Lama in person. A rare moment indeed for this group of friends, who thus received much more than they could have ever hoped for. On learning of the Spanish government's decision to cancel his visit to Madrid under pressure from the Chinese, the Monarch decided to use this time to visit the Bubión centre. The God King of the Tibetans and his Lama reached the village on a Sunday. The entire town had come out to meet them with flowers and music. Ocean of Wisdom walked down the narrow streets, holding the hand of a little girl, to the sound of guitars. In the church, the parish priest gave him the place of honour and the mass that was held was an emotional moment indeed. That day Buddhists and Christians experienced how true religion unites mankind, transcending cultural barriers. As hymns were being sung, the Dalai Lama made his way slowly, stopping to shake hands with all who approached him. Paco Hita, Maria Torres and many others were waiting to receive him. Ocean of Wisdom laughed when he saw the precarious state of the centre, the vegetarian paella they had prepared for him and the village missing fate atmosphere of his reception. His was a direct, spontaneous laughter. It seemed as if there was another person inside him who suddenly came out roaring. After the consecration ceremony, Lama Yeshe, gazing at the Dalai Lama with childlike wonder, announced that His Holiness would give a speech. Against the backdrop of Mulhacen landscape, the region's highest peak, a disparate group of townspeople, tourists, Buddhists and Tibetan masters congregated around a threshing floor. They listened as the Dalai Lama explained in great detail the nature of the mind in its various states. The Dalai Lama spoke of the state of pure light, the deepest mental level that is attained just before death. He explained: "In Buddhism, it is not the reincarnation of the soul that causes the eternal cycle of death and birth. What matters is the living force or vital energy, which feeds on the passions and desires of an entire lifetime. It is these passions and desires that generate, even after the body has expired, another combination of force and energy. In each new life, this combination reflects the sum total of the previous deeds of each individual. Real spirituality, therefore, is to be aware of the interdependence of each and every thing. Even the most trivial of words, thoughts or actions have consequences for the entire universe. It is just like the ripples that are formed when you throw a stone in water. The ripples caused by a tiny stone travel far. So you see, we are responsible for all that we do, say and think, each one is responsible for himself, for everyone, for all that surrounds us."

On the following day, before leaving, the Dalai Lama asked his hosts:

"Do you have a name for this place?"

To tell the truth, nobody had the time to think of one.

"Then I'm going to suggest a name to you. Why don't you call it Osel-ling?"

"Osel-ling?"

"The place of pure light. "

IV

A few months after his visit to the Bubion centre, Lama Yeshe fell seriously ill. For many years, he had been suffering from a heart ailment, which he had developed at the Buxa Duar camp. Doctors had advised him to slow down and give up travelling. But he was a man with a mission, he had to transmit *dharma* across the world and to this end, he spared no effort. He died on March 3, 1984, at the age of forty-nine, leaving behind a network of seventy centres, spread over fifteen countries.

Less than a year after his death, in Granada, a fifth child was born to Paco Hita and Maria Torres, the founders of the Bubion centre. As soon as the father entered the hospital room, he held his newly born son in his arms and said: "His little face is so radiant. Let us call him Osel or pure light." Maria liked the name. What better tribute could there be to the centre they had worked so hard to set up under their master's guidance.

On April 18, 1986, while Maria Torres was making lunch for her large family, she received a phone call from India: "Can you come to New Delhi next week with Osel? We want him to perform some tests." The person speaking to her on the phone was a disciple of Lama Yeshe, reputed to be a monk of great erudition. His name was Lama Zopa. While speaking, he was forced to cut off his sentences because of a breathing problem. His conviction that his master would be reborn in the West to continue his work for the spread of Buddhism in the world had been confirmed by the oracles. More significantly, the Dalai Lama, who had been keeping a watch for signs that would lead him to Lama Yeshe's reincarnation, had received answers while meditating. One name that kept recurring was that of Osel. "We are still not sure, but if he is the reincarnation, will you let us bring him up?" Maria was overwhelmed. She had always cherished the dream of going to India but never had she imagined that it would happen like this. There could be no greater honour than her master choosing to return as a son of hers, proof of the deep bond of friendship she shared with Lama Yeshe, a vindication of her efforts and devotion.

"Yes, I'll come," she told Lama Zopa.

Ocean of Wisdom was waiting for them at the Ashoka Hotel in New Delhi. As usual, he had a rosary in his hand. He bestowed them with a kindly smile, a knowing gleam in his eyes.

"Have you noticed anything special about the child?", he asked Maria

"No, not really. Though one night while I was pregnant, I did dream of Lama Yeshe. That's all."

"In all our investigations so far, Osel's name has appeared repeatedly. But we have to wait until he starts speaking. He will give us the most conclusive proof. "

Maria was relieved. The Dalai Lama's words gave her to understand that there was still time, that the final decision would only be taken after a few years when the child could speak. But Lama Zopa was not prepared to wait. He, like the other disciples, was in a hurry. After all, the purpose of reincarnation is to ensure that work carries on. He wanted Maria and her son to go with him to Dharamsala that very day. He wanted to show the Foundation's followers that Lama Yeshe was alive among them. They spent the whole night travelling. Maria was dazed. The overpowering smells and sounds of India, the exhaustion of the journey and her son's strange destiny were too much for her to take in at once. They

When Horsemen Gallop on Wheels

reached the temple of the Tushita Centre, located in a cedar grove in the upper reaches of Dharamsala, where a large group of followers were waiting for them. Little Osel was wide awake. He threw down his feeding bottle and picked up a small bell, with the correct hand, his followers were quick to point out. Next, he sat on a throne, rang the bell in the same way as a Lama and laughed. Even his mother was impressed: "He was behaving just like Lama Yeshe". Some disciples began to cry. Maria could hardly believe what she had just witnessed. Was this her son or her master who stood before her?

During the next few days, Osel was subjected to the traditional tests, which were carried out in front of various groups of disciples. The Spanish child was able to pick out from a heap of objects those that belonged to his previous incarnation. He seemed to know what to do with the rosaries, bells and *katas* or white silk scarves. It was only after he had undergone all the tests that he was acknowledged as the legitimate incarnation of the deceased Lama Yeshe. Monks, nuns and Western disciples in Dharamsala, who had known their master so well, could not take their eyes of this blond baby with chubby cheeks, running about in nappies. This indeed was their guru, but he had reappeared in such a different body! Osel was made to undergo some more tests in France to satisfy the Western Buddhist monks, who were far more skeptical. At the age of fourteen months, he was declared the absolute and undisputed reincarnation of Lama Yeshe. The Dalai Lama confirmed this recognition, though he was not in favour of making the news public, remembering perhaps the difficult solitude of his own childhood. He preferred that be child be brought up in his own culture. But his wishes were overruled. Lama Zopa was heading a vast organization with thousands of followers; he wanted to keep their hope alive. So he went ahead with the announcement of the reincarnation. The reaction was instantaneous: there was a flood of letters, invitations, and interviews. From that time onwards, life was never the same again for the family from Bubion. The strange phenomenon of the little Spanish Lama got world-wide coverage. Some said it was a political gimmick, others, a publicity stunt. To many it seemed like a fairy tale. "No one was able to understand the simplicity and beauty of it all, but that is understandable," said Maria Torres.

A year later, Maria and Paco returned to Dharamsala with their son. Hundreds of followers — monks, nuns, disciples and journalists from the most influential countries of the world- climbed, on foot, the steep slope that lead to the Tushita Centre to witness a unique event: the investiture of the youngest western monk ever. Osel Hita Torres was about to make his official entry in the world. He was barely two years and a month old. The temple had been decorated for the occasion with mural paintings. The ten feet high throne was wrapped in golden brocade. Two rows of Tibetan Lamas, attired in their ceremonial best, were sitting on the ground in the lotus position. Bugles and oboes resounded across the valley, followed by the clashing of cymbals, the beating of drums and the blowing of conch shells, sounded traditionally to drive away evil spirits and call for the protection of the Buddhas. Osel arrived in the arms of his father. He was dressed in ceremonial robes, wearing the yellow hat with ear covers of the Gelugpa School to which the Dalai Lama belongs. For three hours, he sat still in his place. Sometimes serious, sometimes mischievous, he nonetheless maintained, throughout, a dignified posture for one his age. He treated the ritual as if it were a game. Accepting the offerings with unusual patience, he ate some sweets and played with a go-cart. At the end of the ceremony, he ran to his father. From that moment, his destiny had been sealed.

V

At 7:00 a.m., the Dalai Lama finishes his morning meditation and turns on the radio to hear the BBC world news. The whispers of monks saying their prayers float into his office. Then, he settles himself on his cushion, at the foot of a low table. Through the window, he casts a glance at his birdhouse; no cats around. He opens one of the few holy texts that could be brought from Tibet, thus escaping the destructive wrath of the Chinese. Whenever he manages to spare time from his public affairs, Ocean of Wisdom devotes two to three hours to the study of some of the ancient teachings and scriptures. Going through these books, which contain almost 3.000 years of accumulated wisdom, is an exercise in spirituality. An exercise which is a further proof that brute force can never destroy the human spirit. In the monastery below, bugles are being sounded to mark the hours.

To dive into the past helps him understand the present. The world is getting smaller, more interdependent by the day, a world that worships at the altar of a single god: science. Ocean of Wisdom fully appreciates the value of modern science. Ever since the Austrian mountaineer Heinrich Harrer showed him his first camera and tape recorder, he has always been fascinated by the way machines work. Whenever he received a gift, he liked to dismantle it to see how it worked. As a young boy, he would pull watches apart and whenever anybody from his family, friends or government had a broken watch, they would just send it to him.

His passion for watches has diminished somewhat with the coming of the digital watch but his interest in the sciences is as keen as before. In spite of criticism from several compatriots, he went ahead and gave permission to North American scientists to carry out experiments on hermits. His friend, Dr Benson from Harvard, was fascinated by the phenomenon of internal or psychic heat. With body heat, the monks can dry clothes that have been washed in freezing water, sometimes at sub-zero temperatures. Dr Benson observed that the hermits' body temperature rose by ten degrees, their intake of oxygen decreased and their breathing slowed down to seven inhalations per minute. Fat reserves were burnt through a combination of physical and psychic phenomena, a process which until then was believed to have been restricted to animals in hibernation.

What was of interest to Ocean of Wisdom was not so much the physiological process as the fact that there was ample space for modern science to develop in Tibetan culture. The theoretical knowledge of the one complements the empirical knowledge of the other, and the relationship between the two holds the key to penetrating the mystique that has surrounded Tibet since times immemorial – a task as challenging as it is fascinating. Some of the latest discoveries in quantum physics seem very close to the Buddhist thesis that no duality exists between mind and matter. This can be verified by compressing an empty space. Particles appear spontaneously as if matter was inherent. With these discoveries, a convergence between science and Buddhist theory becomes possible, as the latter states that mind and matter are realities which are both separate and interdependent. Tenzin Gyatso is also very keen on a scientific study of the oracle, who continues to play a key role in Tibetan life.

But he is not willing to believe in the supremacy of science. Science must be totally dispassionate for it to become wisdom. The most important discoveries take place when the scientist is guided solely by his intellectual curiosity. However, the twentieth century belief that science alone holds the answers to everything has eclipsed the quest for wisdom. The spiritual approach is different. It recognizes that human beings are both knowledgeable and ignorant, good and bad. Science tends to get fragmented, losing itself in the endless complexity of matter. Science only accepts tangible proof, whereas spiritualism acknowledges the validity of inner conviction that comes from a life of contemplation. One thing is clear: scientific certainty does not necessarily confer wisdom.

Though most people enjoy the fruits of scientific progress, very few are involved in the development of science. Only a small minority has any understanding of how the universe, matter and life function. But nothing, neither religion nor any utopia, can provide these people with the composure and spiritual peace so necessary to attain happiness. The social utopias that were supposed to have transformed society and created a better man have proved to be disastrous failures. History has shown that they have failed on every score, be it in terms of ethics or human and material freedom, leaving the West with nothing but a void. It is this that explains the renewed Western interest in the quest for wisdom. Today, Westerners are attracted to Buddhism because it speaks of the human being and compassion, because it does not claim to be able to rebuild the world after destroying it, to regenerate humanity after murdering it. As opposed to the chaos and disorder of life, Buddhism suggests the silence of inner experience.

In Dharamsala, the gong strikes twelve. The Dalai Lama has spent the last five hours studying and meditating. It is not very often that he gets so much time, alternating as he does between spirituality and politics, between personal contemplation and altruistic action, between the transcendent and the imminent.

A thin mist lies in the valley below. Monkeys jumps about, squirrels scamper up branches. A monk enters his residence, carrying a bowl of *thukpa* for him. It is his last meal of the day, as monastic discipline advises against eating after midday. After he finishes his lunch, his personal secretary enters the room with his schedule for the afternoon: interviews, visits, audiences. Ocean of Wisdom leaves his apartments, and walks through the flowery garden towards the main hall. The affairs of the world now call for his attention.

VI

If Kathmandu had taken the small group of Tibetan refugees by surprise, the Indian capital overawed them. They had never imagined such a large city could exist, twice as populated as the whole of Tibet. In New Delhi, cars zoomed ahead, oblivious of the chaotic traffic with ramshackle buses, three-wheelers, taxis, motorcycles and cycles jostling for space. Entire families lived in shanties under flyovers. How could anyone spend a whole lifetime in this pollution and dense traffic? But the refugees were dazzled by the many parks and gardens, the majestic colonial buildings and the steel and glass sky scrapers. Much as they would liked to stroll down the streets, stop at the food and fruit kiosks, soak in all the city's vitality, they did not want to run the risk of losing their way or getting into any kind of trouble. So they remained all the time in the office of the representatives of the Tibetan government-in-exile, a small building located in a residential area. There was still the journey to Dharamsala.

Finally, the group broke up. The old man left the same night for the South. From Bangalore he would go to the Bylakuppe settlement where lived his son and grandson, who was studying. His offspring had struck roots on the plains, but the old man remained a son of the mountains, a nomad in body and spirit with neither hearth nor home. At his age, he had achieved the impossible, and this gave him immense satisfaction. How could he die when he still had so much energy in his body? The thought made him happier than usual. As he bid farewell to his travelling companions, his face twitched with emotion. The wrinkles, more visible than ever, seemed to reach his eyes, making them sparkle: "When I reach my grandson's monastery, I shall make an offering for you," he told them. Yandol presented her small rosary to him. The old man was not used to receiving gifts. Shyly, he accepted the beads and put them on his wrists. "I have nothing to offer you," he said, shamefaced. Both the nuns began to laugh. The old man himself had been the best present that Providence could have given them. His serenity had made them feel secure at all times. His stories had comforted them. His songs had made them dream and laugh. They hoped one day they would meet again, if only to listen to that lullaby his memory had saved from oblivion.

The nuns travelled the whole night. In the morning, the rickety bus left the plains and began the climb up. Women in colourful saris walked to and fro, carrying copper jars on their heads. It was a very different world from life in the city, gentle and full of colour. The people and animals seemed to come straight out of a fairy tale. The bus did not stop in Dharamsala, but continued up a steep path. On the way, they saw the purple silhouettes of monks reciting the morning prayer. They passed by the medical faculty, which also served as a clinic, a chemist's shop selling traditional medicines as well as a medical school. It was a replica in miniature of the Chakpuri faculty near Lhasa, which had been razed to the ground by the Chinese during the 1959 revolt. A little later, they saw the residence of the Dalai Lama, a modest house in front of a temple, whose name conjured up all the marvels of Lhasa. The nuns were thrilled. It was an incredible feeling to be so near the man who was the embodiment of their faith and culture; who personified the suffering of exile, who was their flame of hope. For him, they had braved mountain passes, snow storms and blizzards, they had defied the Chinese, they had left everything. For him, they had risked their lives, and for him, they were ready to do it again. Knowing that he was so nearby was a heady sensation. It was nothing short of a miracle.

At last, they reached MacleodGanj in the upper part of Dharamsala. The town is a tribute to the British official who decided to set up a cantonment here to spare his troops the unbearable summer heat of the plains. Situated on the top of a hill surrounded by woods, it consists of three streets, starting from the bus stand below. On the roadside is the store owned by the Nowrojee family, who have been living here for generations. It was at the initiative of one of the members of the fifth generation of this family of traders that life returned to this town, practically deserted after Independence. Aware that the Indian Government was on the lookout for a suitable place to install the Dalai Lama, Nowrojee traveled to Delhi to plead the case of Dharamsala before the authorities. Officials inspected the place and found it suitable. And, thus, was born 'little Lhasa'.

The nuns were confused. It was just like Tibet, yet so different. The narrow, dirty streets were crowded with Lamas, backpackers, hippies, school children, tourists and nuns like them. But there were also the Americans, the Swiss, the Germans and even a Spanish woman, who was known in the

When Horsemen Gallop on Wheels

region for her discipline and devotion. Her name was Eli Pelaez. Born in SaLamanca, she ended up at the Tushita Centre founded by Lama Yeshe. Currently, she is translating texts from ancient Tibetan. Every winter she spends four months in the solitude of her hut, at the foot of a hundred-year-old cedar tree.

Kinsom and Yandol turned the prayer wheels of the temple, situated in the heart of the town. The exiles had built this shrine in memory of those who had suffered the Chinese occupation of Tibet. Later, they passed by the little shops selling handicrafts and clothes. Dirty restaurants offered *tsampa*, Tibetan tea – and also pizzas and burritos. Posters of Bruce Lee and Arnold Schwarzenegger stared down from the walls, a symbol of a community that lives astride two eras, two civilizations.

At the end of the main street was the Refugee Reception Centre. The three-storeyed brick building was a safe haven for all those who survived the Himalayan ordeal. Kinsom and Yandol were settled on the ground floor, a large room in which were arranged rows of iron beds. Entire families were recuperating before being sent to other destinations. The walls of the centre seemed to reflect the suffering of all those who had crossed its doors. Sitting on a khaki blanket, a student recalled how he had been beaten with a cattle prod. A little further ahead, a young mother with two children was hoping against hope that her husband who had been detained at the border would come. Other women, sitting among their scarce belongings, relived the horror of the rape and the forced abortions. An old monk was meditating, eyes closed. He had fled his village after shooting a policemen who mistreated the neighbours. The second floor was reserved for more severe cases. There were nuns from the Drapchi and Gutsa prisons, wounded forever in body and soul, women who could not sleep, tormented as they were by the horrific memories that would not leave them. There were teenagers who had gone astray, fighting both pain and shyness, unable to speak, unable to forget, unable to live.

The only person in whom they all confided was a young Dutch girl. Blond-haired and always dressed in jeans, Francesca Von Holthoon worked for Amnesty International. She would spend days talking to the refugees, taking notes. She was to be the link between their suffering and the outside world. She had heard the most chilling accounts a human being could hear; what amazed her was the fact that her interviewees never once uttered a word of complaint. She had seen them breaking out into sobs, trembling with emotion, heads held between their arms to chase away the images of the past, but no one had any feeling of self-pity. On the contrary, they felt they were privileged in comparison to those who remained behind in Tibet.

Kinsom and Yandol too told their story to the young Dutch girl. They spoke of everything: the Drapchi singers, the Chinese soldiers in the streets, the internal prison organization, the various methods of torture, the number of torturers, Ani Choki's assistance and the border posts. While talking about those dreadful moments of her life, Kinsom felt flushed with embarrassment. But she told her story in full, going into the minutest detail, as if each detail was of vital importance. She knew words were all she had: an accurate description of what the Chinese had done to her would be the best weapon against Chinese oppression. The pain of her memories was nothing in comparison to the pain and suffering of her compatriots. They owed it to their country to tell the truth and so Kinsom agreed to open the wounds of her memory.

When at last Kinsom stopped speaking, night had already fallen. She went out onto the street alone, as if the fresh air could heal the anguish that her memories had caused. She had managed to keep her tears in check while narrating her story, but she could hold them back no longer. The suffering her torturers had inflicted on her would not go away so easily;

When Horsemen Gallop on Wheels

it was like a chronic disease, she would have to learn to live with it. Instead of lying down on her bed, she sat next to the mother of a family, who had also been tortured in Gutsa and who could not sleep. Kinsom put her head on the woman's lap, who stroked her hair as if she was her own daughter. Kinsom wanted to cry, to relax but she could not do so. All she managed was a low lament, like the cry of a bird, which mingled with the sounds of the night.

VII

Barely twenty-four hours after their arrival, they are urgently summoned by the management of the reception centre. Their hearts beating furiously, they climb up the stairs. What can the matter be now? "Nothing serious", the director says, "His Holiness would like to welcome you."

That afternoon in 1993 would become their most cherished memory. They climb down the hill until they reach the Dalai Lama's quarters, in front of the Tsuglakhang Temple, a much more modest version of the Jokhang in Lhasa. In the square that precedes the temple, Kinsom and Yandol find themselves in the midst of a group of refugees. Lay people, monks and nuns wait alike, their hearts quivering with emotion at the meeting that is going to take place. In the past, the common man had hardly any access to the Dalai Lama. The refugees wish they had some mental preparation, some kind of supernatural protection before coming into the presence of the Divinity. To be in the company of a master of wisdom, if only for a moment, is to participate in his world directly, to be in harmony with the benign influence that his presence radiates. And they had not even had the time to consult an oracle about a propitious date and hour. They wonder whether the old protocol is still in existence. In the past, visitors had to leave the room walking backwards so that their backs would not face the Illustrious Presence. People could not stand out on the balcony to watch processions go by because no one had the right to be higher than the palanquin of the Sovereign. Now, the refugees cannot hide behind the strict protocol of the past. The God King, the temporal personification of a divine emanation, has become human like them.

He has chosen to live the life of an exile, less interested in the affairs of this world than in study and meditation. He dreams of being like Gandhi, who, once the goal had been achieved, opted to stay out of government. The Dalai Lama has travelled across the world to plead the cause of Tibet, drawn up a democratic constitution for the great day when he will return, worked out the organization of elections to the first free parliament of his country. On several occasions, he has declared that he will retire from public life after reaching an agreement with the Chinese. He will then devote himself to his real calling, that of being a humble monk. He wants to make his position clear in order to silence his detractors, one of whom had lived the last hours of the Khampa rebellion and is presently residing at a stone's throw from the Sovereign's home. His critics allege that the government in exile is a continuation of the middle ages and the policy of non violence, a ploy for the Tibetan church to maintain its power. What power? ask those close to the Dalai Lama. The only power he has is what he gets in love and respect from his people. But his opponents entertain illusions of grandeur, harking back to the Tibetan empire that existed at the dawn of history. The Dalai Lama is clear in his mind: no one will go and fight for Tibet. Tibet is not going to become another Kuwait.

Many Tibetan youngsters are impatient. They dream of an armed struggle. Forty years of non-violence seem to have brought no results. The Dalai Lama reminds them that even if Tibet gets autonomy, it will still have to contend with a powerful China as its neighbour. Bloodshed is no answer; it will only come in the way of reconciliation. Ocean of Wisdom sees far ahead and acts accordingly. His duty, during this period of agony inflicted by the Chinese, is to stay as close as possible to his people. For this reason, he insists on sharing some time with the newly arrived refugees. He knows how many have benefited from the path of spirituality. This is their only hope and he wants the others to keep the flame alive.

That afternoon, the Dalai Lama receives a number of illustrious guests, gives interviews to the European and American press and accepts an invitation to travel abroad to raise funds. After which he leaves the temple for the public audience. He knows it will be an emotional moment.

As she catches a glimpse of him arriving, Kinsom feels her heart miss a beat. The God King, draped in crimson and gold robes, his schoolboy shoes peeping out, walks up to the group. He has a hearty smile on his face. Surrounded by his secretaries, he exudes energy. His visitors are surprised. Instead of the aura of sanctity they were expecting, he has the bearing of a man of integrity, the simplicity of both a peasant and a scholar.

The refugees stand in line. The nuns can hardly believe their eyes: this is their life's dream coming true, the dream of all Tibetans. In the silence of this unique moment, they think of their families, of those who have helped them and also of those been unable to do so; of their prison companions and the convents; of the city of Lhasa, the villages, the animals and the woods which had been a part of their childhood. Suddenly, they understand just how much these things were a part of them.

While blessing the refugees, the Dalai Lama places a *kata* of white silk around their necks. When Kinsom and Yandol come close to him, they prostrate themselves. But the Precious Protector, paying no heed to protocol, takes Kinsom by the arm and raises her. His small eyes are shining like jet beads, as if he can see all the suffering trapped inside her.

"When did you come?", he asks them, raising Yandol with the other arm to look her in the eye.

Kinsom is too moved to say anything. Yandol answers in a low voice: "Yesterday..."

"Are you the ones who had been detained in Gutsa?"

Yandol nods in assent.

The Dalai Lama turns to Kinsom. "How old are you?"

"Twenty-three", replies Kinsom, "and she is nineteen".

Ocean of Wisdom's eyes tense imperceptibly. He read the report about the new arrivals that very afternoon. Now he knows who the two nuns standing before him are.

"Are you well? I hope you're not injured?"

Yandol shakes her head to say no. Kinsom cannot move. Though she is not afraid of him, she does not dare look directly at the Precious Protector. She is not worthy of it.

Ocean of Wisdom insists: "You must go to the hospital. We have a doctor who specializes in curing mistreated people...", (he does not have the courage to say tortured.) "he might be able to help you."

Then there is silence. Precious Protector looks at them attentively. "Is there anyone from your family in India?", he asks.

"No, no one", mutters Kinsom.

"So your entire family is in Tibet?"

As Kinsom shakes her head, tears well into her eyes. They keep falling, like a Himalayan torrent, made of millions of little drops. Seeing her friend thus, Yandol can no longer contain her emotions and breaks into sobs.

When Horsemen Gallop on Wheels

The Dalai Lama is used to this kind of reaction. His compatriots, who have braved everything for the privilege of meeting him, of being in his presence, cannot hold themselves back. But he does not allow himself any trace of emotion.

"Now you have nothing to fear," he says, giving them a pat on the back. "Now you are free. Don't worry about money, we have a fund to help you. Take care of your health and do your best to develop your mind."

He remains silent for a few moments before asking in a hearty voice: "And where are you staying?"

Kinsom has somewhat regained her composure. "At the Reception Centre. "

"Which convent would like to go to?"

Kinsom and Yandol shake their heads. Ocean of Wisdom smiles at them, his eyes glinting like a constellation of stars.

"I think you will be happy in Dolma Ling. My people will see to everything."

Situated in the valley, the Dolma Ling Convent was built with financial support from the German Green Party. It was expected to become an important centre for the community in exile.

"There you can study and be happy. And if you need anything, I'm always here."

He puts a bright white *kata* around their necks and turns around to exchange a few words with his aides.

After leaving, the nuns slowly climb the hill. For a long time, they remain seated on a stone, looking at the valley that stretches out far beyond to green and ocher fields. Birds sing in the crystal clear air. Monkeys hang from cedar trees. All is calm. The nuns are far too moved to speak. And what can they say? They have no words to describe the plenitude they are experiencing.

As night falls, bugles and oboes are sounded for the last time in the monasteries and convents of Dharamsala. The shops are closing. Only a few restaurants, hotels and handicraft stores remain open. The nuns return to the reception centre and relax in their dormitory. Near Kinsom and Yandol's beds, a mother is feeding her child. A little ahead, an old man is turning his prayer wheel. Before them, a monk is chanting mantras.

A mere five hundred metres from the centre, outside the residence of the Dalai Lama, the sounds of the world have ceased. After a final hour of meditation, Ocean of Wisdom withdraws to his room. As he lies down, he reviews the events of the day. He sees the two nuns, so young, their faces bathed in tears, their silk scarves shining in the reflection of the sun's rays. It is this privileged contact with the exiles of Tibet that allows him to speak in their name, to fight against the mists of forgetfulness and ignorance that threaten to extend like a mantle over the country of his childhood.

Then, in the silence of his heart, he remembers his vows as a Boddhisatva:

> *For as long as space endures,*
> *And for as long as living beings remain,*
> *Until then may I, too, abide*
> *To dispel the misery of the world.*

EPILOGUE

It was the month of February 1994. Thousands of pilgrims were assembling in Dharamsala for the celebration of the Annual Prayer Festival. Some were coming on foot, in buses and trucks; others by plane from faraway continents, or by train from the heart of Asia. In a coach of the *Jammu Mail*, travelled a Spanish child. His blond hair set him apart from the others on that sunny February morning. Each year since his enthronement, Lama Osel has been coming to the Annual Festival from the south of India, accompanied by his father. He lives in the Sera Monastery, a replica of the original where Lama Yeshe, his previous incarnation, had studied. The child occupied a privileged position in the monastic order. He did not share the quarters of the other monks. His was a spacious, comfortable bungalow. He had a doting father and brother, seven assistants, tutors and private teachers to keep him company. Lama Osel was part of a unique experiment, one whose results could not predicted. It was the clash of two universes, two eras. The child accepted his lot readily. Like any other child, he loved to run around and play. But he also knew how to conduct himself like an oriental sage. He meditated for hours without moving, translated texts from ancient Tibetan and participated wholeheartedly in long ceremonies like this Prayer Festival. He was being trained to become a Great Master, one who would spread the message of Buddhism to the West. For the time being however, he was just a wise, mischievous child, who, that day, merged in the vast human ocean of crimson and gold.

More than a hundred monks and nuns, some with *tsampa* smeared on their faces, were crowded in the square of the Tsuglakhang Temple. They were wearing shining new habits, as tradition requires on such a day. Kinsom and Yandol climbed up from the Dolma Ling Convent, where they were living as students, thus, fulfilling the dream they had cherished for so long. They called their new home a paradise on earth. There they read ancient texts and studied English, science and geography. Amidst so much friendliness and natural beauty, it had not taken them long to adapt to their new lives. They felt free as never before. They were even free to demonstrate against the Chinese and publicly condemn the horrors of occupation. They felt privileged and at times they were overcome by a sense of guilt for having run away from the battlefield. That is why Kinsom cherished the dream of returning one day to Tibet to continue the struggle. A dream shared by all refugees.

The ten-year-old child who had been their travelling companion also dreamed of returning home. He had been hospitalized in Kathmandu and was presently living in the Tibetan children's village, located on a nearby hillside. The village had been founded by the Dalai Lama. More than three thousand children were being educated there with the help of donations from European sponsors. The little hero was staying in a house along with twelve girls and three boys, all of whom were being looked after by an adoptive mother. Finally, he had found the warmth and discipline of a home. He told his friends that he had to get his feet cured because he would soon be returning to his parents in Lhasa. A fourteen year old friend of his had made the journey back home on foot, accompanied by two other people. Pilgrims at heart, Tibetan children take risks even the most intrepid mountaineers would not think of. The child still did not know that without the four toes of his feet, he would never be able to achieve this feat.

That day there were many children in the crowd. One of them was a studious little Lama. He had ruddy cheeks and was wearing thick, black spectacles. Along with him were his father, his mother, his uncle and an old, parched Tibetan with an unmistakable look in his eyes. Yandol recognized him immediately. She took Kinsom by the hand and lead her towards the old man, their travelling companion and good friend. When he saw them, tears of joy filled his eyes. He prostrated himself as if before an incarnation of one of the Buddhist deities. Now in the company of his family, he had again met up with his traveling companions. Standing in front of Precious Protector, he lived the best moment of his life. Nothing could have brought more happiness to his soul. Later, the old man confessed to them that he would not return to southern India, even though that was where his only family lived. It could never be his land. He still had the strength and the will to keep moving.

"Aren't you ever going to stop travelling?", Yandol asked him.

"No, never. The day I stop, I'll die.", the old man said, laughing.

He knew that death could take him by surprise anywhere: in the mountains, on a glacier or a rocky trail. He decided, nonetheless, to return to Tibet after the Great Festival, on foot, like in the Middle Ages.

Finally, the familiar figure of the Fourteenth Dalai Lama appeared, followed by his aides, and monks playing oboes. Ocean of Wisdom smiled radiantly at the crowd, which made way for him. Then started a litany of mantras and songs that lasted for many hours. The only time the congregation's attention was diverted was when tea or cold drinks were served by smiling, young monks, happy to stretch their legs. Foreigners, ears glued to their headsets, listened to the simultaneous translation of the prayers. At sunset, hundreds of yak butter lamps illuminated the square. The Great Master of ceremonies bowed before the crowd, and then disappeared, smiling, into his residence. The great prayer for the happiness of all human beings had come to an end. Gradually the square emptied. All that remained were the wind horses, fluttering in the wind, sending their blessings to the four corners of the earth.

FINAL NOTE

In September 1997, I made my last trip to Tibet, Nepal and India to write this book. I had the opportunity to interview, in Lhasa the Abbess of a Convent. Ten of her nuns were locked up in the Drapchi prison. She told me of all the torture they had suffered. The Chinese had changed their methods of torture. In view of the widespread condemnation by the international press, they no longer sexually abused women who dared to shout: "Free Tibet!" or "Long live the Dalai Lama!" Instead, they used pins to prick their tongues. Furthermore, the sentence for any form of protest or demonstration had been increased.

In the Dolma Ling Convent of Dharamsala, I learned from Kinsom and Yandol that Dawa, the nun who had been their cell mate and the victim of the worst kind of torture, had been detained again in Lhasa. It seemed she had taken part in another demonstration.

I also visited the Kathmandu Reception Centre and was surprised to see it full of newly arrived refugees. I was very moved by the number of children in the eight to fourteen age group I saw there. They had crossed the Himalayas alone, without their parents; most of them seemed in good health. The nurse Tsering Lhamo told me that since 1990 there had been a steady increase in the number of refugees, and on some days, they did not have enough staff to attend to the new ones. The Dharamsala Reception Centre confirmed that the number of refugees had tripled in the last three years.

ACKNOWLEDGEMENTS

A great many people have helped in the researching and writing of this book. I would like to express my profound gratitude to His Holiness the Dalai Lama, who took time out of his busy schedule to patiently answer my queries. I would particularly like to thank Kinsom and Yandol. No matter how painful it was for them, they spoke spontaneously and without reserve of the hell they had been through in prison. To the children of the Tibetan Children's Village, who told me of their flight, my sincere thanks and apologies for having brought tears to their eyes.

I am particularly indebted to Dominique Lapierre; without his constant support and encouragement, this book would not have been possible. I am also grateful to my publishers, Mario Lacruz, Leonello Brandolini, Marco Vigevani and Shekhar Malhotra.

My warm thanks to Michelle Parfait, who accompanied me on several trips to India, Nepal and Tibet. These journeys will always remain in my mind because of the extraordinary hospitality shown to me by Vicki and Ang Kami Sherpa in Kathmandu. I would like to express my gratitude to them as also to Lama Osel, his brother Kunkyen and his father Paco Hita who met us with affection and kindness in the Sera Monastery in southern India. I would like to thank all the Tibetans in Tibet who trusted me enough to answer my questions.

I am grateful to Mr. Atuk, the Indian Ambassador in Spain, who helped me get an interview with the Dalai Lama. I am also indebted to the following: Kelsang Gyaltsen, the political secretary of His Holiness, for his patience and efficiency; Tsering Tashi, press advisor; Rinchen Khando Choegyal, the Dalai Lama's sister-in-law and Minister of Education of the Government-in-exile. In charge of twenty-seven thousand pupils, living all over India, she gave freely of her time to me and provided invaluable assistance in procuring the necessary documentation. My heartfelt thanks to Philippa Russel, the representative of the NGO looking after nun refugees, for her kindness and the assistance she provided in facilitating the interviews. And of course, I wish to express my gratitude to the interpreter Lhamo Choeden.

I would like to thank the staff of the Information Department of the Government of His Holiness for allowing me to consult their archives. I am very grateful to John Ackerly, the Director of the International Campaign for Tibet in Washington for having allowed me to reproduce, free of cost, the photographs he had taken at the time of the Lhasa demonstrations.

I am also very grateful for the help given to me in Dharamsala by Stephanie Faber, Bo, Reverend Pema Dorjee and Yonten Chodon in finding the people I was looking for. My thanks to Laura Allen for her hospitality in New Delhi.

I would like to express my gratitude to: José Juan Ortiz for his collabouration; Gloria Rognoni; Jordi Risa who told me the fascinating story of his love for Nepal and the mountains; Alan Cantos, whose advice lead me to discover unknown stories and whose corrections of the manuscript proved invaluable; Maria Torres and François Camus for the long interviews they granted in Bubion; Kia Abitbol for her encouragement and enthusiasm at the time of reading the book; Joan Carol for her invaluable advice; Eugenio Suarez, who spent many hours correcting the manuscript and without whose generous assistance it would not have been completed.

For all the trips I have made in India. I would like to thank the Taj Group of Hotels and Air India for their cooperation.

Dharamsala, December 1994
Finestrat, October 1997

BIBLIOGRAPHY

Among the many books and documents that I have consulted, I would like to make special mention of: *"Les rebelles de l'Himalaya"* by Philippe Broussard (Denoel, Paris, 1996), an extremely interesting account of the same Himalayan journey and an article by Tim McGirk in *The Independent* (12.2.1994). Also "Le *Dalai-Lama. Un certain sourire"*, by Laurence Vidal (Calmann-Levy, Paris, 1995), a sensitive and poetic portrait of His Holiness,

Of invaluable help were *"Freedom in Exile"*, the autobiography of the Dalai Lama (Hodder and Stoughton) and *"The Dalai Lama: A Biography"*, by Claude Levenson (Oxford University Press, Delhi, 1994).

For accounts on the recent history and the situation in Tibet: *"Tibet: Survival In Question"*, by Pierre Antoine Donnet (Zed Books, London 1994), *"In Exile in the Land of Snows"* by John Avedon (Alfred Knopf, 1984), *"Tears of Blood"*, by Mary Craig (Indus, Delhi, 1992) and *"Cavaliers of Kham: The Secret War of Tibet"*, by Michel Peissel (Little and Brown, 1972).

Apart from these works, I would also like to mention *Reincarnation*, by Vickie Mackenzie (Time Books, Delhi, 1992) and *Tibetan Buddhist Nuns*, by Hanna Havnevik (Norwegian University Press, Oslo 1995).

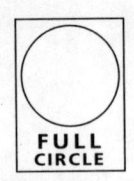

FULL CIRCLE BOOKS ON BUDDHISM & TIBET

THICH NHAT HANH

Old Path White Clouds *Walking in the Footsteps of the Buddha*	395/-
The Stone Boy *and Other Stories*	195/-
Cultivating the Mind of Love *The Practice of Looking Deeply in the Mahayana Buddhist Tradition*	140/-
Our Appointment with Life *Buddha's Teaching on Living in the Present*	140/-
Being Peace *(Hc • Gift Edition)*	295/-
(Pbk)	175/-
Present Moment, Wonderful Moment *Mindfulness Verses for Daily Living* *(Pbk)*	195/-
(Hc• Gift Edition)	295/-
Transformation & Healing *Sutra on the Four Establishments of Mindfulness*	195/-
The Heart of Understanding *Commentaries on the Prajñaparamita Heart Sutra*	140/-
Breathe! You Are Alive *Sutra on the Full Awareness of Breathing* *(Pbk)*	175/-
Interbeing *Fourteen Guidelines for Engaged Buddhism*	195/-
The Long Road Turns to Joy *(Hc)*	295/-
(Pbk)	95/-
जहं जहं चरन परे गौतम के	125/–
बांसुरी	95/–

HIS HOLINESS THE DALAI LAMA

H.H. Dalai Lama **Worlds in Harmony**	195/-
The Heart of Compassion	195/-
Tibet: The Issue is Independence	125/-
दैनिक जीवन में ध्यान साधना का विकास	125/–
करुणाशील हृदय	95/–

To privilege faith over fear,
hope over despair, love over hate,
put a *A Thousand Suns* into your heart,
by reading this new epic
by **Dominique Lapierre.**

From Japanese terrorists in the Holy Land to freedom fighters in fascist Portugal; from spread of Nazism to the liberation of Paris; from Mahatma Gandhi to Mother Teresa; Lapierre delves eloquently into the very heart of the history of our time. Most of all, this international bestseller bears moving testimony to the ability of mankind to endure, to dream, to triumph.

WORLD WIDE PREMIERE EDITION

"...An inspirational book as any. *A Thousand Suns* is a Bible in itself."
The Indian Express

Among the premier journalists of our time, Dominique Lapierre has traveled to the four corners of the globe, witnessed world-shaking events, and met extraordinary people from all walks of life. Now this remarkable man shares his adventures and encounters in a book that aptly reflects a favorite proverb from India: that beyond the clouds, there are always a thousand suns.

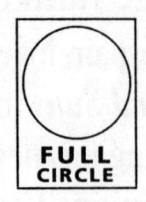

FULL CIRCLE

Full Circle publishes books on inspirational subjects, spirituality, religion, philosophy and natural health. The objective is to help make an attitudinal shift towards a more peaceful, loving, non-combative, non-threatening, compassionate and healing world.

Full Circle continues its commitment towards creating a peaceful and harmonious world and towards rekindling the joyous, divine nature of the human spirit.

Our fine books and music are available at all leading bookstores across the country.

FULL CIRCLE PUBLISHING
Registered Office
18-19, Dilshad Garden, G.T. Road, Delhi-110 095
Tel: 228 2467, 229 7792 • Fax: 228 2332

Editorial Office
J-40, Jorbagh Lane, New Delhi-110 003
Tel: 462 0063, 461 5138, 465 3930, Fax: 464 5795
E-Mail gbp@del2.vsnl.net.in

Music & Book Store
34, Santushti Shopping Arcade, Opp. Ashoka–Samrat Hotels,
Race Course Road, New Delhi 110 003
Tel: 688 1304 • Tele Fax: 688 1306